350/

LANDSCAPE · PORTRAIT · STILL-LIFE

By courtesy of the Earl of Radnor

1. VELASQUEZ, PORTRAIT OF JUAN DE PAREJA. DETAIL

Longford Castle

Juan de Pareja, painter, was a mulatto and the slave of Velasquez

(*p.* 251)

LANDSCAPE
PORTRAIT · STILL-LIFE

Their Origin and Development

by

MAX J. FRIEDLÄNDER

With 41 Illustrations

SCHOCKEN BOOKS
NEW YORK

Translated from the German
by
R. F. C. HULL

1st Schocken paperback edition, 1963

This edition is published by arrangement with Bruno Cassirer, Publishers, Ltd., Oxford, England.

All rights reserved. No part of this book may be reproduced in any form without permission from the publisher, except by a reviewer who wishes to quote brief passages in connection with a review written for inclusion in magazine or newspaper.

Library of Congress card catalog No. 63-13344

Manufactured in the United States of America

CONTENTS

PAGE

FOREWORD 9

LANDSCAPE

The Idiosyncrasy of Landscape 11
The Origins of Landscape in the 15th century 23
The Emancipation of Landscape in the 16th century 46
The Golden Age of Landscape in the 17th century 88
Landscape in the 18th and 19th centuries 109
The Significance of Landscape in our day 142

GENRE

The Nature and Origins of the Genre as a category 154
The Golden Age of Genre 170
Genre in the 18th century 207
The Genre: Present and Future 218

PORTRAIT

Something of the Principles and History of Portraiture 230

RELIGIOUS ART

Religious Art and the Historical Picture 263

STILL-LIFE

Concerning the Still-life 277

INDEX 285

LIST OF ILLUSTRATIONS

PLATE — FACING PAGE

1. VELASQUEZ. JUAN DE PAREJA. DETAIL. Longford Castle — *frontispiece*
2. JAN VAN EYCK. THE ROLLIN MADONNA. DETAIL. Paris, Louvre — 24
3. JAN VAN EYCK. WOMEN BY THE SEPULCHRE. Rotterdam — 26
4. ROGIER VAN DER WEIDEN. THE STAR APPEARS TO THE MAGI. DETAIL. Berlin, Kaiser Friedrich Museum — 30
5. DIERICK BOUTS. ST. JOHN THE BAPTIST. DETAIL. Munich, Pinakothek — 32
6. HUGO VAN DER GOES. THE FALL OF MAN. Vienna, State Gallery — 36
7. MEMLING. PORTRAIT. Florence, Corsini Gallery — 37
8. GEERTGEN TOT SINT JANS. ST. JOHN THE BAPTIST. Berlin, Kaiser Friedrich Museum — 40
9. DIERICK BOUTS. ST. CHRISTOPHER. DETAIL. Munich, Pinakothek — 41
10. GERARD DAVID. BAPTISM OF CHRIST. Bruges, Museum — 42
11. H. BOSCH. ST. HIERONYMUS PRAYING. Ghent, Museum — 44
12. QUENTIN MASSYS. THE LAMENTATION OF CHRIST. Detail. Antwerp, Museum — 48
13. PATENIER. THE BAPTISM OF CHRIST. Vienna, State Gallery — 49
14. JAN DE COCK. ST. CHRISTOPHER. Coll. Frh. v. Fürstenberg — 58
15. JAN SWART VAN GRONINGEN. ST. JOHN THE BAPTIST PREACHING. Munich, Pinakothek — 66
16. ALTDORFER. SATYR AND HIS FAMILY. Berlin, Kaiser Friedrich Museum — 67
17. CRANACH. REST ON THE FLIGHT INTO EGYPT. DETAIL. Berlin, Kaiser Friedrich Museum — 68

PLATE FACING PAGE

18. PIETER BRUEGHEL. THE TOWER OF BABEL, DETAIL. Rotterdam 78
19. JAN VAN GOIJEN. RIVER LANDSCAPE. Priv. Coll. 90
20. J. VAN RUISDAEL. LANDSCAPE . ETCHING 96
21. A. CUYP. VIEW OF DORDRECHT. Coll. A. de Rothschild 106
22. COROT. SUMMER MORNING. Priv. Coll. 118
23. CEZANNE. LANDSCAPE. New York 128
24. JAN VAN EYCK. WOMEN BY THE SEPULCHRE. DETAIL. Rotterdam 160
25. PIETER AERTSEN. THE BIRTH OF CHRIST. FRAGMENT. Amsterdam, Museum 161
26. BROUWER. PEASANT LIGHTING HIS PIPE. Munich, Kaulbach Collection 176
27. PIETER DE HOOGH. THE BEDROOM. Washington, National Gallery of Art 186
28. VERMEER. MASTER AND MODEL. DETAIL. Vienna 194
29. METSU. THE MUSIC LESSON. London, National Gallery 198
30. WATTEAU. A LADY AT HER TOILET. DETAIL. DRAWING. London, British Museum 210
31. CHARDIN. THE WAY TO SCHOOL. Liechtenstein 211
32. JAN VAN EYCK. ARNOLFINI AND HIS WIFE. DETAIL. London, National Gallery 238
33. GHIRLANDAIO. OLD MAN AND BOY. Paris, Louvre 240
34. GHIRLANDAIO. OLD MAN AND BOY. DETAIL. Paris, Louvre 241
35. RAPHAEL. PORTRAIT OF MADDALENA DONI. DRAWING. Paris, Louvre 242
36. A. MOR. ANTOINE PERRENOT DE GRANVELLA Vienna, State Gallery 246
37. TITIAN. ANTOINE PERRENOT DE GRANVELLA Kansas, City Museum 247
38. RUBENS. MARTYRDOM OF ST. LIEVIN. Rotterdam 272
39. VELASQUEZ. THE SURRENDER OF BREDA. Madrid, Prado 276
40. W. KALF. STILL-LIFE. Amsterdam, Rijksmuseum 282
41. VELASQUEZ. KITCHEN SCENE. DETAIL. London 284

FOREWORD

There is no lack of books to instruct us on the development of painting. They resemble ground-plans. But, by following out the genesis and decay of the separate categories of painting—landscape, genre, portraiture, religious art and still-life—I yield to the hope that I may have augmented the ground-plan by cross-sections, just as a work of architecture is only fully illustrated by the juxtaposition of this view and that. The reader will, I hope, not regard it as prolixity on my part if he comes across the same remarks in one case as in the other. Such repetitions are a natural and necessary consequence since the cross-sections belong to one and the same edifice, stand on one and the same ground-plan.

I have already touched on the theme of the various categories of painting in my book *On Art and Connoisseurship*. Now, by following up the historical development, I have endeavoured to make the vicissitudes of the categories more graphic—to the art-lover and possibly also to the historian of civilization.

The illustrations put me in something of a quandary. Completeness could not be attained in view of the quantity of pictures mentioned. I hope that I may have succeeded, through the reproduction of selected examples, in reminding the reader of his own visual experiences and of the originals, thus deepening his understanding of the text.

M. J. F.

I

THE IDIOSYNCRASY OF LANDSCAPE

Looking round the art exhibitions today we get the impression that landscape has conquered all the other categories of painting, though not, perhaps, quantitatively. It is the landscape first and foremost that captivates and satisfies the art-lover. To track down the causes of this triumph of the landscape—a relatively young genus of art—may prove to be a profitable theme for the art historian.

Time was when the categories of painting fell into something of a scale of values, with the historical picture and the devotional picture at the top, the genre and the portrait lower down, still-life and landscape at the bottom. This order of rank has now collapsed. Spasmodic and fruitless efforts have been made to resuscitate the historical or devotional picture; the entertaining or soulful genre is regarded with mistrust. Strictly speaking, what remains the best and most highly prized in contemporary art is the portrait or portrait-like group, still-life and landscape. Besides which, the boundaries between the various categories have ceased to be water-tight. With many paintings one does not quite know to what compartment they belong. Philosophers have defined the enjoyment of art as 'disinterested pleasure'. A slice of reality copied, because not real in the copy, is contemplated with delight, since what we see there makes no minatory move to intrude into the fatality of our lives. The modern cry of 'l'art pour l'art' calls for a high degree of intellectual independence in the artist, since it insulates the practice of art against all other kinds of spiritual exertion, not merely against any concern with active or passive life. Further, the associations of ideas which once played an essential part in the artistic effect are now suppressed and, wherever possible, eliminated. Hence the desired autonomy of art is most readily secured in the decorative picture, still-life and landscape—the 'dumb' categories, as it were. With this in mind one might venture to set up a scale of values in which landscape came first and the historical picture last.

Though the art-lover of our day may succeed in contemplating the Sistine Madonna with 'disinterested pleasure', the pious-minded in the sixteenth century certainly did not glance up at the altar-piece with anything of the sort.

The question remains why this pleasure has turned so decidedly, much more decidedly than in earlier times, to the earth, the sky, water and vegetation; also why in those days the effect of a work of art definitely did not rest on 'disinterestedness'. After all, one's spiritual welfare belonged to the major interests of life. The second question is easy to answer. In the Middle Ages and far beyond them the visual arts served some purpose: they were of service to the Church, and, once become profane, they regaled people, entertained them, amused them, instructed them and in many ways satisfied men's intellectual needs. The proud, so easily accepted cry of 'art for art's sake' would have sounded incomprehensible or frivolous to the Old Masters.

The first question is more difficult. The joy and thrill of contemplating natural landscapes was there right enough in olden times, as can be observed in literature and poetry. But the step from verbal expression to pictorial expression was ventured relatively late. And it was not enough that the artist's vision impelled him towards representation; receptivity had first to be awakened, pleasure had to become widespread before painters could undertake anything in the way of landscape. Nor were there, as now, painters living on the proceeds of parental incomes and working only for posterity, intent on posthumous fame alone, thus incidentally avoiding, luckily for them, the experience of failure.

In classical times the joy and thrill of contemplating natural landscapes passed into mythological beings with human bodies. Sculpture held the field, and men's imaginations were peopled with bodies that had solid bounds to them. Nor could the religious spirituality of the Middle Ages express itself artistically save in human figures. Sculpture still held the field, for which painting acted as a substitute, though bound by the laws of relief. The visible world today arouses pleasure in those of us who are gifted with pure looking. Even a pair of old boots can become an object of artistic realization. The world of phenomena, aesthetically regarded, falls into two parts: the kingdom of complete and measurable things with firm outlines, and the sphere of the seemingly accidental, the arbitrary, the unbounded. Our sense for law and order, our delight in intellectual mastery lead us to the one, our enjoyment of variety and visual adventures to the other. Sculpture tends in this direction, painting in that; here the human body is singled out, there landscape. The land is the earth's surface or a part of the earth's surface; landscape is the physiognomy of the land, land in its effect on us. Using, or perhaps abusing, philosophical terms one might say: land is the 'thing-in-itself', landscape the 'phenomenon'. The peasant knows the land which he cultivates, which nourishes him; he looks up at the sky, sender of light and rain, but the landscape hardly affects him at all: the relishing eye cannot emerge where hard necessity and harder use predominate. Men were far indeed from the age that knew a life of cattle-breeding, hunting, fishing and farming, and nothing more, when the sight of earth and sky awakened stirrings in their souls and the desire to bind these stirrings in an image.

The earth, or any part of it, is an irregular mass humping itself skywards with its weight of vegetation and architecture. In order to grasp the formation, the realness of it, to gauge its heights and distances, land has to be surveyed geographically. The land surveyor, the cartographer, satisfies practical or scientific requirements by furnishing reliable topographical data. But look at the terrain from any vantage-point whatsoever and you will get quite a different picture from the objective statement of the map—a picture that is to the map as a poem is to a report. Thanks to foreshortening, blocking, displacement and hazing, the spatial facts have been transformed, and what we see would be unintelligible did not our knowledge, our experience come to the aid of our visual perceptions. We see, it may be, an isosceles triangle looming above a row of trees and know that it is a church spire; we see objects close together yet know that they are far apart; we espy grey foliage knowing full well that it is green.

Vision is bound in space, according to the position of the observer, and also in time, so far as the appearance of things changes with the position of the sun and the clouding of the sky.

Seeing is a give and take, sensuous passivity and intellectual action, the result being highly subjective and, in a certain sense, our own creation. The French poet and art-critic Paul Valéry puts it like this: observing is in the main an imagining of what one is confidently expecting to see. What the creative artist sees is conditioned by his intention and ability to reproduce the vision, as much as by the means he has of realizing it. Valéry expresses this conditioning factor succinctly in the words: It makes a vast deal of difference whether you see something with a crayon in your hand or without a crayon in your hand. Nietzsche says of the painter: In the last resort he paints only what pleases him—and what pleases him? What he can paint. At any rate, of the innumerable things there are to see, only a few are selected and accepted. The painter imagines that what is there for the seeing is 'beautiful', but he only sees what tallies with his sense of beauty.

Having turned the values of the art-categorics upside down I feel in duty bound to inveigh against the idea that there are 'difficult' and 'easy' art-categories. It was not least on this account that the academies looked down on landscape-painting, because it seemed to them comparatively easy, a spare-time job. A painter faced with the task of portraying the murder of Caesar may think that it is child's play to paint trees. Not a few masters who took their profession seriously—Degas, for instance failed to see in landscape a single object worthy of their efforts. It is easy to discover the reason for this disdain. In the seeming anarchy of landscape-forms the limits of what is possible and permissible are not immediately apparent, and in consequence free rein is given to the artist's caprice. The painter thinks it allowable to lengthen or shorten the branch of a tree at will, while he feels constrained to a certain caution and precision with regard to the arm of a man or the leg of a horse. In this sense and in this sense alone can the landscape-painter's job be deemed an easy one. Strictly speaking, however, things are easy for him only in so far as he can count on more lenient judges and his own self-criticism is lulled. For the seemingly fortuitous disorder of landscape-form hides the inevitability of nature. The very thing that makes the nonchalant artist more nonchalant—that apparent lack of obligatoriness—forces the conscientious artist to stick to the phenomenon as given. Not knowledge, not theory, only the unprejudiced devotion of his gaze enables him to do justice to the inherent inevitability of nature. And to such a one his profession will not seem easy.

If, as Valéry succinctly puts it, observing is in the main the imagining of what one is confidently expecting to see, this is less applicable to landscape than to any other object of observation. Comparing a tree with a column or a human body we see at once how relatively little all our foresight and knowledge help us to take in the tree. A blind man could, at need, outline a human body, but in no circumstances could he sketch a tree or a landscape. Sensuous passivity rather than intellectual action, unqualified fidelity to actual appearances are the things demanded of the landscape-painter.

When the desire and the ability to paint landscapes first made themselves felt, evidently in the North at the beginning of the fifteenth century, there were four obstacles in the path of this young aspiration. First of all there was no occasion, within the range of commissions falling to the painters' guilds, to paint landscape for the sake of landscape. Then the habit inherited from the Middle Ages of seeing bodies with firm outlines—the sculptor's way of seeing things—was but ill equipped to find its way about in the chaos of landscape. Further, there was no knowledge of the laws of perspective. And, finally, objective interest was against the straightforward acceptance of a mode of vision which contained nothing but distorted, misplaced and hazy forms and which seemed to deceive the eye.

I shall probably have to define what I mean by 'objective interest'. When Jan van Eyck painted brocade he thought he was producing something which, seen from every angle, resembled real brocade. When he painted a house in the background of the landscape his aim was to make everything that belonged to the house visible despite the tiny scale. His distant view is really a diminutive near view. Craving for knowledge, paedagogic zeal and a pious reverence for the qualities of things brooked no other way of seeing. Whereas the Italians of the sixteenth century painted things big although seen as if from a considerable distance, van Eyck sees them from close to, no matter how minute (corresponding to their position in depth) they may appear. People speak of van Eyck's 'microscopic' sharpness of vision, but, to be quite accurate, he never magnified the small—on the contrary he diminished the big without impoverishing it.

Just how much this objective interest hindered the growth of landscape-painting will be recognized most easily if we bear in mind the last, or last but one, phase of art. A Monet or a Cézanne never dreamt of thinking that the coloured patch in their field of vision had to give a faithful and unequivocal report as to the form, colour and texture of a thing; looking, they forgot what they knew about the thing in order to take in the visual experience in all its purity. This was an end and aim. Many halting-places along the road, many stages in the weakening of objective interest, and reactions too, are noticeable in the course of historical development.

The land, as a subject for art, is not a whole in itself, rather part of an infinitely big whole and is thereby distinguished from other subjects, the human body in particular. The fragment, the sample, the instance that it is, points beyond itself and stimulates the imagination to roam beyond the confines of the visible. When I see the limb of a human body, a foot or a hand, I complete in my mind the organism whose part I have been shown; but when I see a bit of land I cannot, with my mind's eye, embrace the whole that goes with it. The less the thing directly seen comes to view as a structure complete in itself, the more urgent the necessity to give the section the appearance of wholeness through the art of composition.

About human development and with particular regard to the history of seeing and artistic creation, much is to be learnt by observing the doings of a child. Asked to draw a man, a house, a tree, a child will set to work without misgiving and will, to its own satisfaction, produce in a few strokes and more or less skilfully something from which the object in question can be recognized. If, on the other hand, I ask the child to draw a bit of country, it will get all confused and fail. Hence art on the primitive level is absolutely restricted to isolated things. A mountain (a swelling on the boundless mass of the earth), a river (a groove in the ground's surface), are not things in this sense at all and can only be grasped visually in relation to space. They are unimaginable without their situation and topography. Landscape-painting begins with the artist sharply observing single parts, trees, plants, mountains and making them true to nature, without being able to give verisimilitude to the whole—the relation of the parts to one another. Landscape appeared as an accumulation, a conglomeration of isolated parts until, in the last phase, the particular segment is approached from some vantage-point or other and all the details are arranged according to space-logic.

Since the painters deriving from the Middle Ages were intent on complete bodies rounded off in significant outlines, they longed for the totality of landscape and tried to encompass the whole terrestrial sphere. Such a wish being unattainable, they then struggled to make the part representative of the whole, that is, to display in the segment everything that could possibly be seen on earth.

What they felt to be the primary property of the earth was limitless distance. In order to represent extension in space the eye had to be directed on to the land from above, especially at a time when there was no assured control of linear and aerial perspective.

It is said that the Duke of Burgundy once commissioned his artist to paint the globe, and that a work of this kind, half map and half landscape, was done by Jan van Eyck. Up to a point all the landscapes of the fifteenth century are geographical ground-plans.

Landscape, which is part of an unassimilable whole, is made up in its turn of parts: mountains, trees, paths. The individual items are not like the links in a chain, rather the threads in a piece of fabric. Thus landscape grows into a school where relativity is taught, since here the terms decide the issue less by their own shape and idiosyncrasy than by their relation to one another and to the whole, and are not so much adjacent as confluent.

Continuous space resembles a river, a river without banks, and the things in it resemble the waves.

Sculpture isolates, drawing articulates, splits up and divides, painting combines and unbinds solids, effaces boundaries. Interest in landscape and painting reinforced one another, with the result that painting became pre-eminent. Michelangelo, the sculptor, Ingres and Cornelius, draughtsmen, despised the landscape.

The beginning of the fifteenth century saw the first stirrings of joy and pleasure in the contemplation of the countryside, especially in the North. The art of painting was still faced with the same tasks as in the Middle Ages, only it undertook to solve them in another spirit. Landscape insinuated itself into the religious picture, became the hand-maid of the Church, albeit a somewhat unruly and even dangerous member of the household. But not only was she tolerated, she was also accorded a warm welcome, because the growing urge towards greater realism in respect of the holy figures and biblical events demanded natural space and authentic local colour. What the poet says is true of the saints in mediaeval pictures: 'No place about them, still less time.' Together with the ideal golden background there vanished that placelessness and timelessness which went with orthodoxy. It is true that Bible and legend chronicled place and time, but the pious in the Middle Ages prayed to icons; they did not read the Scriptures. Moreover, it makes a difference whether one reads that the Saviour sojourned at such and such a time in such and such a land, or whether one sees him travelling in the flesh in this land. From its illegitimate liaison with religion landscape acquired seriousness, solemnity and importance—it was necessary after all to illustrate far-away holy places in foreign lands—and the religious picture became profaned, since with the earth itself something of earthly reality penetrated into the temple, and attention was diverted from the holy centre to additional and incidental factors.

The 'where' reminded people of the 'when', and the holy picture turned into the historical picture. In time the reaction came, a defence against the threat of secularization. When Rogier van der Weyden painted his *Descent from the Cross*, a work distinguished by its moving and compelling religious atmosphere, he cut out space and place altogether and set a frieze-like composition on the reredos. And Dürer's *Apostles*, those monumental and strictly religious productions, are likewise done at a remove from all spatiality.

The mediaeval picture, be it framed tablet, stained glass window, sheet of parchment or mural, acted as a plane surface. The more the figures on them were invested with reality the more violent grew the thirst for space, until finally the surface was broken through, the eye went deeper as through a window, and the third dimension was conquered. With this shift in their mode of vision landscape-artists opened the door which had already been shaken vigorously by their love of nature. Thirst for space is the primary thing; the discovery of the laws of perspective only comes second. People were painting more or less correctly in perspective well before the mathematical rules were known.

Landscape invaded the ecclesiastical picture as a sort of setting or stage for the figures and scenes, having to fit in and arrange itself as best it might. Apart perhaps from an inconspicuous strip the whole of the foreground was taken up by the actors, who also covered the middle distance. The one place where the landscape could spread itself was, almost exclusively, the background, and this could only be glimpsed over the heads of the figures. Landscape was thus confined essentially to distant views and mountainous terrain. Since, however, the rising mountains (seen from ground-level) threatened to shut out the background as well, artists were forced to take the bird's-eye view, seeing from the top of a mountain towards other distant mountains. But it was not possible to stick to this vantage-point and adopt it for the picture as a whole, since the figures in the foreground had to appear unforeshortened and upright. This disparity between vantage-point and line of vision was overcome only gradually in the sixteenth century.

I have indicated the starting-point, the aim and the course, also the obstacles with which landscape-painting had to contend as it developed. By throwing light on some of the stages in the journey I may now and again have given the reader the impression of progress. I would like to quash any such optimism in advance. Progress in looking at the world, in the way of seeing and shaping is really only a step towards ourselves. That is why there is not a little presumption in the idea. A Japanese art-lover might well see a retrograde step where we see a forward one. In addition, the historian who is on the look-out for progress easily overlooks the loss that is bound up with the gain. By following almost exclusively the road taken by Netherlands—or as regards the nineteenth century, by French—painting, I hope, despite this limitation, to overlook nothing essential.

II

THE ORIGINS OF LANDSCAPE IN THE FIFTEENTH CENTURY

I begin with Jan van Eyck. How else should I begin? Maybe with Hubert van Eyck? Alas, I don't know anything of him. More than anyone else Jan van Eyck contributed to the shift of vision which opened the way to landscape for the panel-picture. Even in his own lifetime he was honoured with the title of 'inventor'. He is supposed to have invented 'oil-painting'. There is a hard core of truth to this traditional legend. But Jan van Eyck did not paint as he did because he had invented something; rather he invented or discovered certain pictorial techniques because he was unable to reproduce his visual experiences with the techniques he had inherited, because he had an overriding urge to make the lustre, the luminousness, the shimmer of matter, together with an infinity of detail, visible in the small compass of the panel-picture. Love of nature and thirst for space created what we call 'oil-painting'. Jan van Eyck was confronted with the same tasks as his forbears, but through travel and intercourse with powerful, luxury-loving, worldly princes he had broadened his horizon beyond the confines of the mediaeval mind. From sheer delight in the senses and freedom of spirit he gave the devotional picture a happy humanity, an individual stamp to the portrait and spaciousness, depth and air to the landscape.

His interest in objects made him professional in many fields. He was a goldsmith, an architect, a town-planner, or at least had the knowledge which these professions require. And this knowledge did not come from books; he owed it to his love of seeing and his sharpness of vision. It is quite likely that his contemporaries, even his princely patrons, esteemed him more on account of his attainments than on account of his creative imagination.

Jan van Eyck seized passionate hold of the opportunity to put landscape into the devotional picture, so as to praise Creation to the honour of the Creator and buildings to the glory of man. More than once we note how he fairly drags the opportunity in. In the *Rollin-Madonna* the painter himself kneels, praying, before the seated Madonna in a loggia. The theme of the picture in no way requires the prospect of a handsomely built, richly populated town lying on the two banks of a river. The Master has devoted himself with passion to this filling in of the background—a gratuitous gift. The loggia is situated in the upper storey of the palazzo. Our standpoint, at some distance from the columns in the frame of which the far-off town can be seen, does not itself permit us—granting the laws of space-logic—to view the town. On the terrace which, in the middle distance, adjoins the loggia—two men, one of whom is leaning over the parapet, enjoying the noble view. With a stroke of genius Jan van Eyck invites us to share the position of those men. We see not merely what comes into our field of vision; we are made an additional present of what those men are gazing at. Here the double standpoint—unavoidable at the Master's time-level—is used to enrich the picture as a whole. His contemporaries must surely have been grateful to the magician who united in the picture what, in reality, they caught sight of now from here, now from there. Rogier van der Weyden took over the same motif in his *St. Luke* (Pl. 2).

Although Jan van Eyck did not know, or knew only

2. JAN VAN EYCK, THE ROLLIN MADONNA. DETAIL
Paris, Louvre

partially, the laws of linear perspective, his visual experience led him to construct interiors more or less correctly, with the result that it is only by checking his measurements that we can prove the geometrical laws were not known to him. He was acquainted with the phenomenon of colour-perspective, as the aerial blueness of his distant mountains and the gradation of greens in his vegetation show. But he was not prepared to go to logical extremes with the veiling and dusking of his distances. His interest in objects forbad him this, his feeling of obligation to the facts of form and colour—which, despite logical diminution, gradation of dimensions, did not allow him to rob far-off things of their distinctness and precision.

In no other panel of Jan van Eyck's was the need to develop spatiality, landscape roominess, put more challengingly by the theme itself than in the painting of the *Women by the Sepulchre*, which has gone from the Cook Collection to private ownership in Holland. Some experts rate this a work of Hubert's, but all, with the exception of a few sceptics, are agreed about its date and think this work came before the Ghent Altar. A dramatic incident, out-of-doors, at a definite place, at a definite hour. Early one morning, at sunrise, the three women have gone out from Jerusalem to the tomb of the Saviour, find the sarcophagus empty, the three guards asleep and see the angel on the lid of the sarcophagus, announcing the miracle of the Resurrection. The seven figures are distributed loosely over the surface of the picture. The first rays of the sun strike the shining messenger from Heaven, setting off the apparition in a landscape from which the darkness of night has not yet fully departed. The figures, relatively small in scale, the holy women somewhat flattened and weightless, let everything be said by the landscape as well as by the *genre*-like mercen-

aries who have slept through the miracle and now, in blunt contrast to the unearthly angel, make a vulgar and, owing to the combination of sumptuous armament and slothful torpor, a well-nigh grotesque impression. Like Shakespeare, Jan van Eyck frankly and boldly puts sublimity and tragic seriousness cheek by jowl with drastic coarseness. We have a picture in our minds of Christ's grave as lying on a hill, but the town in the valley. Jan van Eyck was unable to see eye to eye with this idea. He shifted the grave to the low foreground, the town in the distance on to a hill. Only thus could he succeed in constructing a picture that was in keeping with his time-level and way of seeing. The horizon had to lie far up, on top of the figures if the chain of mountains and the town were to stand out in sharp profile against the sky. Furthermore, a high horizon is everywhere a sign of the Primitives, just as is the need to fill in practically the whole surface of the picture—which, coming down from the Middle Ages, only disappeared, slowly, in the fifteenth century.
In the picture with the women by the sepulchre waves of earth rise up in the middle distance and jutting rocks, making a wall from which the figures detach themselves, some light, some dark. The illusion of space stretching continuously into the distance is not quite achieved. The mass of the sarcophagus is faultily constructed. The deep, unitive colouring, however, covers up and conceals defects of construction. Colour and light, not so much the linear structure, produce the uniform effect. The dawn-light tips some of the buildings in the distance with gold and stirs the slumbering landscape. There is no other picture of the fifteenth century which achieves so much in point of harmony of place, mood of the hour, grouping of figures, and draws from the landscape so great a contribution to the dramatic narrative (Pl. 3).

Museum Boymans/van Beuningen

3. JAN VAN EYCK, WOMEN BY THE SEPULCHRE
Rotterdam

This step forward is all the more astonishing since in many respects the bond with tradition seems no whit overcome. The curvy, archaic folds of the draperies—legacy of the past—stand out against the textural reality of the stone and the metallically sparkling armour of the sleeping guards.

The *Crucifixion* in the Berlin Gallery, attributed by most experts to the same painter, be it Hubert or Jan van Eyck, and to the same period as the *Women by the Sepulchre*, contains, back of the figures, terrain rising like a wall with broken stones and sparse vegetation, and, high up on the horizon, the town with its solid, serried buildings, a windmill, a pine, a barren tree and undulating chains of mountains. A serpentine path adds somewhat to the suggestion of depth. Mountain terrain, absolutely necessary at this stylistic level as a ground-surface for the figures and as a filling for the plane of the picture, becomes a medium through which the narrator can give the flat-landers the feel of far-off and foreign climes where Christ and the saints lived and suffered. And the pine points southwards.

Thick-studded with distant buildings the land peeps through the rocks in the picture of *St. Francis* at Turin. Buildings, whose actual dimensions are known to us, give us information in miniature about the distance. Of this trick for guaranteeing depth to pictorial space, Jan van Eyck made fairly regular use. The saint and his sleeping companion detach themselves from rock and foliage on a plane running parallel to the panel. This work certainly does not belong to the Master's early period, was done at any rate after 1435 as can especially be noted from the folds of the draperies, which partly fall quite straight and partly crumple up into angles. Despite the relatively late date the dualism between the figures and the landscape—a dualism the Master is always fighting against—is not completely conquered.

Even in the *Madonna* which is in the possession of Baron Robert von Rothschild the figures stand juxtaposed on one plane, while the view of the town is virtually something on its own, as in the *Rollin Madonna*. And this picture is quite late. That the horizon is comparatively low here is one argument, but by no means the only one, for relegating this picture to the last years of the Master's life.

The Ghent Altar—child of sorrows for art historians (not that they lack children of sorrow elsewhere!)—makes plain the crisis in which Jan van Eyck found himself. Disquieting fluctuations of style in this great multipartite work have repeatedly tempted the experts to try to sort out the individualities of two Masters, the brothers. So far these efforts have not been very successful. In the centre panel, the Adoration of the Lamb, the stratification of the parts of the picture, the separation of the groups of figures from the landscape is carried through consistently, with the Primitives' eye. In the wing with the pilgrims and hermits, on the other hand, the pious procession seems to be advancing towards the foreground out of the darkness of the forest, and a more spatially logical connection to obtain between actors and locality. A move might be made here to answer the oft-posed question—Hubert or Jan; it has in fact been broached and the centre panel imputed to the elder brother, the wings to the younger. This solution of the ancient problem is not, however, very satisfying.

The reorganization of the panel picture whereby cubic reality was given to the figures and light and air to space, was already afoot in manuscript illuminations. The supposition, confirmed by the discovery of the Turin-Milan

Book of Hours which originated before 1417, that Jan van Eyck graduated from book-miniatures, makes the Master's attainments seem less miraculous. In book-miniatures dating from about 1400 buildings are occasionally found which, set obliquely and at an angle to the plane of the picture, pave the way for the illusion of spatial depth. Some of the pages of the Turin-Milan Book of Hours contain landscape views that are foxingly close to nature. The step from manuscript illumination to the altar-picture (the latter rests on quite another tradition) was the historically decisive act and called for that innovation in painting technique which was hailed as the *invention* of oil-painting, and recorded as such. The discoverer was honoured, by the pragmatists, as an inventor.

Jan van Eyck was too far advanced for contemporaries and pupils to follow him. He certainly raised the level of Netherlands painting, and his successors learnt what there was to be learnt, above all to avail themselves of the new painting technique; but the boldness and frankness of Jan's visual attack remained inimitable. Though the territory won by van Eyck was not given up, love of nature and thirst for space still continuing to be driving forces with the Netherlanders, his example was thrust into the background about the middle of the fifteenth century by that of Rogier van der Weyden. The Master of Tournai decided the fate of Netherlands art, particularly in the southern provinces. His work, more that of the draughtsman than the painter, was easier to grasp and easier to imitate than van Eyck's. His strong religious sense effected a shift in pictorial expression, amassing it in the movements and heads of the holy men and women and diverting the spectator's regard away from the setting, the stage of landscape. One can discern in Rogier's sternly plastic approach a reaction against the relaxing, enriching, worldly influence of van Eyck.

This contrast between hard, harsh spirituality and happy sensuousness has often been described, so long as only those works which Rogier did after 1440 were compared with Jan van Eyck. But the Master of Tournai was already 40 years old in 1440. His youth, his early period are shrouded in darkness. Recently some savants, first among them Firmerich-Richartz and then E. Renders, have dispatched the so-called Master of Flémalle and annexed the work that was collected under his name, to that of Rogier. According to their opinion, which has of course met with violent resistance, Rogier began with pictures which were erroneously attributed to his nameless contemporary or predecessor. I will not expound the arguments which substantiate this fusion, and would allude to my exposition of the controversy in the fourteenth volume of my *Altniederländische Malerei*.

As far as landscape is concerned the productions of the so-called Master of Flémalle, one or two of them in particular, are quite distinct from those of Rogier, who must have altered considerably if he really was the author of both sets of works.

At any rate the paintings of the Master of Flémalle were done between 1425 and 1438, hence contemporaneously with van Eyck's. There is no lack of grounds for the assumption that they were done in Bruges, hence where Jan van Eyck was resident. The primitiveness in the disposition of landscape space, the faulty perspective, the very high horizon, all are in keeping with this time-level. Surprising effects of light, stunning illusion of material, still-lifelike details, *genre* themes, figures that turn their backs on us, are more reminiscent of Jan van Eyck than of Rogier. The identification of the Master of Flémalle

4. ROGIER VAN DER WEIDEN, THE STAR APPEARS TO THE MAGI. DETAIL
Berlin, Kaiser Friedrich Museum
(*p. 31*)

with Rogier is only possible on the assumption that the Master who was born in Tournai came to Bruges quite early on and was so crucially affected by Jan van Eyck that he only developed his personal style much later. It would be necessary to indicate the gradual changes in the chronological sequence of the works, and this can be done successfully up to a point.

In his mature and generally accepted works Rogier organizes his attainments surely and self-confidently, building rather than looking. He subjects the world of appearances to a spiritual tyranny. Distinctness, unequivocal utterance of religious doctrine, zealous sermonizing: to these purposes bright daylight, diffused radiance and positive, cool local colours are subservient. The landscape contributes little to his pictorial expression. Other Netherlanders have exerted themselves in one way or another, with more or less success, for a harmony of stage and actors, but he seems to give up the struggle in the consciousness of being able to say what he has to say in the ascetically emaciated figures, their movements and heads. Everything stands there with extreme urgency before our eyes, bare, almost naked, unenveloped in any atmosphere (Pl. 4).

Dirk Bouts came from Haarlem, but settled in Löwen and became the leading Master there. The change of place did something to fix the character of his art. He came to Löwen about 1440, at a time when Rogier's style was in the ascendant, and his modest and humble nature could not escape the compulsion that emanated from Brussels. No less church-minded than Rogier, more a mild curate of souls than a disputatious priest, he fell short of the Master of Tournai in monumentality and dramatic energy. His creations make their appearance with a sort of worried air, stiff and uncomfortable, with despondent little gestures. Prone by nature (as a Dutchman) to contemplativeness and quietude of soul, he was forced by his commissions to depict gruesome executions, and he did his job loyally if with a certain pedantry. His martyrdoms are more like surgical operations. If Rogier preaches stridently and vociferously, Dirk Bouts' pictures sound like mournful dirges. And the connection with melody comes from the colouring, which despite glowing local colours gives the picture as a whole a warm harmony and blending of the parts. A passionate feeling for nature and the natural life is apparent in his foregrounds, in the little strips of earth on which he lavishes his sympathy, executing, with loving patience and the observation of a naturalist, the turf, plants, a spring, a snail that leaves an iridescent trail of slime behind it on the brickwork. The localities where the saints dwell he thinks of as a kind of fairyland, where the brook has washed precious stones to the shore. The middle distance causes him embarrassment, presents itself as an empty wall-surface to which the figures stick. This embarrassment, everywhere prevalent at his time-level, is the more acute for him since he observes the human body with anatomical exactitude and lends it the illusion of being cubic, which demands aerial perspective. Up above, on the horizon, he imparts powerful moods to the landscape views and, wherever opportunity offers, gives expression to the weather, time of day, twilight and darkness of night. Nature is the source of his richness; unlike the Master of figure composition, the creator of types, Rogier van der Weyden, he is never threatened with stiffness and anaemia (Pl. 5).

Landscape runs underneath and at the sides, framing the centre, which is the place for the holy figures and happenings. The figures themselves, seen from a normal height

5. DIERICK BOUTS, ST. JOHN THE BAPTIST. DETAIL
Munich, Pinakothek

and stiffly erect, do not seem to be embedded in the bird's-eye view of the landscape. Even so Bouts, with his colour technique, welds the heterogeneous pictorial elements more firmly together than any of his contemporaries. In the *St. Christopher* panel of the Munich triptych, the so-called *Pearl of Brabant*, where the relatively small size excited the Master's courage and enterprise, the water runs from the bottom of the picture right up to the high horizon. The glittering liquid surface, lit by the evening sun and fading away into the distance in tone and colour, and the diminishing wavelets, evoke the impression of uninterrupted regression in space, while in those places where, inevitably, the connection between foreground and background is laboriously established by means of undulating terrain, there seems to be a stoppage in the spatial flow. Bouts' technique—and he was the first, so far as I can see, to make use of it—for creating the illusion of continuity in space was frequently employed in after-times. He himself painted his *Christ and the Baptist* (now in the possession of Prince Rupert of Bavaria) in much the same way as the *St. Christopher*. Here, of course, he could not set the rocky banks of the river under the same angle of vision as the surface of the water, which was seen from above.

Bouts has single trees jutting up over the horizon, their thin trunks standing out against the expanse of sky. A smooth, fairly light-toned wall on top of the dark strip at the lower edge of the picture forms the background for the figures, which are often joined to the scene by strong cast-shadows. Roads wind luminously into distance, which is generally twilit. The sky is not infrequently overcast.

After and next to Jan van Eyck, Bouts, of all the Netherlanders of the fifteenth century, is the discoverer and conqueror of the landscape world. Delightedly he crowds the pictorial wealth of vegetable forms into the narrow compass of the picture. He lights up the painting as a whole according to the position of the sun and the formation of the clouds; he observes reflections as well as cast-shadows. Although in proportion to the figures landscape is not, quantitatively speaking, strikingly prominent, the special creativity of this Master was recognized quite early on: the chronicler Molanus lauds him as *the* portrayer of landscape. Petrus Cristus, who was active in Bruges at the same time as Bouts in Löwen, is justly accounted a loyal follower, a pupil in the proper sense of the word, of Jan van Eyck. As the moon from the sun he takes his light from his predecessor. Diligent and thoughtful, he was able to advance beyond Jan van Eyck in his knowledge of the laws of perspective, and his knowledge came in particularly useful in the correct construction of interiors. It was not so easy to master landscape space with rule and measure. But even in his *Madonna with the Carthusian*, which I hold to be one of the Master's early works and in which van Eyck's form-language appears, albeit much impoverished, Cristus has gone beyond his predecessor as far as perspectival construction is concerned. The horizon comes down relatively low, and the view into the inside of the town falls from above, in accordance with space-logic.

In his early period an imitator of van Eyck, he seems later to have taken Bouts for a model. His landscape backgrounds, scant and lacking in profusion by comparison, are held together by a deep tone, profiling themselves against the sky in mainly horizontal lines. Trees, often like broomsticks stuck into the earth, jut up. He does rocks in the same way as van Eyck, and low hummocks with rotund masses of foliage like Bouts.

Rogier van der Weyden died in 1464, Bouts in 1475 and Petrus Cristus about the same time. The representatives of the next generation that began about 1465 are Hugo van der Goes in Ghent and Memling in Bruges. They have little in common, and nothing in common deriving from extraction and temperament. What nevertheless strikes one as common to both is the contrast they present to the first generation. They burst open no doors like their predecessors, they no longer astonish and are themselves astonished when they break through the canvas. They lack the naïvc curiosity, the wondering regard for nature, the urge to seize hold of anything and everything in the world of appearances and lock it up in their pictures, including the still-lifelike details which often obtrude to the detriment of the painting as a whole. The fields won by their fathers have become a secure possession, firm ground whereon van der Goes erects formidablc buildings and Memling comports himself peaceably and thriftily.

Van der Goes is not so time-bound as Memling. I shall never forget how an eminent connoisseur, when I showed him the Monforte Altar that had just arrived in Berlin, declared that this was undoubtedly a product of the sixteenth century and could therefore not stem from van der Goes. Affected, it would seem, by the Italian Renaissance, so that there is some vague conjecture of a journey to the south, the Ghentsman strains after monumentality, the grandeur of prideful human bodies, and his imagination is so set upon psychological expression that little—progressively less and less—feeling is left for local values. A fanatic of the human and the psychological, this Master seeks no opportunities to introduce landscape. But where the theme demands landscape his superiority, independence and advancedness prove equal to the task.

In the painting of *The Fall* in Vienna, where Paradise, the green, summery, happy home of the first human pair is an essential part of the story, the countryside is closer, denser in its effect than in Bouts' painting. It rises gently, luxuriantly, and spatial depth results without seeming to be visibly sought after, by way of labyrinthine paths and the criss-crossing outlines of hills. The dwindling perspective of foliage enables the Master to give free space to the standing figures, and the discord between them and the terrain seems almost completely overcome. No bird's-eye view is attempted, the vista being shut off in the middle distance. In his understanding of plant-growth he is not behind Bouts, and this gives him the advantage of avoiding all excess and subordinating detail to the total effect. Although it has aroused loud contradiction I still consider the Vienna picture a relatively early work of the Master's. Since van der Goes, in contrast to Bouts, prefers cool tones his atmosphere is coloristically nearer to nature than the latter's (Pl. 6).

Hans Memling was not a Netherlander by extraction. Born in the central Rhineland he may, about 1460 in Rogier's workshop at Brussels, have picked on what he was by personal and racial inclination equipped to assimilate. He then settled down in Bruges, was successful, meeting the demands and needs of one of the most satiated of societies with his mild, moderate and optimistic approach. The heroic age had come to an end with the fall of Charles the Bold in 1477. Memling's patrons included Italian merchants. Nothing is more characteristic of his balanced nature than the fact that van Eyck, whose heir Petrus Cristus was still alive, failed to make any impression on him and could not turn him from his straight and smooth path. The art of van Eyck may have struck him as hostile, unapproachable, perhaps terrify-

6. HUGO VAN DER GOES, THE FALL OF MAN
Vienna, State Gallery

7. MEMLING, PORTRAIT
Florence, Corsini Gallery

ing. With a rooted sense for shapeliness and charm he took far less from individuals and from nature than did his Flemish and Dutch contemporaries. He was the first among the early Netherlands Masters whose work appealed to the soft-hearted tastes of the first half of the nineteenth century (Pl. 7).

His frugal fastidiousness, his aversion to everything wild, crude, violent and elemental persists in his landscapes. Countrysides cultivated like gardens, uniformly serene in mood, are fitted into his portraits, and the sitters come out like the inhabitants of some blessed earth, at peace with their surroundings. The wide open spaces, everything heroic, has dwindled to the narrow and idyllic. The land lies basking in the height of the season; it is always high noon. Van Eyck and Rogier van der Weyden, using a neutral, generally black background in their portraits, concentrate attention on the face. Bouts on one occasion —1462—allowed a little landscape to peep through alongside the head—in the picture in the London National Gallery. Memling amplifies and loosens the portrait's statement by making room for a vista of landscape on either side of the head, and this with some regularity. The sky, setting off the bust, pales towards the horizon which lies fairly low down, just above the sitter's shoulders. Far from thirst for space or even love of nature driving the Bruges Master to this elaboration of the portrait, it was his desire to make the whole surface of the picture a luminous harmony, and uniform lightness is secured by the head appearing to be modelled with very little shading, as though in the open or a light interior. The country with its well-kept paths, pools, swans and riders surrounds the sitter with an air of friendliness and sociability. He is conceived as if standing in the midst of life, not lifted out of it and isolated like a monument.

The sculptor, I've read somewhere, does honour to the hero, the saint or the ruler by placing him in the void. The painter who has emancipated himself from the stylistic laws of sculpture in developing place and environment, sacrifices something for his gain. In Memling's portraits attention is drawn away from the individual personality and is dissipated over the countryside.

In his altar-pieces and devotional pictures Memling models the terrain thoughtfully, but always as a means to an end. Whatever local values belong to the flow of the epic are represented, but nothing else. No lingering over details of vegetation, little interest in natural life or landscape for its own sake. In the *St. Ursula* reliquary the landscape and topographical elements are all part of the story of travel and adventure and are elaborated with loving precision.

Gerard David entered the Bruges Guild of Painters in 1484, at a time when Memling held the field. After Memling's death in 1494 Gerard decided unquestioned —and far into the sixteenth century (he did not die until 1523 in Bruges)—the fate of art-production in that city. With these dates before his eyes, the historian may easily fall a victim to the error of seeing in David the heir and successor to Memling. In reality there is astonishingly little connection between the two Masters. David was born in Oudewater near Gouda, probably towards 1460. Where he received his training and may have been active before coming to Bruges is shrouded in darkness for us. But his art states sufficiently clearly that by disposition and temperament he was a Dutchman, who, in his new home, the sumptuous commercial city, sharpened his sense of dignified good-living. A delicate feeling for beauty is the sole thing he has in common with Memling, whom he falls short of as a story-teller and leaves far behind in the convincing life-likeness of his well-rounded massive figures. His inability to set dramatic action going, and his intensity of feeling, remind one of Dirk Bouts, who came from Haarlem; so that these qualities may be regarded as a peculiarly Dutch legacy.

Even if van Mander had not taught us that it was in Haarlem that landscape-painting first began to bloom, love of nature and sense for space would have been expected of the Dutch-born Master, as his artistic *forte.* And this anticipation is fully confirmed. David's men and women, three-dimensional in themselves, both demanding and creating depth, do not stick to slopes of hills but stand and sit surrounded by air. In his early pictures the horizon is still fairly high, and an overall survey of richly finished backgrounds is presented. But more and more he lowers the line of the horizon and works up the landscape in the middle distance, thickset with dark walls of foliage. Fortunately, he knows how to avoid spatial conflict between landscape and the human figures standing in the foreground. The wooded countryside grows ever bigger, simpler, emptier of detail and attuned to the religious solemnity of the theme. Just how far advanced Gerard David is can be learnt most forcibly from a comparison of his triptych, *The Baptism of Christ*, with Bouts' *St. Christopher*. As there the saint, so here the Saviour stands up to his knees in the water. The advance in space-logic, in fusion of the pictorial elements is astonishing. David's altar-piece was done at the beginning of the sixteenth century, and we can feel that the author is not behind the times. A master of composition so long as he is controlling masses at rest, he frames the centre panel with side-borders of trees, which, with their smooth, column-like trunks, are cut off at the top and send out pointed shoots from the dark clumps of foliage left and right into the empty sky. Wooded darkness over all, with the naked body of the Saviour rising up, dominant. To the left, in front, the angel, to the right the Baptist, but a little deeper in, and between them Christ. The main figure-group is set slightly athwart the plane of the picture. The wood acts as an enclosing interior, and the thrusting trees are, as terms of the composition, of a value equal to that of the human figures. The landscape is no longer read or spelt out: it rings as a whole (Pl. 9, 10).

After noting, in this discussion of Bouts and Gerard David, what the influx from the east produced in the west, we turn with tense expectance to the Masters who remained active in the east, especially the Haarlem painters van Ouwater and Geertgen tot Sint Jans. As to van Ouwater, who was active about 1460, he is praised by van Mander as a master of landscape. We cannot, however, arrive at any view that would corroborate this praise since the only painting of Ouwater's to be preserved, the *Raising of Lazarus* in Berlin, contains no trace of landscape. The incident has been moved to a chapel. This Master made no use of the opportunity to develop the landscape element which the theme offered. But Geertgen certainly did so in his treatment of the same theme—the painting that is preserved in the Louvre. This Master, who was active about 1480 and died young, is, with a series of pictures rightly attributed to him, to our limited knowledge almost the sole representative of Haarlem art during the fifteenth century (Pl. 8). Geertgen's figures are three-dimensional like those of his contemporary David, but not so rounded, more stereometric, built up of planes colliding at all angles. Strongly lighted, they throw cast-shadows. Heavy and massive, standing, sitting or kneeling they all require a flat ground

8. GEERTGEN TOT SINT JANS, ST. JOHN THE BAPTIST
Berlin, Kaiser Friedrich Museum

9. DIERICK BOUTS, ST. CHRISTOPHER. DETAIL
Munich, Pinakothek
(*p. 40*)

at right-angles to the canvas, capable of bearing their weight. In his authenticated masterpiece, the two wings in Vienna, this requirement is met. A stage of some depth in the foreground, a sufficient area for the actors to develop their three-dimensional reality undisturbed. Rising country in the middle distance. The Master cannot dispense with the upper zone of the picture as the place for side-scenes. The horizon lies close to the picture's edge, on top. In the picture of the '*Burning of the Bones of the Baptist*', Geertgen was faced with the tricky problem of fitting several events separated from one another in time, into the picture as scenes separated from one another in space. Such a spatial epic—if the expression be allowed—clashed with the Master's enlightened and advanced view of nature. Four episodes: in front, gravitating to the right, the bloodthirsty Julian with his henchmen and the Burning he has commanded; then, to the left in the middle distance, the Johannines standing by the sarcophagus of the Baptist, taking the holy bones into their keeping; further back, and again to the right, the reception of the relics; and finally, top left, the Saint's interment. The first scene in time appears as the last scene in space. It was easy to manage the separation of the groups by grading the scale of the figures, more difficult to wrest the four theatres of action from the hummocky terrain without impairing the unity of the picture. As the groups are posed alternately left and right the eye is led zig-zagging into the distance. The Master has faced the difficulties with coolness and sound judgment. But the stress and strain of the disposition is still perceptible. More clearly than anywhere else one can see here how the demands which the fifteenth century made of narrative obstructed the natural relationship between the landscape elements already being aimed at, and it is a good guess that chains fell away when landscape freed itself from the devotional picture.

Geertgen's *Raising of Lazarus* in the Louvre displays a less mature spatial outlook compared with the Vienna paintings. The foreground does not have the effect of a horizontal support for the figures. I think it may be concluded from this that the Paris picture is relatively early.

The task set in the Berlin painting of the Baptist—a single figure surrounded by greenery, a theme that licensed and necessitated peace of body coupled with deep expressiveness of soul (a theme, therefore, very welcome to the Dutchman)—is happily solved. Here the sward is not an artificially constructed stage, rather, as a vehicle for the content of the picture, it is of equal value to the figure of the Baptist and contrasts with it significantly. One is tempted to declaim: all's well with the world, and only man is vile! Formally and coloristically the following elements face and complement one another: the saint sunk in thought and sorrow, humped into a triangle, in a cool brown and grey-blue robe, not enthroned but simply seated to one side, and, to the other, a warm, soft, radiantly sparkling slope of meadowland. The old enmity between man and his surroundings has been pregnantly and dramatically exploited, as nowhere else in the fifteenth century. The whole thing seen from one angle of vision. The country rises gently, rounding off at the back in the middle distance, viewed just a shade from above, and the eye seems to fall just a shade from above on the Baptist as well. The zig-zagging line of a brook draws the eye unviolently into the distance.

To find the right place in space and time for Hieronymus Bosch in our historical exposition is a matter of considerable difficulty. This Master resists classification. He died in 1516 and, judging by one portrait, at a good age.

10. GERARD DAVID, BAPTISM OF CHRIST
Bruges Museum
(*p. 40*)

Assuming that he was born about 1450, he was of the same age as Gerard David and a little older than Geertgen. He does not fit at all into the society of his contemporaries. It remains doubtful whether we ought to regard Geertgen who came from Haarlem and David who came from the vicinity of Gouda, as his countrymen in the narrower sense. His native town, 's Hertogenbosch, belongs today to the kingdom of the Netherlands, but lies, as the capital of North Brabant, outside Holland proper. Writers like to contrast the 'Dutchman' Bosch with the 'Fleming' Brueghel. Yet Breda is as little in Flanders as 's Hertogenbosch is in Holland.

Bosch is distinct from all his contemporaries and predecessors in temperament, the ease and speed with which he worked and also the cast of his imagination. Compared with him they are all patient observers and—a little—still-life painters. He is creative, independent of visible data, past-master of his own vision and gifted besides with an astonishingly true visual memory. He seems to lag behind in one respect and forge ahead in another. That his art points into the future can be seen from the fact that it enjoyed a sort of revival about 1550, since at this time second-rate painters were aping the 'What' rather than the 'How' of his work, and the great Brueghel followed him.

The landscape in his pictures, which are in the main higher than they are broad, appears as an empty wall, expressive despite its emptiness. The scant illusion of depth in his wilderness-like expanses is not felt as a defect or awkwardness, because the loosely grouped, relatively small figures have too little weight and reality for them to require a natural *Lebensraum*. The harmony of the whole is assured because, despite his archaic construction, the flat and insubstantial beings in human form—mostly spirits, spooks, demons or ascetics—correspond to the unreality of the scene, fit in with it. One is aware of no need on the part of the Master to break through the panel, or cover it up.

The land and its inhabitants are galvanized by a demoniacal fantasy. Unfruitful, with parched, thorny shrubs, monochromatic, ochreous, the wilderness (seen from above) stretches out, so weird and creepy that nothing that looms up in the way of beasts and monsters or preposterous edifices can possibly astonish us. The unity—sure sign of originality—extends also to his form-language which, precipitate, aggressive and curt, is absolutely in keeping with the world of his thoughts (Pl. 11).

Bosch's creatures move with agility. It is precisely this knack of expressing movement which is lacking with most of the Netherlanders, particularly the Dutch. With Bosch the contrast between the quiescent earth and the fluid action of the inhabitants, the haste, the frenzy of attack and flight dominates the whole picture in complementary relationship, not to be met with anywhere else in the fifteenth century and only in Pieter Brueghel in the sixteenth.

In spite of his antiquated treatment of space Bosch is one of the pioneers of landscape-painting, because his imagination spawns not only demons and monstrosities but a home suited to such creatures, a homeland that strikes a personal, inimitable note no less strongly than the figures of its denizens. For Bosch, man is not a devout child of God, rather the victim and plaything of demoniac powers which reign on earth.

If the lower half, often as much as three-quarters, of the picture is developed preponderantly as relief for the silhouette-like figures (mostly in side-view), at the top, on the horizon, there is unfolded a landscape zone in

11. H. BOSCH, ST. HIERONYMUS PRAYING
Ghent Museum

aerial tones, with mountains, streams and buildings. Tongues of land beckon from the distance like a peaceful shore free of fiends, human madness and misery.
Among the Dutchmen we ought also to count the Master whom the experts have saddled with the name of 'Master of the Virgo inter Virgines'. He was active either in Gouda or Delft between 1470 and 1490, in provincial seclusion. He was less subject to the forces prevailing in the south, in Bruges, Brussels and Ghent, than was Geertgen, as little in fact as Bosch, with whom he has one or two things in common. Having but slight knowledge of bodily form he imbues his creations with fanatical gloom. The tormentors in the scenes of the Passion look scarccly less despondent and woebegone than the tormented and the mourners. This monotonous emotionalism, which makes an unmistakable impression and gives his pictures an ascetic, pathological character, has its counterpart in the landscape, rising up like a wall behind the figures, and the bare tristness of it seems attuned to the stunted, dwarfish human beings. Not rock so much as heaps of sand, clumps of foliage muzzily drawn. His eye takes in only a modicum of the visible forms of nature, and the Master manages his modest estate with circumspection. He makes far less rigid demands of verisimilitude than Geertgen, and his narrow and honest mind knows nothing of the bold, irresistible flow of Bosch's invention. The lack of depth, conforming to the vision in Bosch's works, has the effect here of childish, not to say uncultured primitiveness. Little has been preserved for us of Dutch art during the fifteenth century. We can feel rather than prove that less stylistic compulsion, less conventionality but, instead, more frank originality were at work here than in Bruges, Brussels and Antwerp.

III

THE EMANCIPATION OF LANDSCAPE IN THE SIXTEENTH CENTURY

Interest in landscape-painting fell off during the first half of the sixteenth century. This statement could be violently disputed and proofs adduced that it was just at this time that the genus 'Landscape' was born. The contradiction solves itself. While on the one hand landscape was painted for the sake of landscape, on the other the leading Masters grew estranged from natural scenery, feeling the claims of other and, as they believed, higher tasks. Their conscious striving after form-ideals, with their eyes on Italy, was inimical to the observation of such lawless objects as the formation of earth and the growth of trees. Remember what painters were lording it in Antwerp, the cultural centre of the Netherlands at that time: they are of little significance in our context. Quentin Massys was active in Antwerp between 1491 and 1530, Jan Gossaert came from somewhere in 1503, perhaps from Bruges, to Antwerp, Pieter Coeck van Alost was a Master there in 1527. In Löwen Massys, influenced by Dirk Bouts, kept his interest in landscape at least in his early period—an interest which was later, in Antwerp, to diminish—in this, but only in this, resembling Dürer. Gossaert prefers the mathematical to the irrational, crowding his backgrounds with buildings. In Brussels, where B. van Orley set the tone between 1512 and 1540, things are no different. And even in Holland, where the pretentious art of van Heemskerck gained currency about 1540, understanding and love of natural life were obviously on the wane.

Landscape-painting extricated itself from the altar-piece and stood on its own feet, but was distinct from fine art. Specialization supervened. Nothing characterizes the new state of affairs better than the relationship between Quentin Massys and Joachim Patinir. When Patinir came to Antwerp in 1515 Massys was in high regard there, even though a daring and pushful younger generation may have felt the stolid austerity of his technique as old-fashioned and his sensibility as unmanly and sentimental. Patinir stuck to him, saw in him the supreme creator of figures. The two men fitted in with and complemented one another. Patinir's superiority in the field of landscape was acknowledged by Massys without envy. Sometimes they collaborated. Collaboration, becoming more and more customary, particularly in Antwerp, is a notable sign of specialization. In one instance at least collaboration between the two Masters is actually authenticated—by a note in an old inventory; namely, the painting of *The Temptation of St. Anthony*, now in the Prado in Madrid. According to van Mander, Joos van Cleve, who became a Master in Antwerp in 1511, collaborated with Patinir on a Madonna. Analysed for style, one of the paintings in the Louvre—the Madonna with St. Dominicus—might confirm that statement.

For Massys figure-composition, the modelling of the human form, the expression of feeling in the movements and the heads, was the one thing worthy of ambitious effort; the landscape background was so much trimming, of lesser importance. Collaboration inside the studio was usual, and the landscape element could safely be left to assistants—in Quentin's case possibly to his son Cornelis (Pl. 12).

Proud of his superiority in landscape, Patinir was not afraid to confess his weakness in figures by clutching timidly at Quentin for a model, or asking Dürer to give him a drawing with figures of St. Christopher, so as to use it as a model for incidental figures in his own pictures. When Dürer speaks of Patinir as 'the good landscape-painter', when Patinir is honoured in the literature of art as the founder of a whole class of paintings, it must be said by way of limitation that this Master, with but few exceptions, did not paint pure landscapes at all but religious pictures. It cannot even be said that his figures are uniformly small and incidental in relation to the surface of the panel. His achievement consists in the fact that the effect of the picture proceeds more from the landscape than from the figures. If we compare Patinir's *Baptism of Christ* in Vienna with Gerard David's *Baptism of Christ*, the centre-panel of the Bruges altar-piece, we are amazed at how little these compositions differ from one another—far less than we might expect. And yet, at a remove from the pictures, David's human figures live on in the memory through the noble symmetry and restful solemnity of their aspect, while in Patinir's work it is the expanse of water and the towering, rugged, naked rock that remains. The figures in this picture are fairly large and done carefully in the Massys style, but the landscape, symbolizing the religious import of the event, drowns their languid accents in its heroic harmony (Pl. 10, 13).

By disposition Patinir is no pioneer, rather a legatee prudently administering the inheritance that has come down to him. He is no genius who drives development forward, and he limited rather than created the category of landscape. If he still enjoys high renown he owes title, prestige and influence chiefly to the fact that he understood the demands of his age. The curious pronouncement of the Spaniard Felippo Guevara, who rates Jan van Eyck, Rogier van der Weyden and Patinir as the

12. QUENTIN MASSYS, THE LAMENTATION OF CHRIST. DETAIL
Antwerp, Museum
(*p.* 47)

13. PATINIR, THE BAPTISM OF CHRIST
Vienna, State Gallery
(*p. 48*)

three greatest painters, corroborates the deep impression Patinir's work left behind it.

Historians pay all too little attention to the requirements and demands of the art-lovers on whose taste production to a large extent is, and still more so was, dependent. A painter in the sixteenth century might set loving eyes on a narrow strip of native soil, might even have guessed the pictorial worth of his vision. But unless and until his patrons, the purchasers of pictures, shared his passion the thought of realizing the vision never entered his head. He lived on the fruit of his labours. This is not the case to the same extent today. Consequently too little heed is given to that dependence of artistic production. Dürer was far ahead of his time with his landscape aquarelles. But as understanding and response were lacking, these immediate impressions of nature were without significance in the historical context and remained ineffectual.

In the fifteenth century the form and content of a picture were determined by Princes, by the Church, by ecclesiastical guilds and some wealthy merchants. Generally speaking, there was a commission with a binding programme which prescribed size and subject and put limits on creative freedom. In order to characterize the change that gradually took place in the sixteenth century we employ the disdainful, commercial-sounding terms 'producers' and 'consumers'. A new society was taking shape, above all in Antwerp. A perusal of Dürer's diary offers a colourful picture, a conspectus of the circle of consumers. Busy men who had got around a good deal, South-German merchants, Portuguese, court-officials were all eager to obtain samples of this superior Netherland art. A glance at the Guild lists for the city of Antwerp tells us that painters streamed thither from all quarters of the

Netherlands, and particularly from Holland, to enjoy the benefits of the increased demand. No longer was the rigidly circumscribed commission of some individual taken for granted; the deciding factor was rather the general trend of taste. A market came into being. The Master ceased to wait on an order, he worked on his own impulses, naturally enough with one eye to probable success. He did not have to satisfy definite formulae so much as fall in with inclinations and desires which, in that cosmopolitan society, were multifarious. The social upheavals had altered the economic position of the producer, and also the artistic form and content. It increased specialization. Many Masters limited themselves more and more to a definite sphere—one which, in keeping with their disposition and ability, gave them the prospect of asserting themselves on the market. They made their personal manner known and put it on view. This loosening of the producer-consumer relationship had its advantages and disadvantages. To begin with, it resulted in more freedom for the artist since, in his choice of themes, motifs and pictorial form, he could follow his own instinct, his individual outlook. Earlier, the patron had said: 'I want it like this'; now the painter asked: 'Does this meet predilections which are sufficiently numerous?' Thus Patinir, conscious of his strength as well as of his weakness, could develop the type of the landscape-picture after having ascertained that there was a desire for and an understanding appreciation of his novel talents in the much enlarged circle of art-lovers. Of course, what benefited the men of stronger talent was fatal to the weaker. Subservience and the exigencies of artisanship might constrict, but they also gave support; and, left in freedom, the painter was in danger of becoming a manufacturer. In Antwerp most of all, the city with the widest market and the biggest export, mass-production of art was to become worse than anywhere else in the sixteenth century.

The predilections which Patinir fulfilled, and necessarily aroused and enhanced by fulfilling, concerned the non-ecclesiastical religious picture, which found a place not in chapels but in living-rooms. At a time when religious life was in a ferment and theological dogmas were at loggerheads, faith made itself new pictorial symbols.

So that among the worldly as well as among the pious, approval went out to pictures which, notwithstanding the sacredness of the theme, satisfied people's delight in looking. As the special merit of the young genus of painting they hailed with gratitude the circumstance that, locked in a narrow frame, it offered the eye in comfort what could otherwise be obtained only by exhausting walks or bothersome journeys. Below the threshold of consciousness the impulse stirred to love visible creation in veneration of the invisible Creator. Religion rests on the feeling of dependence. And dependence was deeply felt when contemplating the pitiably small human figure in a spacious landscape.

Patinir did altar-pieces in the traditional manner, though with a preference for—and as something peculiarly his own—religious-minded scenes in which the holy figure or biblical episode is subordinated to and embedded in the landscape. He chooses themes requiring a local atmosphere, like the Flight into Egypt, The Baptism of Christ or St. Jerome, St. Anthony and St. Christopher.

Conforming to the taste of the times his art exerted a wide influence and, gaining currency, was used as a pattern by other painters. He is easily confused with his imitators, and this impairs his prestige. All the more urgent, then, our duty to mark off his 'oeuvre' cleanly.

I give a list of pictures that are indubitably from his hand, without any attempt at completeness.

Madrid, Prado: *The Holy Family on the Flight into Egypt.*

Madrid, Prado: *The Temptation of St. Anthony* (figures by Quentin Massys).

Madrid, Prado: *St. Jerome.*

Madrid, Escurial: *St. Christopher.*

New York, Metropolitan Museum: Triptych with St. Jerome in the centre, the Baptism of Christ left, St. Anthony right; in the outer panels, in grisaille, St. Anne with the Virgin and Child, and St. Sebaldus.

Vienna, Kunsthist. Museum: *The Baptism of Christ* (signed) (Pl. 14).

Paris, Louvre: *St. Jerome* (replica in Venice, Cà d'oro).

Antwerp, Museum: *The Flight into Egypt* (signed).

Amsterdam, Rijksmuseum (Kessler Foundation): Landscape with figures.

Lugano, Rohoncz Collection: *The Madonna on the Flight into Egypt*, resting.

Lucerne, private collection, and London, private collection: Pure landscapes, companion-pieces.

In private possession in Germany: Pure landscapes, companion-pieces.

The art-lover of our day associates the landscape with a definite idea. A segment of space, immediately recorded in the open air from one point of view, is regarded as picture-worthy, all interference in the way of organization being avoided as forbidden, and nothing seeming to be left to choice save the point of view. Anybody who wants to understand and appreciate Patinir's achievement must rid himself of this idea. Observation of nature gave him building material. His organizing mind was set on the stability of the picture as a whole. His starting-point was not visual experience, but religious thinking. He manipulated rocks and trees as a figure-painter human bodies. The remarkable thing is the verisimilitude he actually attains despite his organizing intention.

He favours the broad format as the one appropriate to the landscape. The land stretches out panoramically, often with numerous horizontal features all running parallel. The Master is fond of making the horizon a geometrical straight line by continuing a smooth water-surface right up to the sky. Mountains and houses stand flush with the panel in front and on top of one another, in streaky layers, and the rising foothills criss-cross in the distance, alive with profiles.

Patinir's standpoint is still essentially that of Jan van Eyck and Bosch. His horizon lies high relatively to the perspective plane, but not excessively high relatively to the earth-mass, because the perspective plane is generally set fairly low. Since the figures in his compositions do not cover up much of the landscape, as even where they are comparatively big there is enough room on either side of them, he can devote special attention to the middle distance.

In the foreground mostly stone, the texture of which is worked up into a powerful illusion. A single tree, rooted in the front, towers above the horizon. In the middle distance: soft, rounded clumps of foliage with bright-pointed leaves contrasting with grey masses of rock. The tendency to exhaust all the possibilities of earth-formation in every picture, to display the globe in miniature, as it were, is still active. But the Master's caution, his need of static rest, leaves room for no overcrowding or muddle. Bare jutting rocks are seldom lacking. Yet the Master had no wish to shut off the background completely with them, and in most cases he used the trick of bisecting the picture's width. In the one half, precipitous crags, often brilliantly lit and stabbing the dark sky; in the other, a level plane, cultivated, populous countryside or mirror-like expanses of water. Sometimes this division is not vertical, but diagonal to the frame. So juxtaposed the unapproachable mountains seem all the more grandiose, the flat-lands all the friendlier. With such an arrangement Patinir was able to do justice to the two contradictory demands which had governed painting even in the fifteenth century: the desire to have the landscape rising up like a wall, as a background for the figures, and the other desire to spread out a bird's-eye view of spacious fields like a map. Patinir sensitively shifts the centre of gravity according to the religious theme. In the *Baptism of Christ* the unyielding, bare solemnity of towering rock dominates as a symbol of the sublime, while in *The Flight into Egypt* it is the soft, warm embrace of the vegetation as a symbol of the idyllic.

Technically, Patinir is one of the conservatives. He tries to show himself worthy of Quentin's confidence, who was a patronizing friend to him, by scrupulosity of execution. His paintings enchant with the glow of pure pigment. Will and ability are in nice accord. The harmony of his colouring rests on the cool grey of stone, the dark, warm green of foliage and the aerial blues in the distance. The gradation of colour-perspective is applied masterfully to create depth. One of Patinir's blues works for a distance of 500 yards and another for 1000.

His landscape can be taken as a synthesis of David's and Bosch's landscapes and admired as the successful marriage of elements so heterogeneous. His backgrounds in particular remind one of Bosch, his walls of foliage in the middle distance of David. Now and then he has Bosch in mind with his spasmodic attempts to bedevil the saints. His buildings, solid and credible, show a deep understanding of the architectonic. He is alert and rational compared with the 'dreamer' Bosch.

We must assume that Patinir received his training in the studio of some altar-painter, that he gradually became conscious of his gift for landscape and, by association with Massys, of his weakness in figures. The few paintings from his hand which are altogether free of religious content, of all narrative, are probably late ones. The fact that the horizon is relatively low here would also argue for this, since a low horizon is always and everywhere a sign of advanced contemplation of nature.

Patinir, with his premeditative planning mind was successfully concerned to give each picture a definitive character. To represent a segment of nature as a whole was the more or less conscious aim of landscape-painters at all times. Numerous tricks of composition served this end, such as marginal masses on both sides, accentuation of the centre, and the lowering of sky-line. A painting composed of figures will often come out like something whole, quite apart from tricks of composition. We know that three kings adore the Christ-child, know that Paris is visited by three goddesses, but we do not know whether three, four or ten trees make a clump. Not being guaranteed by the pictorial content itself, the impression of completeness must, in the landscape-picture, be wrested purely from form. The fortuitous, the fragmentary, the imperfect are of the very nature of landscape. The need to represent the segment as part of a larger whole and to evoke the impression of countryside extending laterally beyond the confines of the frame, clashes with the desire to offer something complete in itself. Now this urge wins, now that. In Patinir's case he generally waives a lateral framework to his composition, and his horizontal lines point the way beyond the edge of the picture on either side. The view is open to the left and right. But he undoubtedly uses other means to keep the visual imagination from straggling and to concentrate it on this particular bit of nature, above all by accentuating the centre, where, as though from a vertex or vertical line of division, the country sinks away.

Patinir died in 1524. The effect he had consisted chiefly in the fact that the type of picture he devised was cultivated unsparingly, that landscapes found a market in the Netherlands and far beyond its borders. Of Patinir's pupils in the stricter sense we know nothing. So far as the Guild lists for the city of Antwerp give us any information, he registered no apprentices. Van Mander describes Frans Mostaert as a pupil of Patinir, obviously incorrectly. Mostaert cannot, from all we know of him, have been of apprentice age before 1524. Probably the biographer is here, as also on another occasion, confusing Joachim Patinir with Herri Patinir, who became a Master in 1535 and is most likely none other than Herri met de Bles.

Antwerp production at the time of Patinir's death affords a rich and somewhat confused spectacle. Quentin Massys died in 1530. The place left empty by his demise was claimed by Joos van Cleve who, between 1530 and 1540, had great success in the field of altar-pieces, devotional pictures and portraits, completely satisfying the taste of the age, and by Jan van Hemessen, Marinus van Roymerswaele and Jan Massys. These painters all look to the south and are at exclusive pains, if not altogether to their own good, to show the human figure on a large scale. There was but little interest left over for landscape in the studios where fine art—or what was then considered fine art—was cultivated. It was more off the scenes, like manufacturers, with an eye to the advantages of the much-increased export trade, that the so-called 'Antwerp Mannerists' worked. I have spoken of the looser relationship between producers and consumers. In the work of the Mannerists, for whom this new liberty soon turned into licence, giving rise to frivolous, even slovenly treatment, the perils of the new situation were revealed. As regards landscape these painters are unproductive. It is as though none of them, not even Joos van Cleve, had ever looked at the country with his own eyes, but had contented himself with using the Patinir pattern more or less happily as a background for his pictures. The sole exception is the Master (whose significance has only recently been appreciated) whom we—rightly, I hope!—call Jan de Cock. Although in many respects belonging to the circle of the Mannerists, he looks at the natural life of the landscape with a personal vision, independent of Patinir and unconnected with the professional landscape-painters Lucas Gassel and Herri met de Bles, who must be regarded as the proper successors to Patinir (Pl. 14).

Granted that our hypothetical structure is valid, Jan de Cock came from Leyden, became a Master in Antwerp in 1503 under the name of 'Jan van Leien', was deacon of the Guild there in 1520 and died shortly before 1527, so that he would have been active in Antwerp as a representative of the younger generation and as a Dutchman by extraction, contemporaneously with Massys but in strict contrast to him. Stylistic classification started with a picture of St. Christopher in the collection of Professor Bissing, because an engraving after this picture (done about 1550) bears the signature 'J. Cock pictum'. A number of other paintings was also found, and an imaginative personality came to light with the author. If his

Dutch temper is sufficiently noticeable, the heatedness, shrillness and spiciness of his invention and address are more suited to Antwerp, where in the hurly-burly of competition only a loud and piercing note could be heard. In the circle of bold 'Mannerists' all obsessed with originality he appears as a genuine original. A worthy successor to Bosch, if less spiritual, more coarse and earthy, he makes his demons and devils plausible and shares with him that faculty—rare in the Netherlands—of expressing movement. A storyteller teeming with creative ideas, he turns consciously away from tradition. St. Christopher had always and everywhere been shown as a giant, bearing the Christ-child on his shoulders. Jan de Cock, in a picture now in private possession in Western Germany, has the saint striding through the water and pulling the infant after him on the skirts of his mantle as on a raft. A daring and somewhat *recherché* idea, to be sure. St. Anthony has often been portrayed pestered by devils, borne aloft in the air by monstrous beings and generally tormented. Jan de Cock does this scene most impressively, but adds several other episodes from legend: in a little known picture I came across in private possession in Holland. Here we have an elaborate biography of the saint, with the death scene at the end.

In Patinir's compositions the landscape is the primary and important thing, humans are something else. Jan de Cock on the contrary, more so even than Bosch, effects the firmest possible union of the two elements by speaking of landscape and man in the same form-language. His trees look like old men bewitched. The outlines of his figures undulate like his paths. The draperies trail on the ground like roots. The St. Christopher of the Bissing picture resembles a wave heaving itself off the water's surface. His hermits are embedded in their wooded sur-

14. JAN DE COCK, ST. CHRISTOPHER
Collection Freiherr von Fürstenberg

roundings as though by natural mimicry. Almost windowless buildings simulate bed-rock.

Unaffected by the static peace, the discreet order—the virtues of Patinir—Jan de Cock gives himself up to the urge to contrive exciting, fairy-tale landscape scenery as the setting for portentous and fantastic events from Bible or legend. The dramatic effect rests not least on vivid contrasts of light and dark. His animation of mind enables him to conceive local values in terms of the religious theme, differently in each picture, so that he never succumbs to the monotonous schematization which is the bane of the professional landscape-painter.

After Patinir's death limitation turned in fact into limitedness. The prestige and significance of the pictorial category he had founded failed to maintain its standard in the younger generation active about 1525, while quantitatively speaking the production of comparatively small, low-priced landscapes for the home and the export market was increased. A shallow rather than deep need was satisfied by Lucas Gassel, Jan van Amstel and, most assiduously of all, by Herri met de Bles. Lucas Gassel of Helmont was active in Brussels. He appears to have been born soon after 1500, since a portrait of him engraved by Bink and dated 1529 shows him as a man of about 30 years old. He died in 1560. Jan van Amstel, a Dutchman, who became a Master in Antwerp in 1528, has—erroneously, to my mind—been identified with the so-called Brunswick Monogrammist. Of him we learn through van Mander that his wife flooded the markets of Flanders and Brabant with pictures, probably modest-sized landscapes.

Herri met de Bles, who is probably identical with Herri Patinir, became a Master in Antwerp in 1535. He came from the same part of the world as Joachim Patinir, a supposed relative of his.

The extant stock of pictures gives us a view of Lucas Gassel and abundantly so in the case of de Bles, whereas Jan van Amstel remains in the dark. Cornelis Massys, too, emerges as a landscape-painter with a number of signed pictures. This painter, whose weak spot was figures, no doubt had Patinir held up to him as a model by his father. He became a Master in 1531 and did not die until after 1580.

There is no lack of signed pictures by Gassel, and others could be ascribed to him for style. Since the signed ones are also dated we have a clear view of his development, in so far as so unassuming a Master can be said to have a development. A few engravings published by H. Cock and a signed drawing, dated 1560, in the Berlin Kupferstichkabinett, complete our idea of him.

The signed pictures are in the following sequence:

1538. *Christ healing a Cripple.* Formerly in the Weber and Cremer Collections, Hamburg and Dortmund.

1539. *St. Magdalena.* Augsburg, Private Collection.

1542. *The Holy Family on the Flight into Egypt.* Amsterdam, art-trade, formerly Private Collection, Brussels.

1542. *The Baptism of Christ.* Brussels, sold 7th and 8th October, 1930, thereafter Brussels, art-trade.

1544. *A Mine.* Brussels, Museum.

1548. *Judah and Thamar.* Vienna, Kunsthist. Museum.

1550. *Noli me tangere.* Prague, Butta Collection, formerly in the Schottenstift, Vienna.

1560. Drawing, landscape with figures. Berlin, Print Room.

Since the earliest known picture was done in 1538, though Gassel must have finished his apprenticeship by about 1520, we have no certain clue as to his origins. In 1538 Patinir had been dead these 14 years, Herri met de Bles active for 3 years as a Master in Antwerp. Like Patinir,

Gassel favours horizontal features and the geometrically straight line of water on the horizon. As a rule he frames the landscape segment—at least on one side and often on both—with trees which, rooted in the foreground, rise up to the top edge of the picture. His need to secure his frontiers, so to speak, by some such means was all the more pressing because his countryside, rich in little motifs, would have the effect of slithering and crumbling away without a lateral framework. For this Master disorder seems to be an essential feature of the landscape. The numerous buildings are by no means dead straight by the plumb-line. The incidental figures, often dwarf-like, with huge heads, betray the inability which forced this Master to confine himself to landscape. This whimsical straggling approach, so much in contrast to the taut organization of Patinir, seems to have fallen in with the taste of the times about 1540. Herri met de Bles, Gassel's successful rival, has his own share in this pullulating multiplicity. Interest in such a development concerns not so much the few prominent painters as the then widespread tendency to find pleasure in this kind of talent. Every picture by Patinir arouses religious feelings or feelings akin to religious ones. In Gassel's pictures, on the other hand, the piety of the theme is nothing but a pretext, particularly as this painter builds up the landscape without the slightest regard for the emotional values of religion. His one aim is to gratify the curiosity and craving for sensation of travellers and hikers—or rather, to provide a substitute for people who neither travelled nor hiked. As an ingredient for a picture the landscape had to be rich in modulations. Mountains were especial objects of sightseeing for the inhabitants of the flat-lands, and since they were hard of access and little-known territory the painter could let himself go with a vengeance and *épater* naïve souls with beetling crags. The fortuitous element in the world of landscapc invited arbitrariness and negligence. The natural necessity behind the fortuity was not perceived and so could not spur people to track down the organic relationship. 'Natural' is what cannot be other than what it is. But the natural was not interesting, and art-lovers of those days were not offended by the interesting not being natural.

Gassel lived into a period when his manner was felt to be rather antiquated, and a modest change is noticeable in his later works. The turning to a larger and simpler style, in the manner of Italian composition, is, however, much more conspicuous in the efforts of other Masters. We know of no signed picture by Herri met de Bles. Nevertheless it would be easy to bring his 'oeuvre' together, if van Mander were correct in his assertion that this painter signed his pictures with an owl. Although this gives stylistic criticism and enquiry a welcome clue, it turns out in point of fact that Herri met de Bles was by no means regular with the insertion of his owl, and that there exist paintings by other artists in which that owl can be detected.

The oft-reiterated date of his birth—about 1480—is erroneous. His portrait, appearing in the well-known sequence of painters' portraits, shows a man of about 50 in the costume of 1550 or 1560. Accordingly, this Master can only have been born at the beginning of the sixteenth century; and the fact that he became a Master in Antwerp in 1535 under the name of Herri Patinir fits in with our dating as well as with the style of his incidental figures, which remind one now of this painter, now of that, but always of Masters active exclusively between 1530 and 1550, such as the Brunswick Monogrammist and Pieter Coeck van Alost. That Herri met de Bles is identical with Herri Patinir is confirmed by van Mander's conflicting statements. The biographer says of Frans Mostaert on one occasion that he had been a pupil of Joachim Patinir's, which is obviously wrong, then again that he had been a pupil of Herri met de Bles, which seems entirely possible. The mistake clears itself up if one Patinir, i.e. Herri, is named as his teacher. Also the false statement that Joachim became a Master not in 1515 but in 1535 is understandable owing to Joachim and Herri having the same name. Hopeless as a figure-draughtsman de Bles borrowed, copied and collaborated with others. In order to mark off his personal style we must hold strictly and exclusively to his landscapes.

Van Mander gives a detailed description of a sizeable picture which he saw at Martin Papenbroek's in Amsterdam. A merchant asleep under a tree, while monkeys pillage and scatter his wares. A picture corresponding to this description, moreover signed with the owl, is to be found in the Dresden Gallery. A Holy Family in the Museum at Basel is authenticated by a catalogue note of 1586—'Henrich Blesy Bovinatis'. The relatively large figures in this picture are obviously not the work of de Bles: they are fitted into the landscape by an academician of the time of Lambert Lombard. By the style of the figures this picture cannot have been done before 1540, hence it cannot be part of the effects of Erasmus of Rotterdam as the Basel catalogue supposes.

The number of pictures rightly attributed to this Master is great, but his 'oeuvre' cannot be surveyed without difficulty because little of it has found its way into public galleries. The bulk of it lies hid in modest private collections, or drifts to and fro in the art trade.

His horizon comes fairly low, generally about half-way down the picture. A bird's-eye view is of less concern to this Master than to his predecessors. He gives up the idea of spatial depth and covers the perspective plane in the middle distance with a thick veil. Fantastically shaped mountains sometimes jut up over the horizon. Nature is only worth painting for him to the extent that she can astonish, and he has no scruples about making her astonishing off his own bat. If Gassel spreads his motifs, de Bles crams them tightly into the picture. The outermost profile of his mountains generally runs as a diagonal into the perspective plane.

As to themes, de Bles not infrequently follows Bosch and his devil's brood, with a penchant for the curious, the bizarre, the adventurous. The conception may be daemonic or heroic, but it always appears in miniature form. Herein lies his idiosyncrasy as an artist, which won the applause of his contemporaries. Delicately, with a pointillistic technique, he dots and stipples the foliage, light against dark. His paintings are distinguished by their wet shininess and intense colouring.

At all periods finesse, microscopic execution, was a Netherlands speciality which was cultivated with virtuosity. What was taught and prized at home had the appearance abroad, especially in Italy, almost of magic. We can see from the book-illuminations of the fifteenth century right up to the time of G. Dou and Frans Mieris just how much these powers were appreciated and how appreciation increased them.

Van Mander relates that de Bles sometimes applied his owl so cunningly that it gave rise to elaborate games of hide-and-seek, and that people put bets on each other not finding it. This anecdote affords some idea of the way in which pictures were regarded, as though inviting the eye to go for a stroll.

The Masters who excited people's interest in landscape

all came from the north and east of the Netherlands, with the exception of Patinir and Herri met de Bles, whose home was in the south. Flanders proper contributed remarkably little. This being so, it is amazing that the painters who were active in Leyden, Haarlem and Amsterdam, such as Engelbrechtsen, Lucas van Leyden, Jan Mostaert, Jacob Cornelisz, Jan van Scorel, hardly ever cultivated landscape for its own sake. Not for want of the desire and the talent for it, rather for want of opportunity. In Antwerp, economic and social conditions made for the specialization of production and the creation of new categories of painting. These favourable circumstances were lacking in Holland, which was relatively poor. The wider the market the more varied the stalls. The export of paintings from Bruges to Spain, of big altar-pieces from Brussels and Antwerp to Denmark, Sweden and the Rhineland increased enormously in the first half of the sixteenth century. Even France and Italy showed themselves import-minded. In Holland the market was narrow, export but slight, and since the bourgeoisie scarcely wanted pictures for their living-rooms the painters had to fall back almost entirely on the patronage of their native churches and monasteries. A glance at Lucas van Leyden's early engravings shows that this Master's feeling for space, air and light was vigorous enough, and that originally he had all that it takes to make a landscape-painter. But he never got to the point of developing this ability, more particularly because, in his later years, he cherished Italian form-ideals to the detriment of the specifically Dutch source of his strength. It is the same with Jan van Scorel, who, with his lucent atmosphere, his aerial backgrounds, often seems to anticipate, say, Albert Cuyp, but was turned away from the contemplation of natural landscapes by his modish obsession with the heroic aspect of human bodies in full movement. All the same, his superior Dutch treatment of space is unmistakable. As to Lucas, in his early youth he got the effect of aerial perspective from his burin, and—to return to Scorel—his imagination is instinct not only with distance and spaciousness, but, in the centre panel of the Lockhorst triptych (in the Utrecht Museum) he also composes with a nice regard to the depth lying below the psychological threshold of the picture's edge. Jan Swart van Groningen must be counted among the Dutch, and even though jobs of illustration made powerful demands on his time, in one picture at least he endorses the independence and superiority of the Dutch approach to nature, namely in his *The Baptist Preaching*, now in the Pinakothek in Munich. It was most likely on his journey to Italy, among the foothills of the Alps, that he brought off a landscape impression which, in trueness to nature and sheer immediacy, far surpasses anything achieved by the professional landscape-painters of the time, such as Gassel. Accustomed as a woodcut draughtsman to express the essential in figures, he renounces sensational motifs as a setting for his pictures (Pl. 15). In the Netherlands we can, if put to it, trace the germination and efflorescence of landscape as an historical process —at least we are impelled to make the attempt. But, faced with South German art, the historian lays down his arms. In the neighbourhood of the Alps and along the Danube sudden and exciting spurts occur, yielding results which affect us like timeless utterances. Grünewald's Isenheim Altar and Dürer's landscape aquarelles stand out, exceptions of genius, above the line of historical development, but Altdorfer, W. Huber, the early Cranach and the younger Frühauf, though no dazzling pioneers, still face landscape and nature candidly, with a gaze that was

15. JAN SWART VAN GRONINGEN, ST. JOHN THE BAPTIST PREACHING
Munich, Pinakothek

16. ALTDORFER, SATYR AND HIS FAMILY
Berlin, Kaiser Friedrich Museum

circumscribed to a remarkably small degree by convention and the style of the times. Konrad Witz of Basel gives us, with his '*Miraculous Draught of Fishes*' (a panel of the Geneva Altar) done in 1444, a topographically exact view of the mountainous shore of Lac Leman. The younger Frühauf executed, about 1507 (?), in his Leopoldsaltar at Klosterneuburg, convincingly true-to-nature views of the surroundings there. W. Huber, 1510, drew a profile of the mountains at Mondsee near Salzburg. Altdorfer painted two landscapes clear of incidental figures, but turns more instinctively to etching, where he delineated pure landscapes in a series of prints. He grasped the landscape as a whole by adhering to one point of view—a position which the Netherlanders arrived at considerably later. A significant token of this difference is the horizon, which Altdorfer sets deep down, while his contemporaries in the Netherlands set it fairly high up (Pl. 16, 17).

This outburst of love of nature is confined within narrow limits of time and place, rapidly drying up when the creative naïveté of youth is killed by professional duties and mechanical routine, or withers in the bright glare of knowledge.

Compared with what was going on in South Germany—a desultory, temperamental and dramatic process—events in the Netherlands proceeded step by step, logically, in epic sequence.

Matthys Cock was the eldest son of Jan Wellensz de Cock, whose personality has, so I believe, now come to light. Born in Antwerp in 1509 and thus a contemporary of Cornelis Massys and Herri met de Bles, he must have begun work in Antwerp about 1535 but soon have betaken himself to Italy. In 1540 he registered as an apprentice in Antwerp and died young—1548. To go by van

Mander we ought to attach considerable importance to his appearance. The biographer, who sometimes talks like an art-historian, praised him as the first to have had a better conception of landscape-painting in the new Italian or antique manner. What Jan Gossaert did in van Mander's eyes for the human figure, Matthys Cock—some 25 years later—did for landscape. Whether van Mander actually knew of paintings or drawings under whose impression he assigns the Master so decisive a role, is a moot point. The purifying and strengthening effect of the Italian teachings was the ground-idea of his aesthetic doctrine. That he knew—or believed—Matthys to have been the first of the landscape-painters to have sojourned in Italy may have sufficed for him to draw the conclusion which he announces in such emphatic accents. The material at our disposal when we get down to checking van Mander's thesis with our own eyes, is unfortunately very scanty. Paintings by M. Cock are not known. We are dependent on a few drawings and etchings. The drawings are signed 'Cock', so that, as the Christian name is lacking, we cannot be certain whether they stem from Matthys or conceivably from his brother Hieronymus. Hieronymus devoted himself with energy and great success to the publishing business and, as far as he was active as a draughtsman at all, was probably influenced by Matthys. By studying the style of the drawings we can shed light on the personality of the elder brother.

The radical break which van Mander's words lead us to expect is not strikingly apparent. Before trying to decide how strongly and with what success the South influenced the interpretation, choice of themes and composition of Netherlands landscape-painting about 1540, let us ask ourselves what the High Renaissance in Italy had to offer in a field in which the superiority of the Nether-

17. CRANACH, REST ON THE FLIGHT INTO EGYPT. DETAIL
Berlin, Kaiser Friedrich Museum
(*p. 67: cf. 'On Art and Connoisseurship', Pl. 11*)

landers was acknowledged by the Italians. Marcanton took over a landscape background from one of Lucas van Leyden's engravings. Michelangelo's wrathful utterances aimed at the landscape pictures which had reached Italy from the Netherlands betrays the fact that the imported paintings met with a ready reception. At any rate a landscape-painter from the North could set foot in Italy with a certain self-confidence and not, like Jan Gossaert or Jan van Scorel, be overawed by the unapproachable grandeur of the Renaissance and crushed into servility.

Apart from Venice, interest in nature and landscape had reached its nadir in Italy about 1530. What sort of stimulus could a Netherlander who had stayed in Rome bring back in this matter of landscape? Southern vegetation, southern terrain, topographical information? Not much trace of any of this. Neither is there any evidence of direct contact with the advanced landscape-painting of Giorgione and Titian. But it may well be that the Venetian woodcut presented itself as an approachable model. The graphic arts of the North could get in touch relatively easily with those of the South. Drawings, prints and woodcuts were swift-footed go-betweens.

In the eyes of the Italians Netherlands forms were true to nature as regards detail, but petty, while in the eyes of the Netherlanders southern forms were big, but vacant. Mutual stimulation could not fail to exist when woodcuts and prints migrated northwards, painters and pictures southwards.

The landscapist who crossed the Alps about 1538 and travelled in Italy was goaded into observation in view of so alien a natural scene. Travelling opens onc's eyes under all circumstances. The Netherlander may not have found this foreign scenery quite as different, as astonishing as he had expected from hearsay or envisaged in his dreams. The crags of the high mountains were not so beetling in reality as they were in the pictures of Herri met de Bles. So that a sojourn in the south might pave the way to simplicity, objectivity and unpretentiousness, just as the breath of the Renaissance banished mediocrity and taught people to sacrifice detail for the good of the whole. These are expectations, psychological assumptions which are not corroborated to begin with, at least not altogether by the scant evidence regarding Matthys Cock. His drawings hardly differ from those of Cornelis Massys, they are rich in content, with hilly countrysides, be-mountained strands, with ships, houses, trees—'picturesque' in the same sense that the drawings of his Netherlands predecessors are picturesque. They are distinguished by a loose, mobile stroke, particularly in the foliage.

Van Mander dilates at length on the subject of landscape-painting in his didactic poem, but more as a painter or poet than as an historian. He observes: there are few Italians who paint landscape. Tintoretto, the great Titian—whose woodcuts are a lesson for us—are outstanding. One of the old Netherlands Masters, however, he ranges alongside the Italians—not Matthys Cock, but Pieter Brueghel. Tintoretto, Titian and Brueghel were not professional landscape-painters. Van Mander has picked on these names with sure instinct, even if we would like to substitute Giorgione for Tintoretto. And as a matter of fact we do owe the highest achievements in landscape to Masters who were not landscapists, e.g. Jan van Eyck, Rubens, Rembrandt. Intellectual stature was always the pre-condition of revolutionary deeds and it could seldom remain satisfied merely with contemplating the configurations of earth and vegetation. At least, a limitation of this kind is only observable with the significant figures of a more recent period.

Pieter Brueghel, born about 1525, learnt, according to van Mander, under Pieter Coeck van Alost, then worked with Hieronymus Cock before setting out for Italy in 1551 or 1552. In the service of the busy publisher he drew sketches for the engravers and was thereby led to illustration, to Hieronymus Bosch, to topography and landscape. His connection with Hieronymus Cock who, as a publisher of engravings, had to take account of the tastes and requirements of the broad masses, exercised a long-standing influence on Brueghel's production. Hieronymus Cock sensed how much he might profit by the nimble mind, acute observation and humour of his young collaborator as regards his entertaining, instructive and moralizing publications, and, as his brother Matthys died early, in 1548, he may have looked to Brueghel to make up for this loss.

Brueghel has been written about profusely in recent years, and, as usual, controversy rages. War may not be the father of all things, but it certainly makes for increased understanding. The further removed a creative personality is from the ambitious grasp of our intellect the more divergent the paths seeking access to him. In the past people saw in Brueghel nothing but a buffoon, and the old text-books of art genteelly placed him to one side. By way of reaction against such crass misunderstanding his powers as a creator are now praised to the skies, and it is emphatically proclaimed that Brueghel is a great painter and not the slightest bit an illustrator. Now, an illustrator is a draughtsman who represents the thoughts and ideas of others. Brueghel undoubtedly represented his own thoughts and ideas. But when it comes to elucidating and extolling the Master's form-language and composition as his great and distinctive merit, and running down his ideas, there is a danger of overlooking and suppressing the essentials. Finally, as Fränger[1] has most happily expounded, Brueghel has a predecessor in the South German draughtsman Hans Weiditz, who was properly an illustrator.

By a fortunate coincidence I have become acquainted with an essay by Aldous Huxley—in his book *Along the Road*—and there met with a number of propositions, as apt as they are witty, on the essential achievement of Brueghel. The essay starts off: 'Most of our mistakes are fundamentally grammatical,' and then goes on to define the concept 'painter', which covers now this profession, now that. It is superfluous, says Huxley, to excuse the Master for being 'an anthropologist and social philosopher'. I would rather say: poet of comedies and tragicomedies, a good judge of character and particularly of his own people. Curious change of roles: the English novelist takes up the standpoint of the historian, while German professors of art are at pains to measure Pieter Brueghel by the yard-stick which they apply to, say, Cézanne.

Brueghel was, as Huxley opines, a great painter, not in spite of but because of having so much to say. The urgent need to express ideas, doctrines, mockery of human folly, compassion with human suffering gave his pictures their compelling power. It is a false and futile effort to try to separate form from intellectual and spiritual content.

Controversy has also broken out as regards Brueghel's relations with Italy. People have stressed his national powers of resistance to the Italian Renaissance. Huxley puts it like this: 'Brueghel returned home from the south without the faintest tincture of Italianism'. On the other hand Fr. Lugt tries, in the pamphlet dedicated to me[2], to

[1] *Hans Weiditz und Sebastian Brant*, Leipzig, 1930, p. 58.
[2] Leipzig, 1927, p. 111 ff.

prove by subtle and erudite references that in his youth the Master stuck to Italian models so far as he took up landscape at all. If one thinks of the taste of the times, of the then conditions in Antwerp, of Pieter Coeck van Alost, the Italianizing academician with whom Brueghel is supposed to have studied, if one thinks of the young Master's bondage to Hieronymus Cock and of the model which Matthys Cock unavoidably presented, then the 'tincture' of southern art seems only too natural and the small effects of this contact, and the overcoming of it, all the more remarkable. Influence presupposes a vacuum. And in no Netherlander of about 1550 was there so little of a vacuum as in Pieter Brueghel. Perhaps he was more of a Romanist before he visited Rome than he was afterwards.

Visual experiences in the grandiose world of the Alps were the great gain of his journey, and not any impression of southern art. Putting the antithesis voiced by a witty art-historian to my own uses, I would say: 'original experience' rather than 'educational experience' was what counted. Van Mander has said the same thing drastically and is far from asserting of Brueghel, as he does of Matthys Cock, that he treated landscape in the Italian or antique manner.

From various statements we learn that the Alpine world appeared frightening and savage to the man of the sixteenth and even the seventeenth centuries. Before the construction of main roads and mountain railways the Alps threatened such dire perils to the traveller that there was little room for pleasurable sightseeing. In a painting, on the other hand, the wild, precipitous and hardly accessible world could be contemplated like a chained and conquered foe, no longer with horror, but with delicious, soul-expanding shudders. I have no doubt but that the

visual arts paved the way for the enjoyment of reality which came later and gradually educated people into lingering delightedly among the majesties of nature.
Finally, this question of whether Brueghel is, historically speaking, an end or a beginning, whether the old Netherlands art comes to a glorious end in his work or whether it contains the germs of the art of the seventeenth century. To this question, as to all wrongly put questions, there is no answer. Brueghel does not fit on to Massys or on to Patinir. Hieronymus Cock may have referred his collaborator to Bosch, perhaps also to Jan de Cock. But Brueghel's style is not inherited, it is wrested from his personal way of looking. As to his connections with the future, although a few insignificant painters do stem from him, like his son Pieter and Lucas van Valkenburg, who use his themes, the high-road of development definitely does not run in the direction indicated by him. Frans Floris, Martin de Vos, Otto van Veen, Rubens: these are the names that mark the road taken by Flemish painting, the road through the pass of Romanism. And on this road Pieter Brueghel is not to be found. Strongly rooted in his native soil and therefore a stranger to his own age, which pushed out from its homeland, he stands there isolated with what is essential in his work.
Looking at pictures and drawings we are sometimes tempted to ask where on the known earth the artist stood when he saw these things. Sometimes there is an answer to such a question, whether because an inscription comes to our help or because significant characteristics reveal the spot. In front of a picture by Patinir, Claude or many another Master the question does not arise, since the composition can be seen to be obviously invented or freely put together. Brueghel did a number of drawings on his journey in respect of which that question has been

posed and answered. His itinerary has been ascertained accordingly. He visited the south of France, Rome, Naples and Messina. In the case of other, older Masters topographically accurate impressions of South Germany can be pointed out, for instance in the Geneva Altar by Konrad Witz, in Dürer's aquarelles and in Wolf Huber's drawings as well as in the Brussels tapestries, the so-called *Hunts of the Emperor Maximilian*, which were done about 1530 and were probably the result of collaboration between B. van Orley and Willem (?) Tons. Necessarily bound up with topographical accuracy and objective reportage is a nascent sense for the demureness of nature. Topographical obligations banish the joy of piling up themes and of arbitrary 'artistic' construction. In his most mature work—the 'Seasons'—Brueghel composed freely, of course, but because his feeling for nature was deepened and clarified by immediate impressions this guaranteed the organic relationship of his free composition. We have no doubt that these mountains standing on this ground cannot be shaped differently, that these paths, these rivers run thus and not otherwise, that the vegetation in this spot at this time of the year must look precisely so.

Besides these sheerly immediate impressions there are, in Brueghel's 'oeuvre', especially in the engravings after his drawings, landscape compositions which are not markedly different in treatment from those of, say, Matthys Cock, even though they give the effect of greater credibility and inevitability. Bird's-eye views of spacious country, mountainous foreshores, high horizons. Even his original etching of 1566—the *Rabbit Hunt*—exhibits this kind of organization, and also the diagonal line with which the mountain in the middle distance stands out against the distant plain. It must always be borne in mind that

Brueghel was obliged by Hieronymus Cock the publisher to take account of convention, the taste of the age. He was not consciously a pioneer. That he ultimately did overcome convention—in his 'Seasons'—argues all the more for his genius. Yet where Brueghel applies the pattern then in vogue, accentuating the contrast between mountain and plain to powerful effect, the rock towers up like a cubic mass and curves into the picture's depth, it is not stuck on flat like a wall or a 'set', parallel to the panel. Of the three dimensions height and breadth run parallel to the picture's surface. The eye glides quietly from one link to the next, rising continually upwards. But the eye is dragged into the distance by main force, and receives a violent shock. Breadth and height work statically, depth dynamically. With lightning visual grasp Brueghel takes in movement, and this faculty helps him as a story-teller to describe human beings going about their business, working, playing, dancing, fighting, running and riding. The impulse emanating from his active nature pervades even the landscape. According to the time of the year or the day and the weather, the forces of nature determine the doings of man as they do the physiognomy of place, his joys and his sorrows, his very walk, whether he hurries, strolls or stumbles. The land is not only his home, it is also his fate, and man is more the slave of the earth than its master. Brueghel draws the countryside, which had fled out of the figure-picture and become a thing on its own, back into the figure-picture. He is not a specialist and, by breaking down the barriers between the categories of painting, he founds a new category for which there is no name. He portrays the daily round, religious and landscape subjects all in the same spirit. His narrative is genre-like, but his genre is elemental.

Brueghel views human beings from above, with humour and human sympathy; but he looks up to nature and landscape, all seriousness. The land dominates the more limitlessly in that the people on it display no dignity in the face of almighty nature, neither the spiritual majesty of the saint nor the physical majesty of the Renaissance.

His sympathetic insight into the primitive in man, into whatever is naïve, instinctual, untouched by time and change, is one of the causes why his art was able to keep—or rather, acquire—a timeless validity.

How far removed Brueghel is from the Renaissance was confirmed for me in the most striking way by the remark of a German painter who had lived for many years in Japan, and was visiting the Gallery in Vienna on his return. He assured me that the great art of the West, even Titian himself, affected him as something alien, bogus; Brueghel alone seemed familiar, honest and true to nature.

Brueghel has occasionally been dubbed an Impressionist and the fact stressed that he cannot be fitted into the historical context. This is not without meaning. Now and then, most of all in the 'Seasons', he takes in the totality of the scene and the human figures from one standpoint and at one glance, so that the figures in the foreground stand weightlessly in the landscape, poor in detail, like silhouettes. But he does not adhere to this uniform way of seeing as a conscious rule, it is not infrequently vitiated by his delight in narrative, his interest in things and his didacticism. The *Tower of Babel* in the Vienna Gallery had perforce to rear its gigantic bulk—within the limited perspective plane—far away in the distance. Regardless of this, however, the Master has observed thousands of tiny figures all busied on the building, with meticulous precision like a miniature-painter, not like an Impressionist at all (Pl. 18).

Brueghel had much—for a painter, dangerously much—to say, and since the things he speaks of are all different the means of expression are different too. Technique and form-language subserve the sense of the statement from case to case. It is easy to spot a certain chronological development going on within the relatively short space of his activity, but more important than the date of his pictures is the peculiarity of his pictorial thought. Brueghel hardly ever abides by the customs, let alone the rules, as regards formal treatment. His attitude to landscape-space and the face of the countryside is wholly dependent on the task he has set himself as a story-teller. Sometimes the horizon comes very high, so that the bird's-eye view permits a wealth of themes to be housed side by side, packed close in the primitive manner. On the other hand in the picture in the Johnson Collection, Philadelphia, albeit a copy, a flat empty plain stretches into the distance most impressively, with a shepherd fleeing towards us from the attack of a wolf.

What Brueghel perceived, stored in his visual memory and then portrayed, is the activity of the forces of nature, not the worked-upon world but the working world. He not only extended the possibilities of landscape representation, he tried to exhaust it by making the battle of the elements, atmospheric pressure, falling snow, tempest, the heaving of waves, the procession of clouds, temperature and so on visible, giving us the feel of them. The encyclopaedia of his 'Seasons' was a welcome opportunity for him to illustrate all the phenomena of atmosphere, lighting and weather in the cycling of the year.

Just as nothing terrestrial came amiss to this story-teller with his passion for instruction, so nothing human. His

Museum Boymans/van Beuningen

18. PIETER BRUEGHEL, THE TOWER OF BABEL. DETAIL
Rotterdam

delight in the senses, however, preserved him from the danger of opinionatedness. The universality of his knowledge rested on insatiable visual experience and could thus enter immediately into the world of pictures. Brueghel's *Weltanschauung*—understood not as a philosophical idea but in the literal sense of the word: 'a view of the world'—seems, in comparison with his predecessors, contemporaries and followers, really comprehensive, bounded by no convention, no reserve, no prejudice.

Brueghel entertained, delighted and instructed his contemporaries. Princes coveted his works and, bored by Court ceremonial, amused themselves by mingling in the Fairs or with the populace by way of a change. But it took almost three centuries and a half for this Master's truth to be felt as 'beauty'.

It is not to be expected of a Master who towers above the level of his age like a mountain in the flat-lands that he should have worked expeditiously on his successors. He was imitated, of course chiefly by his son Jan, but a study of the copious productions of this son tells us that what took root was principally the thematic in Brueghel, the crudely genre-like, which remained popular in coarsened form far into the seventeenth century. The wide success of the oafish copies and arbitrary variants proves what was understood in his work and what was not. Highly successful as a professional landscapist between 1590 and 1623 Jan Brueghel, just because he is the son, is regarded as a legitimate successor to Pieter Brueghel. In his tame, elegant and agreeable interpretation of landscape there is no hint of the elemental energy which his father infused into nature. About 1560 the people of the Netherlands were in a ferment of revolt against foreign overlordship, and the fight for freedom was under way. Some people think they can feel the tension of national resistance in Brueghel's work. Later, both during the struggle and after the struggle, there is not much of any heroic revival to be traced in art, just as the militant spirit of the German Reformation is apparent in Dürer's *Apocalypse* but not in the art of Cranach.

The frankness, the eloquence, the daring—not the conscious daring of a van Heemskerck but an involuntary one—the virtues to which Brueghel's creations owe their richness, their timeless validity, vanish with his death. Pusillanimity, spiritual bigotedness, specialization, a discreet marking time: these are the characteristics of Netherlands landscape-painting in the years between 1570 and 1600. Each of the artists cultivates a separate field. One or two Masters like Jacob Grimer, Cornelis van Dalem and Hans Bol are contemporaries of Brueghel, but anything we see of them—in so far as we get to see anything at all—is of a later period and was done after his death.

In more than one way the landscape-picture is now made appetizing and woos the art-lover's favour: by being adventurous and bizarre (in which respect Herri met de Bles was so successful earlier on), then by being decorative and, lastly, topographical. The adventurous element has its champion in C. van Dalem, who has found notice only very recently, and to some extent also in Gillis Mostaert. Jodocus de Momper, a relatively late arrival, about 1585, reminds one superficially of Brueghel in boldness of conception and bravura of execution. On a total survey of his uncommonly prolific output, however, there is revealed a tendency to unnatural decoration. Generally speaking, topography plays the same part in landscape-painting as portraiture in figure-composition. For the matter of that, every locality is individual and unique, and the task of making it unmistakable compels keen observation, demands and promotes an attitude of unpretentious loyalty to given facts. Jacob Grimer was often sober and unassuming as a topographer. His few known pictures, none of them in any way outstanding, contain a healthy seed and point into the future.

Exploiting Brueghel's inheritance, changing gold into copper pence, the long-lived Lucas van Valkenburg got busy about 1560.

Hans Bol of Mecheln, who like so many of his countrymen moved to Holland, is an assiduous and tasteful 'Kleinmeister'. Drawing on the old and vigorous tradition of book-illumination, he executed with uniform care a series of neatly arranged, built-up, populous landscapes in water-colours. With sure awareness of his limitations and his impeccable technique he won, as did Jan Brueghel, the approval of his contemporaries.

Gillis Coninxloo, born in Antwerp in 1544, is fêted in the most recent art-literature as a pioneer, and the praiseful sentences with which van Mander calls him to mind underline the importance, or at least the momentary effect, of his emergence. The eventful story of his life did much to spread his teaching. Scion of a multitudinous family of Brussels painters he was 25 years old when Pieter Brueghel died.

In his youth he travelled to France, became a Master in Antwerp in 1570, but left his homeland in 1585 for reasons of faith and betook himself to Frankenthal, where he founded a colony of painters whose leader he became. In the year 1595 he removed to Amsterdam and died there in 1606. An individual tale, but noteworthy as being typical of the times. Just as Dutch painters flocked to Antwerp in the first half of the sixteenth century, so in the second half there was a migration in the opposite direction. Flemish innovations were imported into Holland, not only by Coninxloo. The Frankenthal episode had significant repercussions, since several painters from the Middle Rhine settled there or thereabouts, and Elsheimer, a native of Frankfurt who had probably been inspired by the Frankenthal colony in his youth (about 1595), went to Rome. Coninxloo's interpretation of landscape won more than national recognition. That is why historians have devoted so much attention to his personality, not in itself very important.

Since Coninxloo's known pictures were all done fairly late, in the Frankenthal and Amsterdam periods, his beginnings remain in darkness. We cannot really tell where he comes in or what he took over from his predecessors, such as Matthys Cock or Gillis Mostaert. Were the older Antwerp Masters better known to us than they are, Coninxloo's prestige as a pioneer might perhaps pale somewhat. His oldest signed work, the landscape with the Judgment of Midas in the Dresden Gallery, dated 1588, stems from the beginning of the Frankenthal period.

In this picture the clean break with the past which we might have expected is not perceptible. The eye is still offered the scenic variety of a walk, there being amassed in the compass of the picture a sumptuous vision of things which, in reality, no single visual experience could possibly afford. Nobody asks where on earth this Master was standing when he saw such a vista. All parts of the composition are ranged in layers like theatrical sets, mostly parallel to the surface. The sides are strongly accentuated by dark flanking trees, truncated by the top edge of the picture. The build-up reminds one of an amphitheatre, the steps of which curve in towards a brightly-lit centre. And the scene in the foreground is reminiscent of an antique stage.

By and large we can distinguish two kinds of enjoyment

of nature: a view from above of the open country, an uncommon experience not to be won without effort, the reward of the mountaineer relishing a prospect marked with a star in Baedeker. The spectator feels himself free, lifted up, face to face with nature and outside her. The other kind of enjoyment comes from lingering in the woods, looking up at tall trees, living *in* nature. Here we feel ourselves snug and safeguarded. The tendency to one or the other kind of enjoyment predominates according to temperament and mood of the times. In the second half of the sixteenth century landscape representation turned away from wide prospects and bird's-eye views. Trees claim more and more space. It is not the single stem that rises in significant outline to the sky, but the leaves of several trees merge in a dense mat. One can no longer see the trees for the wood.

We should now expect, as the natural, obvious and comfortable task for the artist (which Altdorfer solved as early as 1520), the erection of a forest-wall in the perspective plane. And if this treatment was opted for so decidedly quite late in the Netherlands, only in Coninxloo's day, it was because the artist's delight in distances counteracted an occlusion of the view. Coninxloo often leaves a peep-hole open in the middle of the picture into the shining distance, but more and more in the course of his development he covers almost the whole surface with a warm, dark lacing of vegetation.

A Patinir interpreted foliage by light dots on a dark ground. But the thing was to build up the foliage in the foreground or middle distance meticulously, from near-to, since each individual leaf in the picture appeared a few millimetres big. Direct observation was not enough, and where it failed a teachable and learnable manner supervened for which the term 'foliage-painting' emerged. The natural form was squeezed into a formula which, passing from studio to studio, allowed painters to develop the walls of leafage schematically but with a certain degree of verisimilitude. System and doctrine propagated apace, and it was only in the nineteenth century that 'foliage-painting' came to an inglorious end. Coninxloo's forest pictures may well be the oldest to cause the fatal word 'foliage-painting' to rise to the tongue. Every Netherlands landscapist at the turn of the century who set store by miniaturesque scrupulosity arrived at some systematic manner of foliage-representation, like Jan Brueghel, R. Savery and numerous others.

Characteristic of the taste of the age met by Coninxloo's treatment is an eschewing of hard stone, a preference for a soft, luxuriant welter of vegetation. Forest-floors are not flat, not solid, rather wet and soggy. Striving away from the heroic to the romantic, from wide open spaces to homeliness, the ideal landscape assumes the character of surface decoration. Dense foliage makes a curtain which shuts out the distance and reminds one of tapestry.

Working in the same spirit as Coninxloo were the following:

Cornelis Molenaer, who became a Master in Antwerp in 1564 and died there. Not much is known of him.

Anthonie Mirou, born 1570 in Antwerp. Seems to have been active for a while in Frankenthal.

David Vinckboons, alleged to have been born in Mecheln in 1578, moved to Amsterdam and died there in 1629. He distinguishes himself mostly in figures and genre as an independent, cheerful, sometimes waggish story-teller.

Pieter Schaubroeck, born about 1570 in Frankenthal, died 1607. He seems to have been active exclusively in Germany.

Denis van Alsloot, born about 1570 in Brussels, died

about 1626. In landscape he joins on to Coninxloo, for the rest preserves a certain independence.

The landscapists active about 1600, namely Kerstiaen de Keuninck between 1580 and 1630 and Frederik van Valkenburg born 1570 in Mecheln, go in for weird and fantastic effects.

About 1600 the superiority and exemplariness of Italy in the cultural world of Europe was fully recognized, as far as aspiration went out to 'fine' art, monumentality and figure-composition. In landscape, on the other hand, the Northerners, more particularly the painters schooled in Antwerp, were, in their attitude to the South, not only taking but giving. Scarcely any Netherlander could have competed as a figure-painter with the Italians, but the landscapists of the North gained esteem and scope for influence in Rome and Venice. They seemed to fill a gap in Italian art, and the Romans may well have left a profession which they did not rate very highly, to foreigners, and without envy.

Matthys and Paul Bril, and later Elsheimer of Frankfurt, stopped in Rome; Lodewijk Toeput and Paul Fiammingo settled in Venice. A later age was to see landscape-painting coming to brilliant flower on Roman soil, in the work of Poussin and Claude, without the Italians (save, perhaps, for Annibale Caracci) having contributed anything decisive. To begin with the landscape-painters in Rome were only given jobs of decoration, such as church walls in fresco technique, so that the tendency to superficiality, schematization and unnaturalness could hardly be avoided.

Elsheimer of Frankfurt successfully blended the delicacy of the North and a deep feeling for nature with Southern forms. He is the only one to have constrained Italian grandeur into small-scale pictures minutely executed; this

Central Rhinelander brought off a synthesis of North and South.

In Holland Coninxloo's outlook had a great following between 1600 and 1610. Van Mander noted the effect and said: I know of no better landscapist today and observe also that his art is beginning to find very many followers in Holland, and the trees, which stood rather thinly hereabouts, are now beginning to grow like his, though some of their planters might be unwilling to admit this!

One feels in van Mander's 'didactic poem', in the wordy section on landscape where the painter lectures the young in verse on what is 'beautiful' in the landscape world and worthy of reproduction, how fluid the border-line was in those days between painting and poetry. In the more intimate circle of the Haarlem Academy with which van Mander was connected, and in which Cornelis Cornelissen and the engraver Hendrick Goltzius were the leaders, landscape was only taken notice of by accident. Nevertheless some of Goltzius' own colour-woodcuts are remarkable because, despite the 'manneristic' linear treatment, there is apparent a Dutch simplicity of theme which points into the future. But the most revealing of all are the drawings and engravings after drawings from the hand of Abraham Bloemaert. A contemporary of van Mander's, he was active far into the seventeenth century, was resident in Utrecht, a city which, in contrast to the other Dutch cities, always looked to the South. He strives successfully to rid peasant houses, shacks, trees of their natural simplicity by means of an exciting linear game. The fashionable, cosmopolitan manner which never allows the human body to achieve a state of rest agitates even the animals in his drawings, the vegetation and the picturesquely tumble-down buildings. He poeticizes pro-

saic themes with his form-language. Perspective foreshortening acts dynamically and emotionally here.
Bloemaert conceived landscape as a draughtsman. Even the Dutch of the next generation, those born about 1590 with Esias van de Velde and Willem Buytewech among them, avail themselves, when working in the open, of drawing. It was not usual to paint in the open air. Now it makes a difference whether the artist looks with a pencil in his hand or with a brush in his hand. The tool determines the way of looking. Everything branchy or twiggy, bare or scantily foliaged trees, everything that strikes him as 'picturesque' without having a coloristic or tonal value, the *draughtsman* chooses, brings into prominence, keeps a lookout for. And the close ties between landscape and drawing persist far into the seventeenth century, and are noticeable in the work of the eccentric Seghers, even in Rembrandt himself.

IV

THE GOLDEN AGE OF LANDSCAPE IN THE SEVENTEENTH CENTURY

Esaias van de Velde and Buytewech overcome the extravagance and pathos of the Bloemaert manner and push on to a quieter and more portraitesque interpretation of landscape; they also turn away from the orgies of 'foliage' that had swamped over from Flanders. Even so, delight in ingenious linear play is a dominant factor, particularly in Buytewech's work.

The specifically Dutch view of nature sets in soon after 1600, in Haarlem, in the belief that the Dutch countryside, howsoever it presented itself to one's gaze, was worthy of being painted without trimmings or accessories. Despite the presence of popular genre-like everyday themes in Brueghel's work, we feel a latent heroic strength. His productivity falls in the time of Granvella and Alba, when the Inquisition, foreign overlordship, religious intolerance, oppression and misery goaded people to secret resistance and fomented the struggle for freedom. About 1620 this struggle had been decided in all essentials. The northern States had secured independence, religious freedom and a life under their own law. The visual arts no longer create triumphant symbols, are not heroic. The great event is not reflected that way at all in painting. The Dutch soul has roused itself and wards off everything foreign with quiet self-confidence. Protestantism holds its own against the 'universal' Church, the Germanic element against the southern, the bourgeoisie against autocracy, simplicity against pomp, painting against drawing. The cut makes a deep mark in the history of the landscape picture. With other eyes than before the Dutch look at their country, so imperilled, so grievously fought for! Their pride in their own strength which had proved equal to the formidable enemy, their defiant contentment, their holding fast to what their country had to offer, their unsentimental objectivity: these things afford the clue to the attitude of mind and spirit which developed during the struggle for freedom and became productive in painting.

Whatever was close at hand and homely was now worth looking at, and this was precisely the bareness, the non-prodigality of the dune-lands. The urge to travel, to go roaming in the distance, to climb mountains, to haunt the depths of forests seems to have vanished with a suddenness rare in the permutations of taste.

The first and purest phase of Dutch landscape-painting is represented by H. Avercamp (b. 1585), Pieter Molyn (b. 1595) and Jan van Goyen (b. 1596). For more than one reason van Goyen is particularly suited to represent that stylistic phase, which was firmly bounded both in space and time. His advance was steady and untroubled. He worked with ease, was prolific. His 'œuvre' lies wide open before us. He dated many of his pictures, so that we can get an easy survey of his healthy, organic development. He was no genius, nor an eccentric like H. Seghers. His work, having no problems, was understood. Small and middling painters could emulate him with success.

If we compare a mature picture of van Goyen's (done about 1650) with one of Jan Brueghel's, Coninxloo's or with any other Flemish painting of the seventeenth century, the contrast strikes us as uncommonly great. The difference extends to standpoint, choice of theme and line of vision. Van Goyen looks from below upwards. The horizon lies close to the bottom edge of the picture. Instead of colourfulness, harmonies in near-monochrome. He is indifferent to his foregrounds which, nothing but a dark strip, set off the distance all the more airily and luminously. In tones of brownish, ochreous and greenish hues the backgrounds merge into one another, are no longer graded off into the distance. Drawing gives way more and more to painting. Van Goyen drew a good deal, but with the painter's vision (Pl. 19).

If there is any object that is picture-worthy as such it is the expanse of sky, which occupies so large a place in van Goyen's pictures. A mountain, a hut, a tree can always be reproduced plastically and certainly by the draughtsman, but not the sky. In van Goyen's pictures the relation of figures to landscape has changed. We are entitled to speak here of incidental figures in the strictest sense, because peasants and fishermen are unthinkable without this earth, this water, this atmosphere, and, without these people, the country would be incomplete. Skaters belong to a frozen river in Holland, ships to the sea and crews to the ships. In Flemish landscapes we meet with saints, mythological figures, noteworthy occurrences—an attack by robbers, it may be, done small and fitted into the general scheme, subordinate to it; but in Dutch paintings incidental figures are to be found only in a more limited sense, impressions of a populous and native countryside where nothing happens but what is expected and a daily occurrence. We can speak of the tact of the landscape-painter in refraining from all narrative and all whimsy, relying solely on the pictorial value of his home surroundings. It is impossible to imagine a saint or a nymph wandering about in a van Goyen landscape.

His choice of theme, standpoint and vision are so familiar to us that we cannot appreciate van Goyen's achievement

19. JAN VAN GOIJEN, RIVER LANDSCAPE
Private Collection, Holland

without an effort. We incline to think that the camera could give us pictures that would appear similar to these paintings. As to the colour, we see differently, of course. We read often enough that objects in Holland, the Dutch littoral, are in fact colourless, sunless, hazy and enveloped in dark fog. This explanation is facile and only right up to a point. It is correct that the dweller in the flat-lands sees more of the sky than the mountain-dweller. But even in Holland there is clear air, powerful contrasts of light and shade and positive local colours. Potter too was a Dutchman and an objective observer, and he saw other things and saw them differently from van Goyen. If van Goyen with unswerving singleness of vision prefers cloudy skies and dull weather, it is not enough to point to metereological phenomena as the basis of this preference; we must rather infer a certain sort of feeling that was in harmony with the lustreless and melancholy atmosphere. The expression of the countryside was always changing, but only with just *this* expression did it become, for him, pictorial and (artistically) worth looking at.

The salient features in a landscape can only be seen from far-off. The tree-trunk which in reality is three feet across may appear half an inch broad in the picture. The fact that the form, texture and colour of the trunk must necessarily look quite different when seen close-to, was a relatively late discovery. Van Goyen's eye is consistently far-sighted. He de-substantiates things, depriving them of colour and weight. If the 'realist' is an observer who gives the real its due, van Goyen is no realist—his love of truth prevents him from becoming one. The distance with its veil-like strata of air is less material, less earthy than what is near at hand; it is plastic and paintable inasmuch as, itself appearing plane, it fits into the perspective plan of the picture. Distance in space as in time has the effect of idealizing and de-banalizing. Atmosphere and clouds are the least real parts of the landscape world of appearances, they are more elements than things, and van Goyen makes ample room for these particular phenomena by directing his eye from below upwards. We can say: he chooses this standpoint and this line of vision because he loves the sky. A hill, a tree, a house arouse our objective interest, if only to a modest degree. We can climb the hill, fell the tree, live in the house. The sky, on the other hand, arching above us and pouring rain or sunshine over us, awakens feelings akin to the religious. We are unable to intervene in its sphere. Sensing the dominion of the sky van Goyen observes its effects in cloud-shadows and beams of light thrown on earth and water. The physiognomy and expression of the landscape are governed by changing weather conditions. The whole works like a chord, not a sequence of notes.

This conception of landscape is not so much the personal achievement of a Master as an accommodation to time and place. Van Goyen derives from Esias van de Velde, whose pictures bear a resemblance to the earliest we know of his. Pieter Molyn makes a more decisive showing in the twenties of the century than van Goyen did. Salomon Ruysdael's pictures of the thirties can only be distinguished from van Goyen's with some difficulty. Not starting out like a pioneer at all, but steadily and consistently pursuing the goal I have hinted at, van Goyen preserves his style even in an age when all sorts of inducements might well have lured him from his straight path.

Although van Goyen was by nature averse to everything artificially constructed and pleasantly rounded off, he was not unwilling—particularly in the thirties—to abide by the scheme of composition that had then become the fashion. Both directly and indirectly he remained in touch with predecessors like Esaias van der Velde, Buytewech, even Elsheimer, whose beguiling art had been popularized in Holland by Goudt and Jan van der Velde, through the medium of drawings and etchings. With some regularity he fits the land, rising somewhat wearily from the bottom edge of the picture, into a recumbent triangle, the shortest side of which forms part of the lateral wall, the next shortest the bottom edge, and the longest the diagonal which dips down to abut on the low horizon. To one side of the picture the land rises up with a sparse growth of trees, poverty-stricken huts, falling away on the other, not only within the perspective plane but into its depths as well. The earth-mass is so disposed that, fleeing away into the distance, it heightens the illusion of spatial depth: it runs like a wedge into the background. Aerial perspective is put with a sure touch at the service of this compositional scheme, which was to hold the field in Holland for a long time. Van Goyen frees himself more and more from the above formula and lays out the terrain for the most part horizontally, in panorama-like views, portraitesque profiles of towns and expanses of water, giving the eye direct access to the horizon-line or some section of this line.

His brush-stroke, heavy and linear to begin with, still apt to accentuate things in the manner of the draughtsman, gains in fluidity and looseness.

Van Goyen did not paint in the open. The unshakable sureness of his style becomes understandable when one considers that he turned away from the chaos of natural life, trusting to his memory. The homogeneous effect of his pictures is not disturbed by any prominence of detail. Van Goyen drew a good deal and out-of-doors, but his drawings are not studies in the strict sense, being viewed no less 'far-sightedly' than the paintings, to which they are like silhouettes. That he did not, with such a method of work, become a Mannerist, that his vision always remained close to nature testifies to the honesty of his character, the depth of his love for landscape and the tenacity of his visual memory.

The earliest known pictures by van Goyen are dated 1622. The Master was then 26 years old. He seems to have become independent rather late. Those first compositions of his are minutely organized, and would like to entertain with their profusion of landscape, architectural or human motifs, their bustle, their tall trees, the leaves of which are done elaborately and according to plan. In the thirties van Goyen has already overcome this old-fashioned 'horror vacui', his incidental figures are fewer, his vegetation is more economical—his landscape crouches, so to speak. The forties and fifties see an increase in the size and simplicity of his themes. The 'empty' expanses of air are not empty at all, they are rather vehicles of the picture's expression, the Master now having become a painter in the stricter sense of the term.

A number of painters, such as van Mosscher, Knibbergen, Wouter Knyff worked in the spirit of van Goyen but got stuck at some point or other on the road he travelled. No follower of his ever attained the visionary quality of his mature paintings. A worthy successor to him is A. Cuyp, who developed van Goyen's personal style—though it was no less Dutch for that—on a different time-level.

Salomon van Ruisdael, a few years younger than van Goyen, emerges with his comprehensive 'œuvre' as the successful rival of that Master. His paintings of the thirties resemble, in choice of theme, composition and standpoint, those which van Goyen did at about the same time, so that occasionally there is some danger of confusing them. Yet we would hesitate to take dependence or imitation for granted; all it proves is how indigenous, appropriate and welcome the approach was which the two Masters had in common as regards their native soil. Actually their paths diverged. Salomon van Ruisdael's development was less logical, had less character about it than van Goyen's. His temperament was more vivacious and receptive. His colouring became livelier, cool, mostly steel-grey and blue, not brownish and ochreous as in van Goyen. His air is clearer, more limpid. While the weather in van Goyen's pictures makes you feel: it's going to rain, you feel with Ruysdael's rather: it's been raining, a fresh breeze has driven the rain away. Buildings and trees stick straight up into the sky, the leaves are done loosely but searchingly with dazzling points of light breaking through. The streaky clouds and the bent trunks of trees show the horizontal sweep of air. In his later pictures the Master takes care to balance the vertical components—trees, ships and houses—against the horizontal trend of river, horizon and cloud. His incidental figures are comparatively sprightly and engaging, sometimes even elegant. Ready to make concessions to the changed taste of the times, he finds himself a stranger to the peace and simplicity of his youth.

Having spoken of van Goyen as the representative of one generation, I must now single out the personality of Jacob van Ruisdael in the same way, for in him Dutch landscape-painting reaches its peak. In this I am at least obeying the idea of him that has become current—indeed, something of a convention.

At the time when Jacob van Ruisdael, born 1628, was beginning to work independently, in 1646, van Goyen was far from old and was not even regarded as old-fashioned. Generations are like roof-tiles, they overlap.

Those who bend their attention to the growth and efflorescence of Dutch painting—in the stricter sense—may be inclined to look for the peak not in the work of Ruisdael, but in the work of A. Cuyp. Cuyp derives from van Goyen, but Ruisdael does not, at least not directly. The 'naïve' Cuyp seems to have stronger ties with his native soil than the 'sentimental' Ruisdael. His sunny visions are to the misty phantasms of van Goyen as fulfilments to promises. He is more of a painter—in the stricter sense —than Ruisdael.

Jacob van Ruisdael was 20 years old at the time of the peace treaty which put an end to the Thirty Years' War and secured the States-General universal recognition of their independence. Even while that fearful war was going on, destroying Germany's prosperity and debasing her culture, Holland was not threatened, was on the contrary assiduously courted as a consolidated Power and an economically flourishing community. Her favourable position is reflected in the innocent unbuttonedness of Jan Steen and the bourgeois peaceableness of Pieter de Hoogh. At the same time it was no longer an urgent necessity to keep the doors shut and ward off everything foreign—Latin and Catholic—as dangerous. Compared with Berchem, whose friend he is supposed to have been, Ruisdael was a representative of the national art, but an eclectic compared with van Goyen or Cuyp. His melancholy of course is personal, has nothing to do with the time.

In the second half of the seventeenth century people's sensitiveness for the pictorial diminished with their increasing love of polished surfaces and virtuosity of finesse. The tragic fate of Rembrandt is a loud comment on this change. Italianate and finally Gallic elements encroached from all sides, their pretensions and allurements bringing confusion. People grew satisfied and complacent

20. J. VAN RUISDAEL, LANDSCAPE. ETCHING

and began to give themselves up to luxury. Now I am very far from trying to scent any decadence or decline in Ruisdael's development; on the contrary, it should be remembered that this Master, who lived until 1681, was no less impoverished than Rembrandt and no longer met the taste of the age. All the same, his was no robust, aggressive nature, and the stress of the times gave his late works a resigned tiredness.

Ruisdael was understood and acclaimed by Goethe more as a poet than a painter, and that in an age when Dutch painting in general could scarcely count on much understanding. A poet of 'sensibility'—in the eighteenth century sense—seemed to be raising his voice in Ruisdael, a sensitive 'nature' which, weary of the bustle, sought refuge in the solitude of the woods and, sunk in reveries far from the madding crowd, followed with longing eyes the procession of the clouds. His art is symbolical throughout, since form and colour convey the artist's feeling. Occasionally it provides abstract symbols, and his insistence on these borders on the officious. Ruins harping on the decay and transitoriness of all things, storm-tossed trees lying like fallen warriors on the battlefield, graveyards complete with tombstones. And it is just these plangent notes, rhetorical rather than lyrical, that had their effect in a Humanistic and then a Romantic age and were the basis of Ruisdael's fame. We judge from another point of view, without the fame of the Master being any the worse for that. For us he is a painter, an observer of nature and as such a poet. His convincing verisimilitude is the pre-requisite lacking which he could not speak to us so winningly and forcefully (Pl. 20).

It is assumed, and with good reason, that Jacob van Ruisdael studied under his uncle Salomon. In Haarlem Salomon was the successful and respected landscape-painter, hence (being so close) the unavoidable model for his nephew. If we compare the works of the younger Master with those of the older, we perceive not only the contrast of generations but also glimpse Jacob as a personality. Salomon seems innocuous beside the nephew, who was possessed of a higher intellect and a deeper spirit. The older Master's 'views' seem, by comparison, slapdash, put together without thought. His trees and buildings could, we think, stand equally well somewhere else. Jacob constructed his pictures artfully, not, of course, like an architect, but with a loose symmetry, a labile balancing of masses. He composes with light, making a cornfield or a path suddenly gleam in the dark flat-land, thus picking out these parts.

In contrast to van Goyen, Salomon had given much attention to foliage, and his contemporary Cornelis Vroom did so still more. Jacob, especially in his youth, plunged into the dense tangle of vegetation which he set off against the sky in a heavy mass, not letting it grow loose and light like Salomon. He observed the growth of trees more acutely than any of his contemporaries, the bifurcation and ramification of the trunks. Later he overlooked detail to the good of the whole. His pictures gained in poise, in firm structure to the extent that he grew more indifferent to the true-to-nature quality of growing things.

Despite the diversity of themes—which were sometimes taken from beyond the borders of his country—the effect of this subjective art of Ruisdael's was governed by the yearning devotion to sublime nature and her mysteries. Spinoza was Ruisdael's contemporary and countryman, and Goethe found his way to the Dutch painter as a pantheist and devotee of that philosopher.

Again, despite the diversity of themes, the impression

given by Ruisdael's pictures varies little according to time of year or day. High summer, already somewhat autumnal, vegetation in full bloom but near to the fall, seldom winter, never the youthful freshness of springtime—in this way, like all the Dutch painters of the seventeenth century, he clearly expresses the contrast between summer and winter but, apart from that, pays scant attention to the change of season. White clouds, shaded with extreme delicacy, bulge and sail across a sky of mild azure. The expression changes with stronger or weaker clouding.

The incidental figures are inconspicuous where they are not put in by other painters. The reason why they are not excluded altogether may lie with the taste and habituations of contemporary art-lovers. It was in keeping with Ruisdael's inclinations to feel he was alone, beyond reach of the city walls, free to enjoy by himself the virgin peace and solitude of nature undisturbed by the bustle of humanity. He had no desire to have the full and sublime harmonies breaking on his ear interrupted by the banality of the human voice. In some of his master-works, such as *Castle Bentheim* in the Beit Collection or the *Forest Lake* in Berlin, and again in the two *Jewish Graveyards*, there are no incidental figures of any kind. For Salomon Ruysdael country is empty and incomplete without the stir of humanity; for Jacob Ruisdael the presence of human beings is a profanation.

Chary of local colour, but rich in the grading of tonal strengths Ruisdael adheres to a solemn harmony, an eloquent silence, an elegiac mood which an age of 'Weltschmerz' was to greet like a soul-affinity.

The far-off and the foreign, anything different now became worth looking at, like waterfalls, like mountain-keeps. Everdingen, who was a few years older than Ruisdael, settled in Haarlem in 1645 after having travelled in Scandinavia, and diverted his inquisitive countrymen with pictorial reports of his experiences. Frans Post, who had lived in Brazil as far back as 1637, satisfied curious interest with his tales of colonies overseas.

The South exerted a direct and an indirect influence. Historians make a clean division between national painters and the italianizing painters and decide in each case whether such and such a landscapist had been in Italy. Jacob Ruisdael is grouped with the 'nationalists'; Jan Both and Berchem are regarded as representatives of Italianate art. It is perilously easy to imagine that this Master rendered the Dutch scene, that Master the Italian. Now reality, judged by terrain, atmosphere and vegetation, wears a different aspect here from what it does there. There we see stone-pines, cypresses, olive-trees, flora which do not exist here. But it is hardly to be observed that Both, shall we say, perceived such significant features. His pictures are idyllic or pathetic, colourful, warm-toned, spacious—glorifications. Charmingly vivacious scenes, happy and blissful, which owe their existence more to lively expectation and bias than to observation and thus satisfied the yearnings of the Northeners. In their eyes Italy was the 'different' land with different inhabitants, with picturesque terraces, a setting for bucolic scenes, cattle and energetically gesticulating shepherds, not so much specifically Italian as universally ideal, paradisal. The Italians themselves took little part in building up an ideal which was developed at its purest by Claude, a native of Lorrain. In the end the Italians may have come to believe that their country was in fact so constituted as the foreigners showed it. Nowhere is the eye more irresistibly captivated by buildings than in Rome, where the very stones bear witness to vanished grandeurs. Brought up on architecture the Italians, and to an even greater extent the Northeners whose eyes had been opened in Rome, saw in landscape and nature structures which, in pride of bearing, could compete with classical buildings: single trees whose growth was not impeded by anything. Claude's landscape compositions, with their poise, symmetry and well-weighed proportions, are 'beautiful' in the sense that antique temples are beautiful. Ruisdael's landscape does not look Italian. The piety and seriousness of his mind did not allow him ever to go in for the arbitrary effects of a Berchem. But indirectly speaking he was not unaffected by the Southern striving after form. Wherever the land rises skywards as a compact body, and does not flow or straggle away, wherever detail and construction seem immutably right—there you can feel the breath of the South.

On this account, therefore, the urge for spatial depth is no longer a decisive factor, because the land is not conceived as a setting or a domicile. Ruisdael starts by coming close to terrain and vegetation, later he stands off more, but even then it is the middle distance that he develops most. He is the first of the Dutch to express his feelings in pure landscape so positively that we can hear the personal, the unmistakable voice of the man himself. We get to know him, although we know little enough of him and glimpse nothing beyond the country he saw in just that way.

Anybody who has set himself the task of tracing the historical sequence is at a loss as soon as he encounters genius. It does not do to ignore what Rubens and Rembrandt achieved in landscape, not so much professionally as for the love and fun of the thing. Their imagination was too powerfully enthralled by man—Rubens by his body, Rembrandt by his soul—for them to have troubled overmuch with landscape. Rembrandt, an eager draughtsman and etcher, sketched places conscientiously and even with topographical exactitude. Looking at his drawings people have asked themselves—and successfully—where the Master stood.[1] His painted landscapes, on the other hand, have the effect of compositions. Not only did he not paint in the open but he did not even absorb the colour and the diffused light of the open air into his visual memory, as Rubens did. His colour-sense could not do without chiaroscuro, the force and glow of his colouring needed a dark foil. It must, moreover, be remembered that for the masters of chiaroscuro who were busy in the South, for Caravaggio and Ribera, for instance, the country hardly seemed to exist. Chiaroscuro is studio-art. The landscapes Rubens painted are more natural as regards colour than those of the Dutchman who, as a draughtsman, goes to work so objectively. Like Pieter Brueghel in his day, Rubens observes the life of nature, the doings of men and animals in so far as these are dependent on weather and temperature. He watches the land like a country squire, like a huntsman—with optimistic vitality. In Rubens: the sun shining, victorious, giver and rouser of life. In Rembrandt: a valedictory sun, at its last gasp, sending out lightning-beams into the mysterious darkness.

A grand period for painting between 1630 and 1660, a period that tops all for landscape. Ruisdael and Claude busy at about the same time as Rubens and Rembrandt, each a personal creator working on his own. One thing these Masters have in common: light as the medium of expression for free use, investing facts and forms with the

[1] Fr. Lugt, *Wandelingen met Rembrandt in en om Amsterdam*, Amsterdam, 1915.

individual tint of the creator's soul, transfiguring, overshadowing and casting a spell on hard, sober reality. Subjectivity, now set free and grown self-confident, manifests itself in an extraordinary, in an extreme light. Creations issuing from the very depths of the individual's feeling for nature come up against an age that was rather sticky about landscape. Rubens only contemplated his country with enthusiasm after he had vanquished the spirit of the Baroque in himself, or at least the sculptural and anthropocentric element in Italian Baroque. Let us look further afield. Germany does not count, as the great war and its calamitous aftermath had ground down any sproutings of culture. The French feeling for nature seemed only to bloom on Roman soil. The unbiassed objectivity with which Velasquez observed everything was occasionally preserved in landscape impressions. In Italy Annibale Caracci, paving the way for the cool and noble art of Poussin. Otherwise not much, except for the brigand Romanticism of Salvator Rosa.

Overshadowed by Rembrandt, and sometimes doing commissions for him, the Flemish landscapists van Uden, Wildens, de Vadder, Huysmans and David Teniers (overrated for his *genre* but more notable as a landscape-painter) fall over themselves to work in the Rembrandt tempo with showy routine. Jan Siberechts' cool and somewhat sober pictures are distinguished by an independent way of looking. True, he moved to England and thus alienated himself from Flemish convention.

Adriaen Brouwer belongs by descent, temperament and the effect he had to the Flemish School, but became acquainted with the Dutch way of life and vision during his stay in Haarlem. His keen eye for the individual and the physiognomical is admired—how starkly typical Teniers is compared with him, how insipid and petty-bourgeois Adriaen van Ostade!—but his performance as a landscape-painter is not so obvious. He did one or two nightscapes and evening-scapes, warm and soft and harmonious. While he turns an eye of almost malignant intensity on human beings, he looks at the country like a poet, a lyricist. In his short life as a painter he put an incredible distance behind him—all the way, very nearly, from Brueghel to Corot.

As little prone to compromise as Brouwer, as aloof from his contemporaries but otherwise completely different, Hercules Seghers is one of those Masters we call geniuses and immediately regret having bestowed this title on them. There are personalities who are genial by disposition but not talented enough to get to the top. Fränger has analysed, as a psychologist and diagnostician and with the forceful language at his command, in the most graphic way all the morbid, unsociable and eccentric traits in this Master.[1] Seghers is a fanatical draughtsman, possessing himself by main force of the line as a means of expression and struggling with agonized, insatiable zeal to catch wild, pathless nature in a close-meshed linear net. His bleak, extinct wastes are a symbol of his lonely, sick, unhappy soul. The fame of this Master reposes on the fact that he went his own way; his misfortune on the fact that this way resembles a cul-de-sac. The extraordinary rarity of his etchings is enough to show that his closeted labours met with little interest and understanding. True, that Rembrandt should have given an eye to this forerunner of his is an excellent testimonial. But the professional landscapists do not follow Seghers.

Brouwer observed the uninhibited doings of the lower classes more frankly than anybody else. This led to imita-

[1] *Hercules Seghers*, E. Rentsch Verlag, 1922.

tion in Antwerp and also in Holland. His conception of landscape was ahead of his time and could have but little direct influence.

Rembrandt, who trained numerous pupils and enhanced their abilities, found (as regards landscape) an important successor in Philips Koninck, whose panoramas give the Dutch motif of a plane built up of horizontal lines an air of monumentality. Jan Lievens, more highly gifted, perhaps, but less persevering than Koninck, tried to combine the achievements of Rembrandt with those of the Flemish School and painted a number of landscapes which might be taken for Brouwer's work.

The people who had resisted the Baroque spirit—which, in its origins, is the Latin cult of forms—displayed a capacity to give a detailed and objective account of landscape and nature. The Baroque was arrogantly subjective, blatant and pathetic and in the end prodigiously decorative. The Dutch view of the world, taken by and large, is objective, modest and patient. Anybody surveying the whole extent of Dutch activity must marvel at the high level of painting in Holland and also at the receptivity which made production on such a scale possible in that little country. The Masters specialized, limited themselves to this or that province of the phenomenal world. They knew what they were depicting and guarded against depicting anything they did not know. An artist like Saenredam possessed the knowledge of an architect, Potter knew as much about cattle as any cattleman, Willem van der Velde had the knowledge of a shipwright at his finger-tips. Professional knowledge based on profound observation exempted painters from the necessity of starting with a unique visual experience *ad hoc*, that is, when they conceived and executed a picture. Their method of work, which pre-supposed and trained a reliable visual memory, gave them an unswerving assurance of style. Thus an Aart van der Neer could paint moonscapes from morn till night in comfort, undisturbed by changes of weather and lighting. Isolated visual experience stimulates, flurries and demands speedy attack, while professional knowledge and visual memory permit even lesser talents to get to the top with phlegmatic industry and stay there—that is to say the top which they are naturally equipped to attain.

Landscape has this in common with still-life, that the object quietly lends itself to lasting observation. To look and to linger accorded with the Dutch soul—contemplation free of mysticism. One of the greatest of Dutch Masters, Vermeer, who, so far as we know, never did a still-life proper, is a still-life painter in his mode of vision and works wonders with it. The painter who comes closest to him, Willem Kalf, was a still-life painter, the first in the field.

Aelbert Cuyp was not appreciated as early as Ruisdael and was therefore hardly admitted at all into the princely Galleries from which the public collections on the Continent have grown. As a result of this defect he has been badly neglected by the art-historians. During the eighteenth century and the first half of the nineteenth the English possessed themselves of most of the best from his hand. He is represented particularly poorly in his own country. Last century the Dutch made praiseworthy efforts to conserve and enrich their art possessions, going to considerable lengths, when the Steengracht and Six Collections were disbanded, to acquire masterpieces of Vermeer, Jan Steen, Metsu and Terborch for their museums, although these painters were already represented impressively enough. But when Cuyp's masterwork, the *View of Dordrecht*, came up for auction in

Courtesy of National Trust—Ascott Collection

21. A. CUYP, VIEW OF DORDRECHT

(*p.* 107)

London from the Holford Collection, unfortunately nobody took this opportunity to fill a yawning gap (Pl. 21). Cuyp is many-sided and careless, sensual rather than spiritual by nature and not by any means always at the top of his bent. He painted comparatively indifferent portraits and genre-pieces without compunction. One or two seascapes and landscapes, however, which he did in his maturity stand out by reason of the freedom and amplitude of his view of nature. The sunny haze, the lusciousness, the glow and enamel of his blonde colours, the aplomb of his brushwork: here he triumphs over all rivals. Jan Both seems theatrical compared with him, Ruisdael cramped and his colouring opaque and drab. The after-effects of his work are more noticeable in England than in Holland. Wilson derives from him—in so far as he does not derive from Claude.

Ruisdael's heir is considered to be Meindert Hobbema, who can be shown to have enjoyed his predecessor's instruction for a spell in Amsterdam. The connection is clear enough in some pictures. But in his 'oeuvre' as a whole, Hobbema differs in temperament and feeling from Ruisdael. Of lesser spiritual pretensions, far more one-sided in his choice of themes, what he offers is rather fortuitous excerpts than artistically meditated compositions. He pleases with inviting countrysides, mills embedded in luxuriant masses of trees. His colouring is more vivid, more luminous than Ruisdael's. With his sensuality, the pomp and panoply of his summer ripeness, he won the hearts of art-lovers and collectors, particularly the English. His pictures have been quoted at higher rates on the art market than Ruisdael's, and not merely because they came up less frequently. But he lags behind him in spirituality, in power of mood. Nobody will ever call him a poet. On one occasion, in the *Avenue at Middel-*

harnis, the picture in the National Gallery, he surpasses himself, and it is precisely this work that Riegel, who speaks well-meaningly enough of Hobbema elsewhere, regards as a grave aberration.[1] A misjudgement like this may voice itself when great talent becomes—for once—genius.

Contemporary with Hobbema, though dying much earlier, Adriaen van der Velde represents the late flowering of Dutch landscape-painting with a sense for the cultivated, the enclosed, the over-smooth. Nature arouses neither devoutness nor longing in him, she has become man's friend and a home for snug and happy lives. The Master observes things in a tempered frame of mind, while his understanding for the vegetable as for the animal world is faultless, and his execution clean, unexceptionable and even elegant. One has only to examine the brickwork in the paintings of Jan van der Heyden, an artist who stands close to him both temporally and spiritually, to see that the application of sharply-focussing near-vision is something peculiar to the latter years of the seventeenth century. In the views which this Master did of towns you can count the bricks.

[1] *Abhandlungen und Forschungen z. niederl. Kunstg.*, Berlin, 1882, p. 78.

V

LANDSCAPE IN THE EIGHTEENTH AND NINETEENTH CENTURIES

Landscape representation seemed to have come to the end of its resources in the eighteenth century.

In the eighteenth century, taste was ruled by the French Court with its passion for the orderly, the civilized, the park-like. Landscape was observed less for its own sake than as a setting for *galant* merry-makings and erotic pastorals, and was thus adapted to society and its pet pursuits. Nature was subordinated to the human being. In Italy architectural painting came to full flower about this time—in the paintings of Panini, Antonio Canale and Guardi.

Nothing more was to be expected from the Netherlands, and as yet not much from Germany. The eighteenth century French artists, Hubert Robert and Fragonard, turned an attentive eye on nature in Rome, as did Poussin and Claude in the seventeenth century; and it befitted the place and the time alike that they should now pay more attention to architecture than to nature proper.

The origin and growth of the love of nature has been traced through the centuries, on the one hand in poetry, on the other in the visual arts.[1] The historian expects the verbal manifestations of it to correspond both in place and in time with the pictorial manifestations. Now the monuments of painting and drawing would seem to indicate that the Teutonic Northeners viewed natural landscapes with a deeper sense of participation than the

[1] Cf. A Biese, *Entwicklung des Naturgefühls.*

Greeks, the Romans, the Orientals and the Latin peoples. A corresponding inferiority in poetry is hypothecated. Gervinus, who enjoyed a high reputation in the nineteenth century as the universally knowledgeable historian of literature, expresses himself unhesitatingly: the ancient world as a whole found no pleasure in nature. He is categorically contradicted by Alfred Biese, who calls his predecessor's outpourings 'a welter of vapidity and error', quotes the lyrics and epics of the Indians, the Persians, Homer, Dante, Petrarch, but deplores the absence in the *Nibelungenlied* of 'the homely German feeling for nature'. Between 1490 and 1520 the German feeling for nature became surprisingly productive in painting and drawing, but remained without after-effects. A corresponding movement in South German literature is scarcely noticeable. There are hardly any parallels to the efflorescence of landscape-painting in the seventeenth century to be found in the poetry of the time. On the other hand, in the eighteenth century when landscape-painting was at its lowest, there was a perfervid enthusiasm for 'the natural life' in literature (A. von Haller, b. 1708; J. J. Rousseau, b. 1712; Sal. Gessner, b. 1730). It was only relatively late, at the time of Byron and Shelley and German Romanticism (Eichendorff) that painting grew strong enough in England and Germany to follow in the footsteps of poetry, whose richest and deepest chords echo in Goethe's lyrics. Whereas the love of nature evinced by the ancient world and the Latins, eloquent and florid, made itself *heard* earlier than that of the Germanic peoples, the latter's love of nature was *seen* only episodically, but was to blossom afresh in the visual arts after their literature had found its tongue.

Eighteenth-century England entered into the legacy of the Dutch in mastery of the seas, in economic prosperity and finally in painting as well. English art was then more aristocratic than bourgeois; it was also eclectic, being dependent on the model of the Netherlands Masters who had worked successfully on English soil, such as van Dyck, Jan Siberechts—dependent also on the numerous and admirable specimens of Dutch painting which superior wealth and the passion for collecting had brought into the country. At first portrait-painting flourished under the favourable economic conditions, later landscape, but never still-life. Of the landscape-painters Richard Wilson is the earliest. He saw the English countryside with the eyes of Claude and Cuyp. Gainsborough was the only English portrait-painter to have done landscape.

English portraits impress by reason of the aristocratic bearing, the grace and comeliness of an exclusive society, but over and above that their value lies in their free and painterly execution, their select colouring, the loose, open brushwork appropriate to the large scale of the pictures. This encomium applies particularly to Gainsborough. We must assume a certain correlation between the attitude of society and portrait-painting. It is very likely that van Dyck helped to give the English nobility something of the supple *noblesse* of the Genoese aristocracy. Compared with the French the English were dilettantes—in a good sense. Even Reynolds was a dilettante or amateur, which was precisely what protected him from the worst consequences of eclecticism and academic paedogogy. He was a connoisseur of the Old Masters, despite which he often chose a doubtful technique; he was a knowledgeable collector of Masters' drawings, yet his own drawings are remarkably weak. The painter Reynolds was not one of the best pupils of his academy.

The English nobility lived, for choice, in country-houses. Open-air exercise in a temperate climate, hunting and riding promoted a healthy naturalness, made for an easy costume and guarded against effeminacy. The French had their portraits done in the salon, the English in the garden—a 'natural' garden, not one laid out architectonically. Gainsborough, moved by the predilections of his patrons, could give himself up to his love of nature even in his portraits. He sketched fluently, far removed from the stolid objectivity of the Dutch, more in the spirit of the Flemish School in the seventeenth century. But no landscape-painter of the eighteenth century, not even Gainsborough himself, gets over a certain superficial decorativeness and theatricality.

In the nineteenth century landscape was once more observed for its own sake, with earnest devoutness—a reaction against the arrogantly anthropocentric attitude of the eighteenth century.

If it is the landscapist who comes nearest to fulfilling the demand of 'art for art's sake', it is a demand which, strictly speaking, cannot really be fulfilled even by him. The feeling with which he contemplates land, water and sky—a feeling he then conveys to the spectator of his picture—depends on his spiritual relations with the supra-mundane Powers and is to that extent not absolutely artistic. This tie is the closer the more strongly the feeling operates in the artist. In the history of religious faith—not yet written—it is gods in human form who first dominate the imagination of the believer and are fashioned *as* gods: images, idols. The idea of Deity becomes more and more spiritualized. The commandment: thou shalt make to thyself no graven image, was hostile to representation. Men honoured the Creator in His Creation, inferring thence His existence since they despaired of forming an immediate conception of this being. The visible universe, though not completely viewable and transparent, became the symbol of omnipotence. Philosophical pantheism was avowed by a few thinkers in the sixteenth and seventeenth centuries; emotional pantheism stirred in revolt against orthodox belief and against the soulless reason of the Enlighteners. Goethe, who esteemed Spinoza and applauded the landscape-painter Ruisdael as a poet, makes Faust testify:

> *Who may name Him,*
> *The All-upholder, All-sustainer?*
> *Does he not hold, sustain*
> *You, me, and himself too?*
> *Do not the heavens arch above?*
> *Does not the earth lie firm below?*

For religious longing, so hungry for representation, nothing remains within its grasp save Creation and, within the realm of created things, landscape as the thing that is boundless and limitless. In the nineteenth century the real religious painter is Millet with his peasants in the field, not Munkaczy with his pretentious and theatrical pictures of the Passion of Christ.

When I stand in front of St. Peter's I admire the work of man, maybe I criticize too, think that this or that might have been done differently. Everything that man's mind devises, man's hand makes, is known to me after the manner of its inception and is subject to my judgment. But when I observe a tree, a flower, a blade of grass I stand before a miracle. Everything natural and inexplicable in its inception, everything that has just 'growed' and is not made to a purpose bears witness to the divine creative Power and becomes an object of devotion to those whose faith is a spiritual one.

Perhaps I shall be met with the proud retort that the enormous strides made by science have explained the origins of everything natural. But the situation is like this: in the past aspiring and optimistic scientists may have thought that a refinement of the methods of investigation, an improvement of the instruments would one day solve all the problems; now, after the methods and instruments have been refined to a degree never before imagined, the mystery seems not so much not yet solved as insoluble. Successful investigators become sceptical, modest, not to say pious, and put limits to the field of rationality. For the Fundamentalist the creation of the phenomenal world is 'explained'; the unbeliever is faced with a puzzle which excites his imagination more powerfully than any explanation. If science has become astute enough to halt before the ultimate questions, its perspicacity has nevertheless discovered perfection and purpose where formerly men felt only chance and caprice. Science has thus changed dull gaping into lucid admiration.

Landscape representation in the nineteenth century, however multifarious its developments in England, Germany and France, derives from the pantheistic view of things, not philosophical pantheism but from the emotionality which agitates that doctrine.

When the scales fell from our eyes—I speak of my generation—Manet's sun was in the ascendant, with the result that a great many things were plunged in darkness. This experience gave us the standard which we applied to all the artistic manifestations of the nineteenth century; everything anterior to that was judged historically. By and by, however, we had to admit that the acquisition of this firm standpoint, gratifying though it was, was offset by a loss, inasmuch as we were deprived of the faculty of doing justice to German art. For the eyes which Manet had opened, C. D. Friedrich was not a weak painter, he was no painter at all. But we feel that with this verdict the German Master is not finished and done with, that there are values to which we have made ourselves blind.

After the French Revolution with its political, economic, social and philosophical upheavals, the nineteenth century contrasted acutely at first with the eighteenth century, even in the matter of art. The reaction against the past was particularly acute in France, less acute in England. In Germany there was hardly any dominant tradition that could be broken with. The veteran of the German landscapists is supposed to be A. J. Koch, born in 1768, who, in Rome, cultivated the ideal landscape and translated Poussin into a four-square, hard-and-fast language. Between Poussin and him comes Anton Faistenberger, a native of Salzburg and still a child of the seventeenth century. The fact that Rome was the centre of German art during the first decades of the nineteenth century (so far as we can speak of a centre of German art at all) is something of an anomaly, on the causes and consequences of which it is highly instructive to ponder. The chief cause, apart from the German longing for the South, is the lack of any receptive society in the decentralized home country—a defect exacerbated by the circumstance that the painters in Rome loosened the spiritual ties with Germany.

Turner, Constable and C. D. Friedrich were contemporaries who were active at the turn of the century, dedicating their labours to landscape—the English full of the self-confidence that flourished mightily after the defeat of Napoleon, the German isolated, on the frontiers of the Reich (like Koch on another frontier in the Tyrol), far indeed from any nourishing and absorptive art-centre.

Ruskin, his countrymen's authoritative mentor for many a decade, was proud of having discovered five painters: Botticelli, Carpaccio, Luini, Tintoretto and Turner. A singular choice, which fails to indicate any fixed standpoint in that eloquent enthusiast. Turner left one of his pictures in his Will to the nation on condition that it should hang between masterpieces by Claude. He wanted to prove to posterity how successfully he had emulated him so that his own work could endure alongside that of his illustrious forbear, even if he did not entertain the wild hope of emerging victorious from this contest. In his late works the eclectic virtuoso outvied his predecessor in boldness of execution. That we feel a certain amount of arbitrariness, pyrotechnics and Bengal lights in his paintings does not prevent us from recognizing that he was a painter in the strictest sense of the word like Constable who, sounder than he, sought refuge from eclecticism in naturalness. For the rest, John Crome, Constable's senior by a few years, had already begun his simple and large-visioned views of the English countryside. There were no painters in this sense either in France or Germany about 1810. For this reason Constable acted on French landscape-painting like a pioneer. Turner's work remained a jealously guarded national treasure. Constable is a virtuoso only in so far as his love for the natural scenery of his own country loses something by his delight in technique as such. One is conscious of the satisfaction he felt in his ability to express himself in a free and easy way. The delightful English reproach 'over-painted' applies to his late great paintings, but not at all to his colour-studies in regard to which nobody dreams of asking how they were done.

The German painters of the first years of the nineteenth century, more draughtsmen than painters, face nature with coy devoutness. All of them have a liaison if not a legitimate alliance with Romantic poetry. Each of them works either for himself or a narrow circle of patrons, not for the public. Often they get as close to nature with their timid precision and painful meticulousness as Constable did with his bold, sure grip. In this circle C. D. Friedrich is a poet in his own right, his eye a magic wand that gives everything an air of faëry. One thinks one can espy sunken cities, forests haunted by hobgoblins. Visions are brought to life with a pendantic, timorous, crabbed hand. This mixture of unreality and sharp focus is a characteristic of dreams. The originality of this Master, who was later to be acclaimed as a representative of German view of art, is proved by the fact that his manner of painting seems to fit in with the substance of his fantasy. The world of the fay should not be spoken of in louder, bolder tones. Of course Friedrich, who was a preacher and German patriot, comes perilously close to the border-line where literature begins and occasionally transgresses against the commandment: *Bilde Künstler, rede nicht* (the artist shall do, not talk). . . . But this danger hangs over most of the German painters of the nineteenth century.

Eccentric, unsociable, with a modesty of manner behind which there not infrequently lurked a spiritual arrogance —such were many of the German painters, Wassmann, Runge, Fohr, Rohden, Olivier, all forgotten until discovered quite recently and now, in some cases, unwarrantably praised. The Viennese Waldmüller is an exception. Worldly-minded and of superior talents he ran the risk which his contemporaries did not run of conforming all too easily to the sentimental taste of a bourgeois society.

The French love of nature awoke late in painting. Corot was twenty years younger than Constable and Turner, Diaz was born in 1808, Dupré in 1811, Millet in 1814, Daubigny in 1817, Courbet in 1819.

Rousseau's enthusiasm for outdoor scenery had scarcely

perceptible effects on the visual arts of his day. Like a parson preaching to the infidels he extolled wild nature beyond all bounds, loathing the tamcness of civilization. Laprade, who wrote a book entitled 'Le sentiment de la nature' in which he claims to have demonstrated his countrymen's lack of feeling for nature, says in explanation of this lack: 'Le génie de la France est le génie de l'action!. . . l'âme humaine est le but de la poesie'.[1] A right judgment, in so far as such sweeping assertions can be right. It seems to befit the period about 1810 when the imagination of the French was intoxicated with world-conquest and antique grandeurs. No constant tendency in the racial or popular will is observable in French art. In the Middle Ages the genius of the French was attested by architecture and monumental sculpture, later by construction and draughtsmanship, with a sense for order and pure limit; finally, in the age of so-called Romanticism, there was an unexpected upsurge of love of nature which availed itself of a superb technique. The esteem for Corot has survived all fluctuations of judgment, all changes of standard and programme. Art-lovers who diverge widely in their opinions of nineteenth century production meet in their love for the unproblematical and enchanting work of this Master. It is difficult to extract the essence of his work with the tweezers of words, because all definition depends on what has been willed and intentionally aimed at, whereas Corot worked completely free of all tendencies. Or else the historian is at pains to set up a goal, proving how far this, that, or the other Master has come to this goal of his. But a goal that is reached is a goal no longer. As far as this concerns Corot, in him will and ability coincide, and he does not put his mastery of paint on show as did Constable or

[1] Quoted by Biese, p. 331.

By courtesy of Paul Cassirer Ltd.

22. COROT, SUMMER MORNING

(*p. 119*)

Turner. Only in his late works is a certain manner observable (Pl. 22).

The French landscapists who met with success towards the middle of the century—the Masters of the Barbiçon School—adopt the same standpoint in interpretation and approach as Constable. They frequent the woods, not, like their forbears, the gardens, and not the wilderness and the mountain wilds of Rousseau: a wood that lies not far from Paris. The French tradition of form gives their compositions and the lyricism these express a disciplined and measured air. Their colouring is in the spirit of the Old Masters. It is a time when the French began to understand Rembrandt. Koloff's book on Rembrandt appeared in 1854. Delacroix had already ventured to predict that Rembrandt would soon be rated higher than Raphael. Millet, who with the serious bent of his mind towers above his contemporaries as a personality, sees the country as the home of the peasants. The biblical solemnity that pervades his whole work reminds us of the first human pair, ejected from Paradise and having to labour in the sweat of their brows. Millet is the first artist in the nineteenth century to have expressed from the depths of his heart a feeling of sympathy with the poor and needy. It was in this way particularly that he accomplished his mission and left a heritage of ethical obligation to posterity—the generation of van Gogh, Jos. Israel and Max Liebermann. Millet—and Corot too—mean more to us than Courbet, who has been looked up to as a pioneer in painters' studios, especially German studios. Personality survives changes of manner; but mere trueness to nature, Courbet's trump card, is an ephemeral thing.

When I acknowledge a picture as being true to nature I am comparing the impression it makes on me with the impression nature makes on me. There is a certain presumption in this judgment—without some presumption there is of course no judgment—since I discern the painter's merit in his having seen as I see. But the impression which nature makes on me is in its turn largely dependent on art, above all the art of my time. Every new art-form to win our approbation becomes the dangerous rival of all the art-forms that have convinced us hitherto. If a Courbet painting which appeared astonishingly true to nature in the eyes of painters and art-lovers about 1870, appears less so to me, I judge as a pupil of Manet's. Our grandchildren will weigh and measure things differently again. Even so, there is no choice but to stick to our own point of view, even after we have realized that instead of having firm ground beneath our feet we have nothing so much as an ice-floe.

The relativity and time-conditionedness of all opinions about truth are fatal to the reputation of painters, particularly those who have aroused an outcry as 'realists', and afterwards enthusiasm. The historian must, however, say a word in Courbet's favour and remind people how manfully this artist overcame convention in his day. Nowadays the art-lover looks at his lush, massive, blackish-green and monotonous colouring, his powerful manner, and thinks that it lacks finesse and shows an unfastidious taste.

Many painters were greeted by their contemporaries as discoverers of truth while, in historical retrospect, they appear significant and commendable for quite other merits. Even Giotto was once a 'realist'. By striving for truth he brought something other than truth to light for posterity, namely his spiritual relations with the object, and this in a form which we do not call 'true' but 'beautiful'. However ephemeral our judgment regarding verisimilitude, we still do not abandon the quest for a universally valid criterion. Take the invention of photography. Nature, in the imitation of which painters have struggled with doubtful success is, as it were, her own illustration, without thc by-road of the eye and mind of man. The significance of photography in the history of seeing and artistic creation has not yet been estimated sufficiently as yet. If we compare a painting with the report of the photographic apparatus on the one hand and our own artistically-trained ideas on the other, we shall find judgments resulting which differ very widely. Our need of verisimilitude is not satisfied by the account rendered by photography.

Since photography has affected our way of seeing more strongly than is generally admitted, the following results are to be observed in artistic creation.

The cautious artist checks his work with the aid of photographic impressions and may thus achieve rather more correctness. As a rule he conceals the methods he has employed (Lenbach). The conceited artist has no wish to be mistaken for a photographer, departs deliberately from verisimilitude and devotes himself to a traditional or else fashionably *recherché* art-form (Picasso). The strong artist, who loves nature more than his art—itself a sign of originality—does not give up the struggle for truth despite the compromising competition of photography, and finds his truth where photography cannot go: in colour, life and movement (Manet).

When he first appeared Manet was called a photographer by people who did not understand him; other critics accused him of being only able to sketch but not produce any real pictures. The two verdicts are contradictory and cancel one another out, since the photographic apparatus cannot do sketches. Sketching implies, to a particularly high degree, subjective choice: overlooking things and leaving them out. Manet could justifiably have turned the reproach that he was a photographer by retorting: Much of what was done before the invention of photography seems to me to be more photographic than my paintings.

A number of French painters who started their work about 1860 are enumerated under the rubric 'Impressionists'. This nebulous concept is supposed to designate what is common to these Masters. Were the term more precise it would soon collapse, seeing that the bond they had in common was a loose one. Manet, Monet, Renoir and Degas, to name the greatest of them, did not understand each other at all well. What united them was their common fate. Incomprehension and, later, recognition came to them from the same critics, the same art-lovers and collectors and more or less at the same time. They felt themselves allied together against the enemy: the Academy and tradition. About 1880 Paris awoke to an understanding of their art, soon afterwards America, later Germany, and still later England. In Germany writers had to prepare the way—here ears were more open than eyes.

'Impressionists'. At all times artists have received impressions. In our case 'Impressionism' can only mean that those painters received impressions willingly and without prejudice, and to a degree so high as to be novel. They clung to the single, unique visual experience, whereas the Old Masters relied on all the visual sensations they had experienced. The accent falls on the passivity of the visual process. Since Manet does not tell a story, does not say anything remarkable, curious, affecting or diverting, since he paints a portrait even when the task in hand has nothing portrait-like about it, the mind's *activity* seems to have no part in his work. At least, it seemed so when the idea of Impressionism first arose.

The impression which the Impressionists receive is momentary, fleeting; it must be caught hold of quickly, as if in flight. The tempo of painting adjusts itself accordingly; colour becomes primary, put on with aplomb. Conceiving and finishing the whole picture from one standpoint, the painter overlooks detail. Somebody has drawn attention to the fact that Manet ignored finger-nails. He certainly was aware that finger-nails existed, but guarded against supplementing the impression with what he knew. Manet, though not painting out-of-doors, still painted in such a way that his pictures with their diffused light, luminous shadows and flowering local colours look *as if* painted out-of-doors. By way of reaction against the convention of the Old Masters, the facile harmony produced by their glazes, the veils fell away which had spread themselves opaquely over the prismatic world of appearances.

The patchy, loose-knit, even mosaic-like image of the Impressionists was recognized and acclaimed as superbly true to nature after the alarm and bewilderment had died down. Approbation is time-conditioned; there can hardly be a judgment valid once and for all time, even though we think we have a fixed criterion, an objective statement in photography. Antonio Canale may have seen Venice no less rightly than Monet—more rightly, perhaps, judging by the corroborative evidence of photography.

Yet in the last resort the active mind, ready to conceive, and bound up with the individual, with time and place, is decisive. Manet painted what he saw, apparently without discrimination; but he saw what he expected to see, what he was on the look-out for, what he loved. The more positively a painter gives himself up to the natural impression, the more of his personal being, his own idiosyncrasy he brings to light in his work. The pictures of the academicians are more alike than those of the Impressionists.

As Frenchmen, more conservative in art than in politics, the Impressionists did not appear so inimical to tradition as has sometimes been represented. Manet derived from Courbet, learnt from Frans Hals and Velasquez. Degas never ceased to speak of Ingres with veneration. Monet, to begin with, allied himself closely with Manet. Each of them worked out his independence organically, at the same time separating himself more and more not only from his predecessors but from his contemporaries as well. It is more an evolution than a revolution that we have to describe.

In a rationalistic age the country afforded the Parisians and bourgeois society opportunities for walks, excursions, recreation in a holiday mood—if the weather was good. When it rained, or there was a storm or some other meteorological catastrophe, the city-dwellers, including the painter, stayed at home. The age of heroic aspiration —that of the Romantics—and of sentimentality lay in the past. The mysteries of nature no longer aroused an earnest piety, the countryside failed to convey epic or dramatic values, but even so it did, like every work of art, convey emotional values inasmuch as radiant light heightens one's vitality or mild harmony soothes the soul. Form informs, colour delights; form is the text, colour the melody. A black and white reproduction of a picture by Ruisdael or Claude still preserves the salient features, but much less so in the case of Manet, Monet or Renoir. This is doubtless one of the sources of incorrect judgment, seeing that most judgments on art are formulated at the writing-desk, in front of reproductions.

What Everyman knows, what the uneducated philistine sees, that is banal. In every age the Masters have, each in his own way, eschewed banality, selecting, intensifying, composing, leaving out. In objects that were always there for the seeing, Manet saw colours which nobody had seen before. As to the winking, nictitating eye, so to him the object seemed flickering, flashing, visionary. Manet shied away from the banality of sharply-focusing vision.

The sun affects the world of appearances in two ways. It models things in black and white, furthering the illusion of the cubic, that is to say, of spatial depth. In this way it served the Old Masters. But when the sun is in the zenith, and with the sky clear, it thaws all fixity to a continuous flow of colour-values. And that was how it served the Impressionists. Of all the effluences of nature which work on our feelings, none is more enchanting, more vitalizing and heartening for the man of our day than that which is lavished by a sunny landscape. The Old Masters were unable to satisfy their longing for strong light, because they did not paint in the open. Switching cause and effect round, I could also say: they did not paint in the open because that longing was not sufficiently strong. Even Claude and Albert Cuijp avoid open sunlight, contenting themselves with a sunlit haze. The passion for intensive lighting which comes to the fore in the paintings of the Impressionists has a secret connection with certain physiological facts. Invalids no longer visit southern strands in winter, but in the summer; in winter-time they seek the healing powers of the sun in high mountains.

The Impressionists' programme and way of looking, the dictum 'art for art's sake', their long-sighted approach, all fell out to the good of landscape. In their mature period these artists turned to landscape for choice. Sisley and Pissarro were professional landscape-painters.

Only Degas who, unyielding, obstinate, the intellectual superior of his somewhat naïve contemporaries, stands alone in more than one respect, avoided landscape. The straggling, haphazard, arbitrary element in landscape seemed to offer him no task worthy of his efforts. Laprade's pronouncement that 'le génie de la France est le génie de l'action' applies to him. His work, an unendingly difficult one whose results never completely satisfied his high and exacting demands, was primarily concerned with the movement of the human and animal body. Fastidious as regards his object, he never tired of drawing and painting dancers, not by any means for the sake of their grace and feminine charm, and not because he would have liked to soak himself in the amorous atmosphere of the world back-stage. It is likely that he hardly spoke to the ballet girls. For him they were nothing but models. He was keener-eyed than Manet, a good judge who became more and more of a misanthrope, and in his early days a first-class portraitist. On the doings of his time, even on the work of his companions he may have looked with sceptical mistrust, feeling a lack of seriousness, of responsibility, a frivolous drifting. Many had cause to fear the mordant wit of his judgment.

He found landscape too natural. The object he took such agonizing pains for, the bodily movement he struggled to catch, were essentially artificial. The ballerina does not act naturally, she is more drilled—dancing is art—and race-horses are overbred. Riding too is an art. His dancers are like female heavy labourers. Their muscles and sinews are taut, their bodies not lax as, say, those of Boucher's naked women.

If he drew and painted dancers over and over again this stubborn perseverance is neither intellectual laziness nor infatuation with this particular theme. Each impression was an experiment, and he thought that the two-hundredth experiment might get closer to the goal than the hundredth.

For an Impressionist—if he may be called so at all—Degas was too much of an analytical draughtsman, also he had too orderly a mind.

Of course he does not compose with an eye to symmetry and balance of masses, but his seemingly freakish slices of life, with their studied overlappings and blockings, add to the impression of continuous action: they are calculated and weighed to a fine point. His figures seem to have stepped into our field of vision at this very moment and on this precise spot, and to be turning just *there*.

Manet hardly lived to experience his fame. His healthy and unproblematical nature would have enjoyed fame with great gusto. Degas only died in 1917 and saw his pictures fetching the highest prices. Success made no impression on him. He remained unsatisfied with the work which was so much admired by others.

Degas with his logic and *esprit* is a Frenchman in his intellect, Renoir in his sensuousness. From his ancestors Degas inherited, or rather acquired by hard struggle, his mastery of line, Renoir his charm, his sense for feminine grace and attractiveness. Manet hunts his object down with virile strength, Degas outwits it, Renoir receives it with tenderness. When Degas portrays a wedded couple you have a suspicion that the man and the woman bore one another or do not get on; Renoir's couples are happily married or happy without being married. His are sociable folk, much alike and somehow related.

Claude Monet, who in his latter years painted almost nothing but landscapes, adapted his technique logically and systematically to the principles of the *avantgarde*. In his loosening up of forms he goes beyond Manet. It would be a misunderstanding to call his pictures 'sketches'; had he done paintings on the basis of these sketches the essential and valuable thing would have been destroyed. His aim was to catch the impression that emanated from flowing water, from vegetation moved by wind, from buildings tremulous with light. Monet's fear was that if he gave much time to observation he would fail in his object, because the phenomenon changed with the position of the sun. He sought the open with several canvases in hand and painted several pictures from one and the same standpoint, spending about an hour on each. This was logical. But logic is often dangerous for the creator. At any rate it would have been more logical had he done a picture every second, like a snapshot. Monet's views, all glimpsed from one vantage-point at various times of the day—of a haystack, a bridge, a cathedral, a pool—were exhibited together to the instruction and edification of art-lovers. It was demonstrated before their eyes that the point was not the haystack but what the light made of the haystack at any moment. Monet's aim was to get closer to nature, but in the result he too, objectively speaking, avoided the banality of the objective and, by seeing what seemed 'beautiful' to him, eventually brought the art-lovers and collectors to finding it equally 'beautiful'.

What Monet came to see (and we must stress the active character of this kind of seeing) was an incomplete, allusive, whimsical statement about something objective, a statement which stimulated the imagination to fill in the gaps. A man who takes several pages to describe some happening in circumstantial detail will, despite a few sentences falling short, attain his objective; but a man who contents himself with a pithy sentence must weigh each word and hit the mark with each. So that Impressionism

By courtesy of the Bignou Gallery

23. CEZANNE, LANDSCAPE
New York
(*p. 129*)

is not, as misunderstanding probably expected, a source of perfunctoriness and carelessness, but, on the contrary, if not exactly a school of analytical study then certainly a school of intensive and unbiassed dedication to appearances. For the Impressionists a bit of land was the object; for the Old Masters it was made up of objects. In earlier days people made hardly any distinction between thing and appearance, and thought that 'being' was caught in 'seeming'. But after Kant had put the antithesis of 'phenomenon' and 'thing-in-itself' at the very heart of his philosophical system, the phenomenon began to acquire, even for painters who had not read Kant, a life and value of its own; and they increasingly avoided filling out the individual optic experience and thereby falsifying it. Formerly the thing was to create something of which the appearance gave but an incomplete report, and artists succeeded in this with the help of knowledge, experience and visual memory; now the painter felt under an obligation to reproduce appearances and not worry about 'being'.

It can hardly have escaped those who have followed the writings of the savants, and observed how the terminology changes in the course of the nineteenth century, that concepts like 'being', 'matter', 'the static' were compelled to give way to 'becoming', 'force', 'the dynamic'. The artist working towards the end of the century was less concerned with the material state of the created world than with the momentary effects of light which, only *now*, at this unique instant, produces, as if by magic, all these patches and splashes of colour (Pl. 23).

Cézanne is of the generation of Manet, Monet and Renoir. But those who do not know the dates think him younger than he was, and in art-literature he is presented as the follower, continuer, perfecter or transcender of Manet. He pushed Manet's art to its extreme limit, at least in one direction. Zola, an energetic champion of Manet, saw in the labours of Cézanne, his countryman and the friend of his youth, nothing but aspiration that had taken the wrong turning and tragic failure. Cézanne was a genius and a dilettante. A genius with all the genius's originality and unswerving certitude of direction, a dilettante not only because every schoolboy can easily throw his drawing mistakes back at him, but because he was incapable of doing what he set out to do in his youth and what the others could. Consequently he began to proceed warily along unfamiliar paths. His incapacity for the high road forced him to seek out a road of his own. His mature works offer little variation. The single picture contains everything that the Master had it in him to give. 'L'art pour l'art' was carried to extremes. He betrays not the slightest interest in psychology, the destiny of man, or any of his doings.

So as not to misunderstand this painter, three things have to be kept firmly apart. Firstly, a number of exceedingly unclear oral pronouncements which have been handed down and from which an anti-naturalistic programme has been deduced. While he was painting he never gave such a programme a second's thought. Then, his conscious intention as an artist, which aimed at imitating nature. Lastly, the individual vision he experienced while struggling for truth, the realization of which vision was the militant work of his life.

Whether Cézanne painted still-life, portraits, genre or landscape, his psychological and visual attitude remained the same. The object was for him nothing but a colour-phenomenon. One can easily imagine him forgetting as he worked that he had a human face, a tree or an apple in front of him, and then, waking as though from a dream or an ecstasy, suddenly realizing from the result that a face, a tree or an apple had come into being. The things or people he portrays are completely at rest. His card-players do not play, they just sit there with cards in their hands. Cézanne did not, like Courbet, paint ocean waves rearing up to the sky. With his exacting demands on trueness to nature he would probably have opined that Courbet's waves do not move—and, placed alongside a picture of Cézanne's, Courbet's flood strikes us as being frozen. Although, or precisely because, the object does not move, Cézanne overcame the rigidity of the picture to a higher degree than any other Master. The exciting animation that streams out of his pictures with their opalescent, chromatic surfaces comes at bottom from the frenzy and heroic struggle of his creative approach. Just as Degas had difficulty and was never satisfied with his abnormally sensitive eye for form, so Cézanne had difficulty and was never satisfied with his hyper-sensitive eye for the nuances of colour. Where others saw a homogeneous colour-surface, he saw a congeries of colour- and tone-values. The landscape disintegrates into a fandango of chromatic splashes seen as if through a vibrating layer of air—a dance, not a confused whirl.

It is no accident that sensitive art-lovers, at a loss to put this exciting impression into words, speak of music. The juxtapositions within one plane have the effect of a succession in time, of a melody. The patches of white between the patches of colour—paper or canvas—are like pauses in the sequence of notes. But with all this wealth of unalloyed and lambent colours following hard on one another there is never any jostling or garishness. There are no dissonances in this unending melody. The Old Masters obtained sumptuousness of colour mainly with the help of a dark neutral ground, and harmony by toning down the local colours through their use of glaze or some other means. Even Manet was still heightening the luminosity of his lilac with the help of a dark neutral ground. Constable and the Barbiçon Masters more or less habitually place their walls of foliage against the sky, thus adding to its brightness and luminosity by this rather facile method. They compose with light and dark, less with local colour. With the uncompromising one-sidedness and consistency of genius, Cézanne managed to constrain the brilliant, scintillating play of positive local colour into an harmonious pictorial whole without contrasting shadows.

It was not without sacrificing something that Cézanne put all his spiritual energy into *looking* and paid more attention to the appurtenances, the texture, the skin of things than their skeleton, their structure, their body. Yet no one would dare to call his work decorative—in the pejorative sense. Never has the surface been less superficially observed. He does not seek out the pleasant, the ornamental or gorgeous; it was the truth he was concerned with, in so far as appearances contain truth.

His still-life seems to lack nothing, his portraits leave out psychological interpretation, his genre is dumb. His landscapes rouse emotional stirrings in us, though the stirrings are all essentially the same. The artist's frame of mind, tense, alert, steadfast, his rapture and wonder and the urge to become master of what was revealed to him—to *réaliser la sensation*—these things communicate themselves to us in a wizardry of colour which we have never noticed before but which we now acclaim as the beauty of nature, and not pyrotechnics or decoration or a freakish fancy of the artist's.

Cézanne's pictures show more personal idiosyncrasy than do Manet's, which seem more 'natural' in the ordinary sense of the word. There is a tendency to speak of Cézanne's 'style' and people have deduced a programme from his form and contrasted it with the programme of the Impressionists. Cézanne lived in the south of France, far from the Paris studios, exhibitions and museums, in an isolation that favoured the development of his idiosyncrasy and its powerful character. His 'style' goes partly with his dilettantism, with his nervous efforts to overcome awkwardness. It is the result of a glorious struggle. Cézanne never aimed at style consciously like Degas. Certain dicta of his, which express yearnings for an art 'solide et durable comme celui des musées', have been taken a little too seriously by the literati. In general, one should not take the pronouncements of painters over-seriously. Delacroix speaks of nature with partiality. Such utterances reveal less the essence and character of the man than the wish to pass into history in that way. All the same, compared with Renoir or Monet, Cézanne does arrive at durability, avoids everything vague, sagging, nebulous. He sets hard-and-fast linear bounds, feeling the need to set the torrent of colour as one 'sets' jewels. He probably guessed that chaos threatened Impressionism in the end, and sought a hold in stoppages which sometimes have the hardness of geometry.

Colour is nothing but an attribute of form, form nothing but the locus of colour. The development of painting up to Cézanne resulted in the second definition becoming more apt than the first. Cézanne sees colour and is at pains to find its locus, to hedge it round; the Old Masters saw forms and endued them with the appropriate colours. Among the Old Masters there is one who reminds us of Cézanne in many respects. That is El Greco. He and Cézanne are perilous neighbours in a Gallery, because by the side of their work all the others seem dull, drab, conventional or untrue in colouring. It is no accident that El Greco has been acclaimed by the admirers of Cézanne.

Together with Cézanne, van Gogh is reckoned among the 'switchmen' who gave a new direction when Impressionism had come to a dead-end. The modern cult of genius has appropriated van Gogh with especial zeal. The many letters he wrote to his brother afford us a glimpse of a touching fate. Since his *via dolorosa* has all the appearance of a novel written by Dostoievski and is more readily accessible than his *œuvre*, his pictures are regarded as illustrations to his biography.

Born in 1853 and thus considerably younger than Cézanne, he was barely affected by the great art of his time. And this aloofness certainly did not lie with his circumstances. His brother, who looked after him with indefatigable loyalty, gave him advice and, as a successful art-dealer, was both in a position and willing to put him in touch with the world of art in Paris, holding out opportunities enough for adaptation. Neither was it van Gogh's intention to set himself apart; he was modest, painfully aware of his helplessness, wanted to learn from the art of others, struggled to produce marketable pictures and with astonishing uncertainty of judgment saw models which he thought quite out of his reach now in Millet, now in Daumier, Mauve, Herkomer as well as in the work of completely indifferent painters. Manet admired Velasquez and Frans Hals to the advantage of his own development, but van Gogh showed himself incapable of learning anything to the point from the work of others. Herein is disclosed the originality of his talent, so certain of its goal. It was not defiance or arrogance, not faith in his mission that isolated him, it was rather the intensity of personal vision that prevented him from profiting by the attainments of the Old Masters or his own contemporaries, although he had to wrestle with awkwardness every time he tried to realize his vision.

Even Millet, who was near him in spirit, influenced him to a barely perceptible degree with his form-language, and not at all with his colouring.

The muddle and wretchedness of his life derive not from difficult circumstances but from the cast of his character, from the ascetic absoluteness of his will, which made him hard to get on with, unsociable and headstrong. His family, his surroundings had much to suffer from him and conducted themselves patiently in face of his excessive boorishness. Van Gogh became a painter by devious and erratic routes. Of a profound religious orthodoxy in his youth, given to good works, ready to sacrifice himself for the suffering and needy, minister to the sick, missionary, he was subsequently infatuated beyond measure—albeit fitfully—with a woman unworthy of him, and not genuinely infatuated either, but rather chained to her by pity. In the end, casting all this behind him, religion, love of women, family, friendship, he put the whole energy of his soul into pure looking. Words like 'beauty', 'happiness' or 'peace of soul' occur in his letters in connection with the landscape. He painted and drew human wretchedness, to mitigate which had been the urgent wish of his youth. What drove him to art was a fanatical love of nature which, in this extreme case, clearly reveals itself as a substitute for lost orthodoxy. Van Gogh is an orthodox pantheist, a martyr to his worship of nature. He painted with the maniacal fervour with which the pious have prayed, mortified themselves and suffered a sacrificial death. Naturally such extremes are pathological, as the painter's end shows.

No matter what van Gogh did he never undertook anything that might have been useful to him in any way, that might have 'advanced' him in the ordinary sense. He possessed that 'objectivity' which, according to Schopenhauer, is the mark of the genius and the saint. Although he proved incapable of mastering life, he expresses himself in his letters in a manner that is neither thoughtless nor high-flown, on the contrary with lucidity and often with shrewdness. His brain worked for his interests, to which his far more powerful instincts, governing his actions, were inimical.

One can read in the letters how van Gogh wanted to produce 'marketable' art; from his 'work' one can see how—and why—he was unable to do so. Today his pictures are not only marketable but fetch exorbitant prices, since intellectual snobbery has turned honest enthusiasm into posthumous fame, as a sure sign of which various falsifications have emerged.

Deep in the south of France, far from exhibitions, museums, art-schools and literati, there van Gogh, like Cézanne, created his mature works, though 'mature' has a different application in this case. It is hardly possible to conceive that, dying in his thirty-eighth year, he could have advanced further along his road. His pictures are far from being 'mature' in the sense of finished, completed, clarified. He created portraits and landscapes which emit a raging torrent of force, not Cézanne's ravishing melody of colour but a shrill clangour rich in dissonances, a terribly stammering if intensely suggestive language. Nature has never been seen so eruptively. His pictures remind one of battle-fields, the brush-strokes seem to have left welts and wounds behind them.

We can imagine how Menzel would have judged van Gogh—certainly with wrath. From his point of view he could have seen nothing but mistakes. But it is precisely what, in his eyes, was faulty that makes van Gogh's style. Perhaps the following statement may be hazarded: van Gogh made a virtue of necessity, to wit, his style, since it is the effort, the exertion, the laboriousness of his work that throws up what is personal and peculiar to him. The fact that his style never strikes us as a manner lies in its not being derived from conscious will, and also because van Gogh never wavered in his fanatical devotion to nature.

His religiousness, rooted as it was in a Calvinistically puritanical faith, turns into pantheistic emotionalism when confronted by nature and into ascetic compassion when confronted by human beings. Not that van Gogh might have become a politician or a party-man. In his epistolary outpourings there is no trace of hostility to or arraignment of the rich, the well-fed, the snug and secure. Sympathy and with it the creative urge were aroused in him at the sight of poverty and hard physical work. He sought his models in homes for the aged, orphanages, poor-houses, among farm labourers. Gnarled, wrinkled figures bent and blunted by fate were the natural—and picturesque—phenomena of the landscape, the ones worth looking at, the only fellow-creatures that existed for him; while he looked—without hatred—past the indolent, the well-washed and well-dressed. One of the few things from Holy Writ to retain its validity in the nineteenth century was the commandment: in the sweat of thy brow shalt thou eat thy bread. Social conscience became a source of strength for creative work first for Millet, then for Israels, Liebermann, Meunier and other Masters, but never did it obtrude itself so powerfully, so crassly and at the same time so untendentiously as in the work of van Gogh.

In the interpretation of landscape the governing factor is not merely the observer's standpoint but, equally dependent on his spiritual state, his line of vision. Without shifting his standpoint the observer can alter his line of vision. Van Gogh's eye is directed earthwards. He sees the ground at his feet, the furrows in the field, patches of grass, flower-beds, fallen leaves, paving-stones. Occasionally he may have viewed nature from above, from a window, but wherever the standpoint does not entail looking *upwards* the painter's interest is caught mainly by what lies at his feet. As a rule the horizon shifts to the top of the picture and not infrequently beyond it.

However shrill the open vowels of his colour-surfaces may sound, as though there were no enveloping atmosphere, the consonants of his violent, sizzling or jagged line quell the orgy. The skeletal pen-drawings go against nature's simplicity less than do the paintings.

The realization of van Gogh's personal and inimitable vision has so little of anything inimitable about it that his pictures can be falsified by copyists with astonishing success. Pieter Brueghel among the Old Masters reminds one very distantly of van Gogh, with his sense for the dynamic. Historians will probably delight in this connection, since they love to stress indigenous values. Brueghel came from the Dutch Brabant where van Gogh also grew up.

Cézanne and van Gogh succeeded in putting pure colours side by side in splashes, streaks or points which, at some remove from the picture, coalesce and bring about a stronger illumination and airiness, suggest life and movement to a higher degree than an unbroken expanse of mixed pigments. This was in keeping with their manner of seeing and feeling. The so-called 'pointillistes', Seurat and his imitators, made a manner of this naturally evolving style, and dotted away on principle, carefully and cold-bloodedly. The result leaves an impression of arbitrary fooling. Here, as also in so-called Cubism, we have a short-lived mode which owes its success to snobbish craving for novelty.

German painting in the nineteenth century offers a confused picture. The history of it is written afresh every ten years, and always new personalities are thrust into the foreground as the real representatives and misunderstood talents zealously discovered. Nevertheless it is invariably the painters who achieve fame in their own day who, through their work as well as their teachings and influence, determine the character of their period, at least for the student of culture. Owing to powerful decentralization there was no centre of German art. Dresden, Munich, Vienna, Düsseldorf, Berlin, each of these cities laid, for a time, fruitless claims to leadership.

The public museums, exhibitions, the mounting flood of art-literature, reproductions, then the German zeal for learning and the German itch to travel combined with better travelling facilities—all this brought the danger of eclecticism nearer. Once upon a time the apprentice started out from the art of his master and trod a relatively straight path; now the multiplicity of movements, each contradicting the other, ended in confusion and finally scepticism or nihilism. 'Affinitive' models were sought and often—far off in space and time—found. Such contacts with the Old Masters rested more often than not on crass misunderstanding, as in Makart's liaison with Venice.

Rising from indigence and provincial stuffiness there grew up an economically prosperous society which, lacking any tradition of form, pestered art-production with its tastes and likings, and favoured the affecting, the entertaining, the anecdotal and pleasant in painting. The school-master who, it has been said, conquered at Sédan, was pre-eminently responsible for this penchant for the 'intellectual' and the 'cultivated'. German painters cocked an eye at literature. First Carstens and Cornelius with their heroic cartoons; the 'Nazarenes' with their quite unsensual faith, striving—in vain—to revive the religious picture; then Kaulbach with his ambitious ideas about world history, Piloty with his histrionics, Makart with his operatic splendours: all of them fashionable sensations which proved sterile in the result. Less successful on their appearance, but of more lasting significance for that, is the aristocratic and exasperatingly idealistic art of Feuerbach, arrogant, cool, and the choicely fastidious art of von Marées, which displays more artistic understanding than creative power.

About 1880 the idea gained ground, in Munich to begin with, that there might be a valuable style of painting independent of sensibility, intellectuality and erudition. The bearer of this message was the Frenchman Courbet—not, as it happens, Manet. Let us stick to Leibl whose work, in the eyes of stern critics, is of lasting validity. In his later years he aspired to something like a synthesis of Courbet and Holbein, and in one or two of his portraits may have triumphed over the Frenchman. Thorough to the point of pedantry, he puts up a display of mastery in his genre-pieces which arouses no correspondingly powerful effect in us. We admire a *tour de force* of prolonged, persistent observation. But the spiritual contact is missing, because the painter regards human beings neither with humour nor with contempt, nor sympathy nor pity, seeing them only as models. The dubious juxtaposition of life-size and near-sight in his approach, with the result that no detail is overlooked, cripples the spectator's imagination. Van Gogh's comparatively botchy figures contain far more life since each was done in an hour or so, whereas Leibl, spending an infinity of time on a picture, loses psychological sympathy with the object and is unable to catch the spontaneous movements of life. The 'correct' in art lies close to the trivial. A man who expresses everything is a bore.

I have not voiced these suspicions, these protests against Leibl, in order to decry this rightly admired Master, but to adduce a broad lesson from the experience that a man so conscientious, so highly gifted and so systematically trained is less important than a painter of questionable talent like van Gogh. The moral is: good painting is not enough. After education, deep thoughts, anecdotes, decoration have all failed, visual art is nourished by springs of forcc flowing to it from the emotional values which have retained their validity. There remains the interest in personality (which keeps portrait-painting alive), and with it social feeling, sympathy for our suffering fellow-creatures—and finally, in a world from which the gods have vanished, the miracle and enigma of landscape.

VI

THE SIGNIFICANCE OF LANDSCAPE IN OUR DAY

Courbet is supposed to have remarked: How can anybody paint an angel when he hasn't seen one? This proposition must at least be supplemented by the following two riders: Those who believe in angels see them and: Even those who are not convinced of the existence of angels but can see them with the mind's eye, can also paint them. Böcklin did not believe in the existence of mythological creatures—at least not in the ordinary sense—but saw them so corporeally that he was able to give them credible form. It's the faith and imagination that decide. This is true of religion, mythology, and in the end of every other object as well. Nowadays of course no honest painter would dare to depict the murder of Caesar. Nobody looking at an attempt of this kind could allow himself to be convinced that the murder went off in quite the way that the clever painter has contrived and arranged. If Menzel's historical pictures convince, it is because Friedrich II was relatively close to the Master in time and space, and also because Menzel combined erudition and imagination to a peculiar degree. Böcklin and Menzel are special cases. But in general Courbet's sober observation holds good of his rationalistic, sceptical, enlightened age. The mind's eye saw only what is conveyed to it by the senses, and the activity of the imagination was limited to individual formulations of what that eye sees.

Of the things conveyed to the senses anything *human* will,

if plausibly portrayed, turn towards us with eloquence, since all human suffering, joy, action is—potentially—our own, and hence can be understood without difficulty, fathomed, felt. It is different with landscape: it rises up before us like something mysterious, a melody rather than a statement. The moods which the landscape-painter conveys to us, such as melancholy, longing, peace, exaltation, awe, solace, are not specific moods differentiated as concepts, like those emanating from the doings of humankind. The landscape is on the further side of life, and in the final phase of its development in painting has ceased altogether to be a setting, it no longer reports topographically. What music is in the categories of art, landscape is in the categories of painting.

Though independent of life's interests, the landscape still affects our emotional life indirectly, delicately, as though from far-off. A genre picture brings us diversion direct, because we are participating in the diverting process as spectators. In the landscape the contrast between, say, inorganic rock and organic growth symbolizes some conflict which reminds us of spiritual conflicts. The sky-pointing tree points to the victory of the forces of life over the force of gravity. The clouds awaken longings for the unearthly. The emotions proceeding from the landscape imply that our sensibility is meeting them halfway. In the poetry of the eighteenth and nineteenth centuries—Goethe's lyrics, for instance—the correspondence between natural phenomena and the state of the mind and heart has been put into words. But form and colour may also strike emotional chords in us which are just as richly modulated. Since Beethoven and Goethe were both Germans, a general talent for lyric, music and landscape-painting on the part of the Germans might have been expected. This expectation has not been fulfilled so satisfactorily where landscape is concerned. We look round in that very prolific productivity and are not as a rule altogether satisfied. The causes preventing an organic efflorescence, after the germination we detected in the works of C. D. Friedrich and his contemporaries, are not far to seek. At the beginning of the sixteenth century and of the nineteenth century the Germans were ahead of the French in their love of nature, but in the course of the nineteenth century the relationship is reversed, since there are hardly any German landscapes to be found comparable with the creations of Corot, Daubigny, Monet and Cézanne.

Schools, education, half-understood metaphysical aesthetics made for abstract thinking to the detriment of naïve looking. Apart from the harmless lack of taste displayed by the buying public, art-production was guided by the wayward, miseducated taste of art-critics. I am afraid that Lessing's *Laocoon* is still being read in school. The Academy still clings to the *fata morgana* of fine art, which today is not rooted in any living soil and only galvanizes a defunct ideal. The works of the Old Masters are easily accessible in the museums and are copied assiduously. Deriving as they do from a world of completely different philosophical ideas they can only be studied, without deleterious effects, by those who possess a powerfully independent and active mind, like Manet or Max Liebermann. For most people they are more dangerous than useful.

Acquisitiveness and ambition now govern the choice of object, the standpoint and the interpretation. Painters struggle to please and to astonish. In the exhibitions dimensional greatness wins the day, the uncommon, the 'effective'; and the man who can produce something that seems 'difficult' to the pundits carries off the medal. A

Judgement of Paris—a composition of nude figures—is 'difficult', a landscape 'easy' in the view of academic authority. In reality the academic prizeman had an easier time of it painting his *Judgement of Paris* than Cézanne had painting an apple. It is not the task that decides but, within the artist's make-up, the relationship between his ability and the demands he puts to himself. Once we are clear on this point we have only a derisive smile for the distinction between 'difficult' and 'easy' as regards the object to be done, and we cannot avoid quoting: Easy though it be, the easy is difficult.

Black-and-white is essentially part of the heritage of German education. Most of what Goethe knew of fine art came out of folios of etchings, just as most of what the art-historian of today knows comes from book illustrations, photographs and the magic lantern. Students in the academies have the habit of regarding drawing as one thing, painting as another. Their teaching goes from contours to modelling and so over to the grading of tones, with colour thrown in. But the untutored child with sound instincts is always in a hurry to get to the paintbox. Colour-sense wilts under academic training. It is with colour that appearances address our feelings, our receptivity; with form that they address our active mind. The Germans have always honoured mind more than feeling, fearing its degeneration into sentimentality. Even the musician Wagner had to resort to words in order to get himself heard. The painters most esteemed for a while—Menzel, Klinger, Böcklin—were witty or at least accounted as such. Looking at their works, people could think thoughts. Landscape affords no opportunity for such displays of mentation. To the extent that painters were regarded as landscapists they had first to legitimize themselves by achievements of another kind, like Thoma with the worthy meditativeness of his genre pieces. The Impressionists overcame the dualism of form and colour, drawing and painting which was natural and necessary to the Old Masters, thus making colour predominant. Van Gogh, the *enfant terrible* of his contemporaries, who pushed everything to extremes, heightened the power of positive local colour far beyond the natural impression, living as he did in the sunny land of the south. He intoxicated himself on colour. The letters in which he orders tubes of paint from Paris read like the clamant cries of a dipsomaniac who needs strong liquor in the belief that he cannot live without it.

Another dualism the Impressionists broke with was that between the 'study' and the 'finished painting'. It was the custom to regard impressions made from nature as hack-work with the aid of which one could then execute the final picture in the studio, in peace and undisturbed by exciting and rapidly changing visual experiences—to one's own satisfaction and also to the satisfaction of the buying public. In this transaction gold was changed into paper-money, which is to say: a lasting value was sacrificed for a temporally valid one. The impression was rounded off and put into 'effect', schematized. Many of the 'studies' of the successful German landscapists, such as the brothers Achenbach, surprise by their freshness and simplicity, whereas their once hotly desired pictures only arouse boredom. The Impressionists put the first last, took the sketch for the final thing and waited until their 'sketches' were recognized as works of full value.

The historical critic, at pains to avoid misjudging the Old Masters in terms of his own age, falls into the other error of demanding that the art of his time should give what the Old Masters gave.

Formerly painting encroached on territories now claimed by science and literature: it reported, described, instructed, told stories, preached, moralized; was a means to intellectual ends. All these duties and tasks have gradually been stripped from it without the artists themselves being aware of this impoverishment, which was at the same time a burden removed. And the critics had difficulty in adjusting themselves to the change.

The supreme example set up by the works of the Old Masters still tempts cultivated and aspiring painters to try to revive a monumental and spiritually significant art, tempts them to notable efforts which fail to come off because there is a lack of religious receptivity, of psychological readiness—in the painters as well as in the art-lovers.

Visual art has marked itself off from science and also from poetry, and withdrawn into the regions that are the core of it. The slogan 'l'art pour l'art' is an announcement of renunciation and limitation, and at the same time the hope of cultivating one's own self-contained garden and reaping a rich harvest. But it is not to be translated as 'good painting for good painting's sake', which could only mean impoverishment. When I stand before a picture representing the *Judgement of Paris* I think of the mythological adventure; other interpretations of that project come to mind. The naked beauties present an unusual spectacle. In the heads and gestures of the figures I read the story. My knowledge, my understanding are taken up and engrossed. If, on the other hand, I stand before the picture of a bouquet of flowers or a meadow with a single tree jutting into the sky, all intellectual interest is shut off. Nothing remains but a segment of familiar reality and the impression: I have seen this before, but never just as the happy eye of the artist has seen it. But in order to convey this effect through my eye direct to my feelings, the Master must have concentrated his observation upon the phenomenon more intensively than the painter of the *Judgement of Paris*, who was concerned to convince me with invention, composition and narrative. One cannot do both things at once to the same degree. By confining himself to the object given, the painter refines his colour-sense, obtains a richness of nuance; and at the same time his delivery acquires an accelerated tempo, a vibrant livingness, since all elaborate and protracted preparatory work is spared him.

In Germany too, despite powerful resistance, the idea of the painter's profession changed. It is no accident that the great ones who were celebrities in their day but later dethroned, such as Piloty, Makart, G. Max, painted historical, decorative or ingenious figure-compositions; no accident either that those who formerly worked in the dark and were appreciated after their death, above all Blechen, were landscape-painters. It was certainly not lack of feeling for nature that inhibited the flowering of a successful landscape art; more prejudice on the part of authority, the art-critic and the buying public, and on the part of the painters themselves lack of self-confidence and instinct. In Paris the misunderstood painters received comfort and encouragement in the society of comrades who shared a common fate, and were able to endure unsuccess without letting themselves be put off their ideals; but in Germany every artist born out of his time had to battle with the obtuse world in isolation, and sooner or later he succumbed. Even Blechen who might, judging by his make-up, have become the German Corot, was sometimes driven to theatricality and decoration by demands coming from outside. If C. D. Friedrich and his contemporaries are now being hauled into the limelight so zealously, and our grandfathers honoured more than our fathers, this preference only goes to show that the German feeling for nature had not spent itself fully in the second half of the nineteenth century.

For us, historians in paint are over and done with, and poets in paint only keep alive with an effort. If Böcklin has not ceased to fascinate unprejudiced art-lovers, even eclipsing our appreciation of the high aims for which we have to thank Masters like Feuerbach or von Marées, the attraction comes chiefly from the landscape with which his mythological and symbolical figures are closely and harmoniously connected, often like embodiments of the elements.

Bleakness or opulence of soil, gentleness or ruggedness of mountain-profile, exhilarating or oppressive atmosphere set the chords of the soul vibrating. It is precisely in the *commonness* of moods so aroused that their effect lies; they resemble variously shaped vessels which, according to our individual disposition, we fill with our experience. A serene landscape perhaps calls up memories of bygone youthful days, of some place where I was happy. Just as wordless music stimulates the imagination without limiting it, gives it direction but not a definite path, so with landscape. We set our own text to the melody, whereas everything human in the picture prescribes the text for us.

As an object, the land has something in common with ornament, which likewise operates as a visual symbol and entirely meets the requirement of art for art's sake. The completely unintellectual art of the East lives on ornament and colour and, as a symbol, works less on sentiment than on the senses.

Experience teaches that people have developed a higher degree of receptivity for impressions emanating from nature unadorned than from artificial, geometrical or architectonic ornamentation.

Released from the service of the Church, visual art by no means lost all touch with the world of religious feeling. The painters of the sixteenth century contemplated landscape in the same frame of mind with which they were accustomed to linger in their capacious churches. All metaphysical thought in the Middle Ages was netted by orthodoxy, guided, but also cramped; later, become free, it sailed out into poetry and art yet without giving up its heritage of devout meditation. Since the world as Creation, or rather as the result of Creation, was glorified in veneration of the Creator, especially in the seventeenth century, it remained hallowed even when the relations between Creation and Creator became open to doubt. Indeed, reverence for the phenomenal world gained in depth when the creative Power, worshipped from time immemorial as divine, was sought in nature herself. The personal longing for belief, the ever-active need to worship by looking, turned to landscape. In the nineteenth century C. D. Friedrich and van Gogh avow in the clearest possible terms that they look at nature in religious ecstasy. Knowing such extreme instances as this, to be met with in the puritanical North, we can trace the religious element even where it is less loudly voiced and works unconsciously—as in the frankly sensuous art of the French sun-worshippers. The painter may be worldly-minded and a freethinker, but he will always gratefully applaud a beauty which, if not of God, is certainly not man-made. Gottfried Keller's

To thee, thou wonder-working world,
Thou beauty without end,
I write a little billet-doux
Upon this pergament . . .

radiates, with optimistic faith in nature, a sort of non-ecclesiastical exaltation of soul, like a painting. Treading the precincts of the church a man shakes off his egocentric narrowness. Or he experiences relief from the load of his daily interests in travelling, in holiday mood. By the sea-shore Heine put questions which had once been answered categorically by the Church. Art has not ceased to unriddle these questions if not for the understanding then assuredly for our intuitive feelings, and has thus become the refuge and sanctuary of religious needs—in a scientific age. Intellectually gifted persons try to fill the vacuum which the vanished belief in the Bible has left behind it, with philosophy; the visually gifted find a substitute for what they have lost, in surrendering to the marvel of the world of appearance. Nature, in her incomprehensibility, has become the symbol of God who, according to Lichtenberg, is 'incomprehensibility personified'.

The word 'Weltanschauung' with its double meaning (philosophy and world-view or outlook) establishes the bridge from visual experience to metaphysical dogma and points out how dependent the history of looking, and hence the history of art, are on the life of the mind and its permutations.

So long as belief in the Bible ruled unshaken, the 'Maker', Himself made in the image of man, was regarded as having fashioned the cosmos, meaningfully and planfully, with organisms that are God-willed and immutable in form and substance. But when the world was regarded as having evolved, when the cause of the evolution was lodged in nature, the eye fastened itself on coming-to-be, growth, passing-away, change, on the relations of things to one another, for instance the relation between soil and growing vegetation, terrain and the course of rivers, the might of the elements and their effects. In all Being the 'having become' was detected. At last, the existent having become questionable, and even the object without a subject dispossessed of existence, the vision that depended on the subjectivity of the observer gained in significance.

Thus Being was superseded by Becoming and Becoming by Seeming. And this development, which loosened the ties with religious feeling, is clearly reflected in the history of the visual arts and particularly clearly in the history of landscape-painting. There was no lack of love of nature in the Middle Ages, but in art it expressed itself differently from the way it does now. The sculptor of the thirteenth century observed the existing organisms of plant and animal life with devoutness, inasmuch as he introduced them as symbols or decoration into his *dogmatic masonry*, which is how we are to conceive the garment of the cathedrals. But within the scope of the tasks allotted him the sculptor lacked occasion and opportunity to pay much attention to landscape.

The programme of the Impressionists is no longer regarded as generally valid. The reaction in favour of solid form, in favour of 'objectivity' is unmistakable. In numerous ways, with theorems which all sound more or less plausible, ambition courts attention and sensation. After all our experience of novel art, first condemned and then applauded, something of value is expected principally from the repulsive and the preposterous. But amid the welter of experiments and excesses one thing seems to stand firm for the present and the immediate future as the legacy of Impressionism: strong, open local colour. Less decisive is the fact that painters have habituated themselves to painting out-of-doors: the sun can also hold sway in the studios, and *plein air* can become convention and be accepted as 'beautiful' just as, in the old days, *chiaroscuro* or warm, gentle harmony. Reaction against the war-cry 'l'art pour l'art' and a longing for an intellectually expressive art are to be observed. Under that slogan art fled more and more from the sphere of the intellect to that of the feelings, and finally to that of the senses, avoiding all ties. As regards landscape—and still-life—it was a change for the good, and as regards painting, too, in the technical sense, since every object attracts the means of expression most suited to it. On the other hand the historian may point cautiously to the fact that art, grown mistress of a limited field, was once a handmaiden, industrious and happy in her work. The fact, too, that a highly esteemed painter like Degas avoided landscape—and still-life—and struggled to put the whole of his intellectual and spiritual powers into his work, may arouse a certain mistrust of the self-limitation and complacency that reigned in the studios. But that he was unable to satisfy his longing in the profession of painter and, despite all his success, grew more and more embittered, shows how difficult it is to combine visual experiences with the demands of the intellect.

The sense-delicacy required of the painter absorbs his other faculties. People gravitate towards specialization, division of labour and one-sidedness. And where might forces be found powerful enough, as once the Church was, to drive the artist back into subordination? In a new faith, perhaps, political or national passions, or hero-worship?

VII

THE NATURE AND ORIGINS OF THE GENRE AS A CATEGORY

Genre is a vague term with uncertain limits, easier of negative than of positive definition. Whatever is *not* of historical, religious or mythological significance in a picture dealing with man and his activities, whatever is *not* characterized, exalted or consecrated by knowledge, thought or faith, falls in the category of genre. I would say that the 'common' is the proper field of the genre, were it not that this word had sunk too low in the course of time. Goethe would still have been able, without misgiving, to define the 'common' as the field of the genre. At any rate the idea of genre has an all-round limitation in the idea of the 'uncommon'.

The made-up German word *Sittenbild* ('custom-picture') has a richer content than the accepted term 'genre', but is scarcely preferable for that since it says something without saying everything. Custom means: the form of life to which we are used, to which we have been educated, which is enjoined on us. But the genre-painter is concerned with what people are accustomed to do not merely because custom prescribes it but from instinct and inclination as well.

The idea of genre can be envisaged as a disc which is defined at its sharpest towards the centre, while towards the periphery it takes on more and more of a questionable character. The disc is traversed by the arcs of other ideas, with the result that fields arise in which the genre appears tinged and adulterated with historical, biblical or portraitesque elements.

The interest which an historical event arouses rests on its extraordinariness, its uniqueness. Man as an individual is unique and to that extent not genre-like. Genre means genus, species. In the genre-picture the particular case points to other cases, so that a certain happening or state is illustrated as an example or, to put it philosophically, as an 'idea'. The historical picture says: *that* happened once; the genre picture says: *this* happens often, this is how peasants behave at such and such a time in such and such a place; or: this is what happens when belligerent horsemen meet.

Somewhere or other I came across the definition: anonymity is the genre's idiosyncrasy. Because we do not know the names, are not interested in them, the common human condition is revealed and, within that condition, class, sex, age, mother, child, soldier, lady. The individual makes us enquire the name.

Seeing is recognizing. An expanse of green is interpreted as a tree and thus catalogued among our empirical concepts—beech, oak—and knowledge relates it to genus. The artist diverts the flood of individualities pouring in upon him into the canals of species, intent on intellectual mastery. Objects facilitate or aggravate this work in that they differ from one another in degree of individual physiognomy, or to the degree of our interest in individual physiognomy. An apple engrosses the painter as representative of this species of fruit although, strictly speaking, no two apples are alike. The higher we ascend in the scale of nature the more markedly the individual triumphs over the typical, the generic. The more resolutely painters begin with ideas the more thoroughly they destroy the individual, stylizing or caricaturing it, above all the human face; whereas an apple, which for them is *an* apple and not *this* apple, they reproduce purely and simply because in the apple idea and appearance coincide. It is clear enough that artists in the Middle Ages started out from the idea; in more recent times the typical conflicts with the particular.

The Golden Age of the genre is the seventeenth century. Then, it was in the main the Netherlanders who arrived at the point of view from which the doings of man—quite independent of the significance of the action or situation—became a choice object of artistic creation. Reality-sense, aiming abstractly at the typical, created the genre-picture.

The germ of the genre, its initial and preliminary stages, may be observed in mediaeval art. The swing towards the profane, resulting in the disruption of the ecclesiastical tradition in painting, came in the fifteenth and sixteenth centuries after certain clandestine stirrings had shaken the limits of the orthodox view of the world.

The God-fearing man who regarded his earthly existence as loaded with guilt and as something to be overcome could not, with a good conscience, take innocent pleasure in the portrayal of reality. And even after rigid dogma had loosened, everything earthly remained a snare and a delusion for a long time, an object of suspicion which required some pretext or other to be admitted into the domain of art.

Opportunities for smuggling in the profane were seized all the more eagerly since the Christian outlook had never been able completely to extirpate man's *joie de vivre* and his delight in the senses.

Faith, according to the doctrines of the Church, endows us with the capacity to see the invisible. Thereby the activity of the artist was brought into line with faith, his imagination stimulated. Since, however, artistic imagination drew sustenance exclusively from reality as given, and could only exemplify the invisible in the visible, the spiritual in the corporeal, the divine in the human, the abstract in the concrete, the image became a symbol, an allegory or a hieroglyph. Something was indeed formed, but something else asserted.

The mediaeval way of thinking was homogeneous and all-embracing. Artists were faced with the duty of making the grandiose architecture of the spirit accessible to the eye. Believers saw the work of art as a tenet from the doctrinal texts of the Church. The earthly was built into a scaffolding that reached up to heaven, as dependent—according to faith—on divine rule as—according to superstition—it was on the stars. A sculptured relief amid the ornamentation of a cathedral may show a man wielding a scythe. Undoubtedly a genre-like theme. What is meant, however, is a month. The calendar gave book-illuminators a welcome opportunity to describe country life in detail. The block-printed books of the fifteen century, which go back to the earlier miniatures, contain illustrations of professional life. Here, too, man's doings depend on threads manipulated from above. The industriousness of country-people is subordinated to the cycle of the seasons, the months.

This circumscription of intellectual activity and artistic imagination by a sovereign faith drove reality down to a deeper level and checked the desire to reproduce the data of immediate observation; it made for purification, intensification, idealization, but it also forged strong links with tradition in painting. The traditional tie explains the impersonality, the persistence of the mediaeval style. Form was regulated by the grand and monumental art of sculpture which, in the nature of things, is chary of the genre. In the service of the Church the artists, devising objects of devotion, took over something of the world-shunning attitude of clerics, while, conflicting with that, the work of their eyes familiarized them with visible reality.

In the fifteenth century painters had almost exclusively the same tasks to solve as in the Middle Ages, but they solved them in another spirit, since the need that was brewing for the illusion of reality sharpened their observation of the things of this world. Genre-motifs encroached on the devotional picture. Everything that man's activity offers to the physical eye is so much grist to the genre-painter, material in which he can discern the typical, whatever is peculiar to this or that kind of man. Anybody observing the battle of Waterloo as a truth-loving eye-witness, like Stendhal, sees nothing but genre. The painter can turn the battle-picture into an historical picture if, looking back from his knowledge of the decisive significance and results of the event, he sets about it with hero-worshipping imagination. Without the 'pathos of distance' (in time) the historical picture cannot thrive. Observed with the unspoken thought: 'This is how it always is', the event becomes a genre-picture; observed with the knowledge that 'it was like that at one particular time and place', it becomes an historical picture. Strictly speaking, nothing is *in itself* genre-like or historical, only thinking makes it so. So also with religious or biblical themes.

Since for the believer everything earthly, hence visible, is at once squalid, evil, unredeemed, the admitted themes drawn from the visible world as given take on a character bordering on caricature, contrasting and enhancing the impression made by the holy and the divine. Worldliness becomes picturesque as a contrast to other-worldliness. Jan van Eyck paints the sleeping soldiers in the picture of the *Women by the Tomb of the Saviour* with whimsical delight, as genre-like, even humorous figures, thus heightening by sharp contrast the ideal apparition of the holy women and the angel who announces the resurrection. Seen reality enters the ecclesiastical picture by a narrow door (Pl. 3, 24).

In the sixteenth century the profane interpretation of biblical scenes hazarded a bold frankness, intent on overcoming iconographic tradition through visual experience. The icon becomes the historical picture when time and place are borne in mind, and the historical picture approximates to the genre-picture to the extent that the painter sticks to reality as given. Pieter Brueghel 'profanes' his *Christ Carrying the Cross* by choosing a point of view from which the Saviour, barely visible, far-off, seems submerged in the mob pressing forward to the spectacle of execution, curious and all agog for sensations. In the foreground of course, on an elevation, the lamenting faithful ones—but this group, done more out of a feeling of obligation than anything else, fails, despite its relatively large size, to stand out against the turbulent mass of people in the effect as a whole. The tragedy is illustrated as the triumph, the mass-weight of stupid insensibility.

The Netherlands predilection for reality went so far in the sixteenth century that the biblical study was used as an opportunity to put genre—and still-life—on wide view in the foreground. What the painter did not see with his physical eye often comes out pale and spectral in the distance, has to be looked for, is rather the title and apology of the picture than its content.

Pieter Aertsen supplied his contemporaries with altarpieces containing large-scale figures, most of which were destroyed by the iconoclasts. His talent aimed at direct apprehension of the visible. He did genre-pictures in which the emotional effect of size and monumental scale is at loggerheads with their spiritually trivial contents. He shows himself stronger in still-life than in genre, since the physical movements of human beings and the psychological relations between them are inadequately expressed, while his powerful painting technique did full justice to dead things and animals. He painted a *Birth of Christ* in which the most powerful impression is made by the head of an ox, formidably true to nature. His still-life had a more exemplary effect on the painters who succeeded him and, indirectly, on the seventeenth century, than did his genre-like narrative (Pl. 25).

We hardly notice that a painter may be lacking in intellect and imagination, at least where the Masters of the fifteenth century are concerned, because Church and tradition make up for that lack. The painters who worked free of the Church in the sixteenth century had to overcome banality on their own resources—which a Brueghel succeeded in doing, but not a Pieter Aertsen.

With his gorgeous profusion of dead things which he violently obtrudes upon the biblical scene, thus violating its meaning, Pieter Aertsen prepared the way for the monumental still-life of the Flemish School developed by Frans Snijders in the seventeenth century. Similarly Jordaens has an ancestor in Jan van Hemessen, who excels in rash foreshortenings of massive bodies and seizes every opportunity—in particular the parable of the Prodigal Son—to give a drastic account of dissolute goings-on. Van Hemessen presents us with disguised genre on a presumptuously large scale. The crisis of taste in Netherlands painting is here—round about 1540—at its height, since worldly-mindedness, religious themes, out-and-out carnality and half-digested Southern ideals of form all come into head-on collision. Working to a small scale, altogether milder and more endurable, the so-called Brunswick Monogrammist (who is per-

Museum Boymans/van Beuningen

24. JAN VAN EYCK, WOMEN BY THE SEPULCHRE. DETAIL
Rotterdam

25. PIETER AERTSEN, THE BIRTH OF CHRIST. FRAGMENT
Amsterdam, Museum
(*p. 160*)

haps none other than van Hemessen) gives himself up to representations of the banquet, the carousal and the bawdy-house in so naïve a manner as to please the pious and the children of this world at once.

The so-called 'Master of Female Half-figures' made a regular business—obviously to the satisfaction of his contemporaries—of portraying graceful young women who, like Terborch's women, are engaged in such lady-like occupations as writing letters or making music, though he never omits to put some receptacle on the table as the attribute of his Magdalena, as if the worldly antecedents of this penitent, like the evil-doings of the Prodigal Son, afforded a welcome opportunity to smuggle in a bit of genre.

St. Jerome in his study as portrayed by Marinus van Roymerswaele, with a head finely modelled by intellectual work, becomes the professional type of the learned thinker.

Brueghel came to pure genre late, only with his *Peasant Dance* and *Peasant Wedding*, the master-works in Vienna. He had much to say, and his comprehensive mind strove after encyclopaedic completeness. His picture of *Children's Games* is the apotheosis of childish vitality; his picture of *Proverbs* as final and comprehensive as a lexicon. However drastically it presents itself there is always an idea in the concrete, a doctrine. Brueghel aims at illustrating the idea not by one example but by many. The sharpness of his observation, the gusto with which he enters into the bustle of human life, his familiarity with the spirit of the people enabled him to grasp the things of this world in all their infinite multiplicity; but the task set him by the taste of the age, the moralizing intention, subjected the individual perception to intellectual planning, and the processes, actions and conditions to some idea, thus illustrating some saying or other, some instructive or jocose tenet of popular wisdom. Popular imagination had made itself vivid precepts, and out of these precepts Brueghel made vivid pictures.

No doubt there are genre-paintings—in the strictest sense—done before Brueghel's time, such as Lucas van Leyden's pictures of people playing chess or cards in company. Older still is the genre-like element in the engravings of Schongauer, the 'Hausbuch' Master and others. Even genre-pictures by Jan van Eyck are mentioned in old descriptions. Of these nothing has been preserved. There is talk of naked women in the bath. It would seem that Jan van Eyck was not unwilling to seize the chance of painting unclothed femininity. A picture of this kind is also mentioned in the fifteenth century under the name of Rogier, in Genoa. Particularly in Italy, princes and aristocratic gentlemen went in for such things. We must reckon with the possibility that the deeper meaning, the symbolical significance, was not understood. We also hear tell of an 'Otter Hunt' in Venice, which was accounted a work of Jan van Eyck's; but the authentication is the less certain since the picture is supposed to have been painted on canvas, an unusual technique for van Eyck.

As to Lucas van Leyden, though his creative intention aims at pure genre, his feelings, which govern the expression of the heads and the movement, still live in the tradition of the ecclesiastical picture, with the result that the predominant impression is one of solemnity and surly ill-humour, unsuited to the genre. At least, this applies to the Master's beginnings.

When Quentin Massys shows a merchant at his books together with his wife, he was probably saying, over and above what he saw, something moral which escapes our understanding; and as a rule he depicts humanity as something rather low, deforms and pillories it. The tension between good and bad in his work is broad and strong. Sexual love throws up waves and eddies in the current of human life, and fascinates as the exciting element in nature, as something that works eternally, beyond time and place, always sure of universal interest. The erotic, coarse and open, veiled or masked, has, in all its gradations, engrossed the genre-painter throughout the centuries. The paedogogic sixteenth century which loved contrasts and caricature liked to pick on the curious in the relations between the two sexes, associating the aged suitor with the young girl and the old woman with the young man. The unnatural within the natural excited laughter through its astringent comedy, but it also warned and frightened. As form-symbols, comeliness was appointed for youth, ugliness for old age; and for the ideas of good and bad we have the manifestations 'beautiful' and 'ugly'.

Worldliness for its own sake only came into its own quite late, nor did it cease to be suspect until religious faith became iconoclastic and relinquished its hold on visual art. In the Protestant North there grew up a view of things in which everything human was deemed pictorial, was regarded no longer as something spicy but as meat and drink, with neutrality, open-mindedness and benevolence.

If the germs of pure genre are clearly observable in the work of Brueghel, Pieter Aertsen, Jan van Hemessen, Martin van Cleve, they underwent no very happy development in the Netherlands, chiefly because of the dominance of southern ideals. The line of development was interrupted when the Netherlanders were taught to go in for big form, monumentality, invention and composition in the spirit of the Italian Renaissance; when

Lambert Lombard, Pieter Coeck, Frans Floris, Heemskerck and Martin de Vos took over the leadership. The data of the physical eye were accepted in so far as they guaranteed the individual correctness of a portrait. Artists struggled for a universally valid kind of beauty, for heroic attitudes, for a fine art which despised everything to do with genre. The Here and Now, whatever was near to hand, specific, homely, was sacrificed to internationalism. If the development of the genre as a category had formerly been inhibited by faith and the Church, now it was the taste for pretentious form, the studied and sophisticated aspirations of the successful and the pundits that hampered an unprejudiced acceptance of the visible world.

Genre could not flourish in an age when Michelangelo and Raphael were regarded as models by the Northeners. The Renaissance and the Baroque faced reality critically, with fastidious hauteur; and to divest it of vulgarity was considered the duty of art. Not that genre-motifs were avoided entirely; but a survey of Italian and Spanish production tells us how much, and for what reason, the interest in the quotidian (which is the mood that produces the genre) is lacking there, or, to the art-lover from the North, seems to be lacking. The big size, the big scale, the pathos of dimensions are themselves enough to deny little, unassuming, unimportant subjects.

The painter of devotional pictures roots out everything individual as base, unsuitable, accidental, fallible, in order to honour the divine and the holy by 'beauty'; the genre-painter roots out the individual in the interests of the generic. The artist who conceives the characteristic in the abstract comes near to caricature, which somebody has aptly called the measles of genre-painting.

The point was to portray the peasant, the cavalier, the

lady in terms of costume, custom and conduct, not the person. Now long-sight combined with small scale allows the typical characteristics to emerge by glossing over the individual ones, as distinct from near-sight, big scale and the sort of vision appropriate to the portrait. The genre-painter can extract the typical from visual memories and is dependent on unique visual experiences to a relatively small degree. Life-size figures call for individualization. The genre-pieces which Velasquez painted, probably the highest achievements of the South in this category, appear, compared with their Netherlands counterparts, as if done from models, portraitesque, lacking in intimacy. More audibly than the big picture the small picture says: 'I am a picture, not reality.' Here the object is close to us psychologically, spatially it is far-off, withdrawn, and thus emptied of banality. If even the 'realist' Velasquez invests the common man with an heroic aura, how much more pose is to be expected from the other Southerners! The extraordinary, the sublime could assume an impressive and monumental repose, but the ordinary and the trivial generally only claimed attention when it moved and thus made itself noticeable. On top, the eternal, the enduring; down below, the fugitive way of the world, restless, fleet-foot mortality.

For the retrospective eye the genre-picture of former days acquires more or less the character of an historical and cultural document. Costume, custom, conduct, the popular spirit, the human stamp, household equipment say their say about time and place and satisfy our desire for knowledge. In these pronouncements the genre contrasts with landscape, which, in itself everlasting and immutable, is subject to the permutations of the historical process by exclusive reason of our subjectivity of vision.

The visible nature and the activities of men are modified

by time and place. Their elementary instincts are kept under, strongly or feebly, by changing customs. The intellect varies, not the 'will', to speak with Schopenhauer. The countryman, the child, all creatures who are close to nature are less affected by change than the higher classes, than civilized society. The painter who feels the universal human constant naturally inclines to the lower classes, whose doings and behaviour are not regulated by education and ceremonial. Children play today not much differently from the way they played in the sixteenth century. The peasant at his work, in his jollifications and squabbles, presented much the same spectacle in former days as he does now; also his dress, his home and his gear have altered comparatively little. Consequently Brueghel's, Brouwer's and van Ostade's genre-pictures affect us directly, whereas the conversation pieces so favoured in the second half of the seventeenth century, with their modishness that has ceased to be modern, strike us as something of a curiosity and a masquerade. The eternally human was, towards the end of the seventeenth and in the eighteenth century, sought primarily in eroticism.

Pictures of life gone by instruct the historian of culture not only in the formal being of a period, they also tell him in what situations and processes people were interested. According to the mood of the time and the political and economic circumstances interest was gripped now by the rough life of the soldiery, or by brigandage; now by festivities, comfortable domesticity or the elegant mode of life of the upper classes. The historian's interest has turned, very noticeably, away from deeds of war and political bill-sticking to changes of outlook, of intellectual life, which reveal themselves in custom and social form. For scientific efforts so orientated genre-pictures bear witness to the history of mankind.

To all appearances the genre-painter paints what he has seen with the physical eye. Strictly speaking, he did not see it, at least, not all hanging together. The crucial thing is the impression: he—and we in his place and time—might have seen it in the ordinary run of human life. Thus far the genre-painter is a realist. But it is always a typical situation, a typical event characteristic of the time, the place, the social class, the man's age, his profession that is vouchsafed us, that amuses or touches or entertains us, but instructs and warns too. Thus far the genre-painter is an idealist. He starts with an idea, or subordinates the visual experience to an idea. It's the outlook, local, temporal and individual that directs him to the object and point of view.

An optimistic outlook is a pre-requisite in the absence of which what can always and everywhere be seen seems not worth painting. The man who expects nothing but misery and wretchedness in this earthly vale of sorrows or, as a philosopher, has seen through the nugatoriness, precariousness and two-facedness of human life, will avoid the genre or burst its bounds as judge, critic or accuser. The affirmative positivism which gave rise to the genre is not only an individual view but a time-view as well. Since the fifteenth century the value of earthly life had been more deeply appreciated. This value could, as in the Italian Renaissance, be invested with aristocratic optimism or, as in the seventeenth century in the North, it could be acclaimed by democratic optimism.

It turned out well for the genre that earthly things gained in importance, that man was no longer afraid to acknowledge his joy in life, that he could contemplate his image with satisfaction; but what also turned out for its good was the fact that the object no longer needed to be valuable and important as such, since the representation of it could be recognized and gratefully welcomed as a task independent of any spiritual statement. Interest shifted from pictorial thought to pictorial form. Now it is one of the more facile tags of aesthetics that everybody can understand the What of a picture, but that only the gifted and the sensitive can understand the How, and the How alone determines its value as art. These apophthegms must be supplemented and limited by the experience that in a work of art there is no clean line of demarcation between the What and the How. The successful solution of the job in hand rests on the pictorial thought having begotten the form appropriate to it. A thought that has not entered into form puts us out as much as the form that says nothing. In the former case we speak depreciatingly of 'literature', in the latter of frivolous decoration. An English writer has remarked: To ignore the content of a work of art is like somebody who doesn't know Latin enjoying Latin verse for the sound of it.

As a story-teller, the painter cannot keep abreast of the poet or writer. He is restricted to an occurrence which expresses itself in the passive. The painter of religious or historical pictures has the advantage of the genre-painter in that he can count on knowledge of biblical, sacred or historical proceedings, while the genre-painter has to make himself intelligible exclusively in terms of data immediately seen. The painter cannot compete with a Dickens. Superior to the verbal artist in description, he lacks the ability to make the time-sequence, succession, becoming, the chain of cause and effect visible. He can at a pinch illustrate how a man acts in such and such a situation, but not how he behaves in numerous situations all different from one another; hence he can record his knowledge of men only as an aphorist, not as a dramatist, being forced to choose a situation which shows the event in an unambiguous light and reveals *character*. He scores a bull when he catches that state in which the happening is at its peak, when he hits the fruitiest spot in the line of occurrence. The poet plays with an equable daylight, the painter can only illuminate in flashes. Drawing and the graphic arts stand in a different sort of relationship to poetry and literature from that of painting. The thoughtful, witty, acute or meditative spirits among the painters, such as Dürer, Brueghel, Goya, Menzel, Daumier, Blake or Toulouse-Lautrec were drawn to engraving, etching, woodcuts, lithography by their need of self-expression, whether they were getting their own or other people's thoughts illustrated and multiplied in this way. An artist like Daumier could never have unburdened himself of his wealth of imagination in painting. With its sets and sequences of illustrations graphic art enters into competition with the epic and the drama; it can follow the flight of thought more readily than heavy-footed painting. Black-and-white is, compared with true-to-nature colouring, non-sensuous, idealistic; it offers a silhouette of reality rather than a similitude, and may venture into regions which painting never treads unpunished. Manipulating its visual memories more freely, less rigidly controlled in respect of trueness-to-nature, it can go in for abstraction on a comparatively large scale without danger. The genre, reporting, story-telling, instructing, mocking, found a welcome medium of expression in the graphic arts. But to the intellectual activity of the painter narrow limits were set—indeed, as history shows, ever narrower.

VIII

THE GOLDEN AGE OF GENRE

The genre-picture flourished when the successful battles waged by the Dutch against Spanish overlordship had strengthened their self-confidence and summoned up a feeling of satisfaction with the political conditions they had brought about on their own resources. The men regarded one another with well-liking, proud of their robust proficiency, looked with contentment at the community that had held its own and done great things. Paintings commissioned by the Guilds, such as Frans Hals did, are like triumphal celebrations. Genre-painting about this time—1630—has a virile air, full of the strength and joy of life.

As religion grew iconoclastic, painting detached itself from the international tradition, and the closing of political frontiers promoted national independence both as regards subject-matter and form. Holland showed herself the nutrient soil of portraiture, landscape, still-life and the genre. Doubtless stimulation had come in from the West; Flemish temperament had allied itself to Dutch contemplativeness. Immigration, migration and miscegenation were fecund incentives.

Frans Hals, born about 1580, came to Haarlem about 1600, probably from Mecheln; David Vinckboons, born in Mecheln in 1578, moved to Amsterdam where he died in 1629, and brought an hereditary trace of Pieter Brueghel's art to Holland, whither also the forebear of the multitudinous painter-family of the van de Veldes had come from Antwerp.

The Dutch-born Masters, distinguished as pioneers of the genre in Haarlem, were born round about 1590, so for example Willem Buytewech and Esias van de Velde. In the drawings, engravings and paintings, above all of Buytewech, one can trace how interpretation and formal language worked free of the academic manner, as the representatives of which on Dutch soil Cornelis Cornelissen, Abr. Bloemaert and the theoretician and teacher C. van Mander had held the field. In the few conversation pieces of Buytewech's which we possess there is something of a theatrical dash, reaction against the seriousness of the religious picture and the solemnity of Italianate compositions, colourful, flaunting costume in contrast to nakedness, so unnatural in the North.

At the time when painting took on its specifically Dutch character and rejected everything academic and Southern, Frans Hals was wielding a superb mastery. By disposition he was a portraitist and so intent on individual traits, whether physical or psychological, that they also determined the style of his genre. He painted the toper, the market-woman, the musician, the fisher-boy and the child, heads and half-figures as representative of their professions, classes, times of life not so very differently as regards size, composition and technique from the way in which he did his portraits: to life-scale. They are all individual to the extent that they are not strictly typical in their effect, anyhow not as typical as Adriaen van Ostade's peasants who are all alike, and thus express the generic character at its clearest. For Frans Hals the individual personality is the object, the human type less so. The world at large, the space in which men live he hardly observes at all. His people talk in monologues. He goes in for dialogue but seldom.

Among the greatest portraitists to which Hals is reckoned

together with Holbein and Velasquez, the Dutchman is distinguished by his dexterity in catching the spontaneous impulse, the sudden flash of mood. His approach is too instantaneous to be monumental. To immortalize the essence of personality by selecting and sifting out a permanent state of soul, as Holbein could, is not his affair at all. With Hals the sitter seems to be caught in this or that action—for instance, in conversation or in some sudden emotion. As a portraitist he is something of a genre-painter and as a genre-painter something of a portraitist. I once heard a painter say: 'If you see a painting by Frans Hals you get the desire to paint; if you see one by Rembrandt, you lose it.' With this remark, not only witty but coming from the depths of a modern painter's experience, the historian cannot, of course, agree. Frans Hals and what is essential in his work influenced the next generation surprisingly little; indeed, strictly speaking, he was, like Velasquez, only understood in the nineteenth century. In art-literature one naturally reads that Adriaen van Ostade, Terborch and other figure- and genre-painters were stimulated by Frans Hals in their youth, but by way of proof of this relationship there is little that is plausible. The Master's sons and then Judith Leyster, Hendrik Pot, J. M. Molenaer, occasionally show signs of successful emulation, but they soon branch off, take refuge from the stormy seas in peaceful harbours or strike out into narrow side-tracks. Rembrandt put pupils under his spell and heightened their faculties far more powerfully than Frans Hals, not to speak of the tyrannical rule which Rubens exercised. Only in old age did Rembrandt stand estranged and lonely as regards his contemporaries and the taste of his time, but in all the phases of his long, consistent and glorious career—so far as we can survey it—Frans Hals remained inimitable. This is not to say that his genre-pieces were not copied, that deceptive copies do not lie hid in his work. Worth-while efforts inspired by his example, such as we know from the hands of Rembrandt pupils like N. Maes, Jan Livens, Philips Koninck or Aert de Gelder, are seldom to be met with in the pupils trained by Hals.

As touching the genre in particular, Dirk Hals, his less gifted brother who was some ten years his junior, seems to have had a more positive influence and to have determined composition, interpretation and treatment more readily than Frans. Here, as is so often the case, we can observe how a more mediocre talent comes closer to the average taste of the time and the people, and can supply what is demanded and applauded more easily than the Masters of genius. Dirk Hals seems to depend not only on his brother but also on Esias van de Velde and Buytewech.

It is of the nature of the genre-picture, as distinct from the portrait, the biblical or historical picture, that composition and form are moulded to a lesser degree by the theme. The Annunciation, the Adoration and pretty well every illustration taken from the Bible are all prescribed by iconographic tradition, however variously the artist may develop the pictorial idea within the set pattern. Social scenes, on the other hand, and what goes on in a tavern, a peasant house, allow more incidental caprice, more selectivity of invention. The artist who has to represent a unique, historically memorable event will be guided, if not by tradition, then certainly by what he knows about the historical circumstances: he illustrates. From all such references the painter who depicts a typical happening in everyday life is free. Consequently the art of the genre, both in its spirit and its form-language, is characterized by a licence which expressed itself exuberantly enough, more particularly in its youth.

In the second half of the sixteenth century Dutch life had groaned under the oppressive yoke of foreign overlordship. After its victorious resistance the national genius burst forth with triumphant defiance in a spate of plebeian coarseness and lickerishness, not even fighting shy of the scatological—a reaction against pomp, bogusness, gravity and ceremonial, against Spain, against Rome.

The Netherlands Romanists like Pieter Coeck, Heemskerck or Floris had been at pains to overcome the rigidity of the religious painting with the help of studied, heroic poses and gestures; but now observation of life yielded a wealth of movement never noticed before. Pieter Brueghel had gone on ahead in the timelessness of genius.

Every object teaches the artist and inclines his intellectual development to one side or another. The portrait awakens and intensifies his knowledge of men, his psychological astuteness; the animal-picture trains him in zoology; the genre bends his thought to the social situation. In the rationalistic and pessimistic nineteenth century the genre ended in satirical or accusative social criticism. But in the beginning—in the seventeenth century—the new world of earthly happenings was greeted with abounding relish as the playground of freedom and energetic will. One is sometimes tempted to speak of genre-painting 'sowing its wild oats'. Haarlem, at least for a short time, saw another genius besides Frans Hals at work—Adriaen Brouwer, who was born about 1605 and lived there in 1626 and 1627. He too is listed as a pupil of Frans Hals, though he cannot by any means be seen as his imitator. Wilfully revolting against academic ideals of form, he sets out with a wild, not to say rude, address. He shares Frans Hals' vitality, his unconcerned frankness and his keen eye for the physiognomical. For him the object is not so much the single individual as the common life of people living in close community. He is a genre-painter in the proper sense, and with sure instinct he chooses the modest size, the small scale. He is the dramatist among genre-painters (Pl. 26).

In his early days Brouwer cannot do enough in the way of grimaces, boldly overstepping the limits of decency and decorum. With hard local colour and the accent on line he describes an animal populace giving itself uninhibitedly up to its instincts. Primitive gusto does away with all triviality. In his mature period the Master gains in restfulness and moderation without leaving his low social milieu. More and more he catches the individual and avoids caricature, but prefers extreme moods, physiognomical curiosities. Crude in the realm of the psychological, he acquires visual delicacy and introduces a wealth of fastidiously chosen notes of colour into his warm harmony and limpid chiaroscuro. As a painter and colorist he goes a long way in his short life. His interest remains attached to slap-and-tickle gallantry, the fun of gaming, the joy of smoking and drinking. The fug in his ill-lit rooms envelops and befogs the figures and tempers the crudity of the proceedings. Squalid reality is ennobled by colour. The older biographers read the Master's way of life and his character out of the content of his pictures, telling all sorts of anecdotes about this pot-house genius. But, in the world of his pictures, we sense a half-cynical, half-stoical wisdom. He did not by any means pillory these rough goings-on; he may have been swayed by the thought of the pointlessness of all ambitious striving after decency and dignity, when precisely the same needs, passions and desires are to be met with in the social depths as at the top, save that what is hushed up in the one is on full view in the other. Brouwer seems to say with Mephisto: *Die schlechteste Gesellschaft lässt dich fühlen, dass du ein Mensch mit Menschen bist* (the worst company makes you feel a man among men).

The bourgeois society that took pleasure in contemplating the manner of life of tramps, tipplers and brawlers—and without this pleasure the genre could never have developed nor Brouwer's work been imitated by enterprising painters—this polished society felt the contrast between the classes, and the glee with which they looked down their noses at these dubious curiosities was not unmixed with delicious shudders and self-complacency. The brutishness they avoided in life had an exciting charm about it in the picture: 'What in life disgusts and cloys/ In the picture one enjoys.' Brouwer's relations with the bourgeoisie resemble Brueghel's with the princes. Looking at the pictures, one could shake off court ceremonial and the conventions of one's class.

Brouwer's influence is noticeable in Holland as well as in Antwerp. David Teniers derives from him, changing gold into small coin. The fact that a Master who certainly accommodated himself to the requirements of his patrons chose Brouwer's motifs and types, in order to pass them through the sieve of his niceness and politeness, only shows how popular the theme was of the 'small' folk, whose harmless and unassuming pleasures, when viewed from above and at a distance, afforded such a delectable spectacle. Joos van Craesbeeck keeps closer, in interpretation and treatment, to Brouwer than Teniers does. He loves slapping great figures, noisome types and he sometimes, in free treatment, gets quite close to his exalted model.

Of the Dutchmen, H. M. Sorgh and other painters translate Brouwer's style into a softer and duller language.

What Frans Hals painted before his thirtieth year is unknown, perhaps remained unrecognized. It seems very possible that in his youth he did conversation pieces whose

26. BROUWER, PEASANT LIGHTING HIS PIPE
Munich, Kaulbach Collection
(*p. 175*)

bold bacchantic tone might have found a faint echo in his brother's pictures.

Festive gatherings with swarms of people, the figures poorly individualized, done to a small scale but unconstrained in their movements and adroitly grouped: such is the type of picture set up by Dirk Hals. Pieter Codde, his junior by ten years, fulfilled similar wishes, but gave his figures a portraitesque slant, also going in for proper, if miniature-like, portraits. The painters who, like Pieter Codde, were born round about 1600, all somewhat mediocre—Jacob A. Duck (Utrecht and The Hague), Simon Kick (Delft, Amsterdam), Willem Duyster (Amsterdam) and Anthonie Palamedesz (Delft, Amsterdam)—satisfy the requirements made of genre-painting about 1630: the current of familiar life, but whipped up, with froth on it. Exciting interludes, such as pillagings, attacks by soldiery, etc., satisfy the demand for sensation. The great war was raging beyond the frontiers; its horrors could be vicwed as a play by the unimplicated Dutch. Billeting, foraging soldiers, bumptious officers, guard-rooms: the trooper's life writ large. The woman in her place, as trollop or serving-wench. The sort of life that bourgeois society at this period wanted most of all to see reflected in the mirror of art was permitted violence if only it offered variety and departed from domestic monotony. Something *different* engaged the imagination. People looked for highlights in the habitual sphere, something that did not happen every day but *might* happen daily and hourly—not the regularly recurring but the occasional incidents which often have the charm of the forbidden. The picture did not say: This is what generally happens; but: This is what might happen. It was inevitable that the urge to extract entertainment from everyday life should direct the painter's eye to the worldly stage which about 1600, and not only in England, became more lively. As an agent whose force does not as a rule receive sufficient attention, boredom excites the need to fill out the vacuity of space and time. The genre-painters provided entertainment in the way of quarrels, mêlées, adventures. The bottle-party for an evening celebration dispels workaday sobriety, cards wrest an immediate decision from drowsy fate, dancing sets bodily movement free of purpose, and all combats the monotony of indolence by instantly reaving us away from the wearisome regularity of work, profession or duty and, if only for the moment, gives the bond the delectable feeling of freedom.

Seldom are forays made from typical happenings into the province of the short story or anecdote. An unexpected motif is contained in that picture in the Berlin Gallery, done about 1630, catalogued under the name of the Haarlem Master H. C. Pot: a brutal wrangling by heirs for the valuable effects of the deceased, the gold and silver utensils piled up on a table by the coffin. A variant, an echo of the moralistic theme that all is vanity—a bourgeois tragicomedy. Possibly this far from outstanding painter imagined the idea in terms of still-life. The Dutch always felt surest with still-life. Hence not only the excessive number of admirable performances in this category but the mania —already noted in the work of Pieter Aertsen—for arranging vegetables, meat, pots and pans into the foreground and the human beings on one side or at the back. An apple is nothing but the exemplar of its species, so that in still-life the Dutch reality-sense could, without fatiguing the imagination, embrace the individual instance and the 'idea' at once. Only a Dutchman could claim so high a rank as a still-life painter as is accorded to an artist like Willem Kalf. As early as the beginning of the sixteenth century the Holy Family's meal was often represented in the manner of a still-life. The bourgeois delight in the possession of useful objects lasted a long time in the genre-picture, as can be observed in the paintings of H. M. Sorgh, C. Saftleven and other Dutchmen. For Brouwer the fuggy living-room with its crude gear is nothing but the domestication proper to the human species; the more modest painters, on the other hand, linger with fond circumstantiality over inanimate objects, giving them undue preponderance in the effect as a whole.

Always, if with less frequency than in the sixteenth century, this proneness to visualize the abstract in terms of the visibly concrete. The five senses are exemplified in the single figures of peasants smoking, drinking or otherwise engaged.

It is with some hesitation that I turn to Rembrandt, bringing him in here not without alarm. There are steep steps to be climbed. Apart from this, Rembrandt has been written about so copiously by seeing, feeling and thinking authors that one is in danger of turning paradoxical in order to avoid repeating what's been said. Every age has created its Rembrandt. His personality stands clearly outlined in the light of our day before the eyes of art-lovers. If I limit the field of vision by asking: What are Rembrandt's relations to the genre? something worth while may yet come of it. The optic data of environment and immediate neighbourhood were deemed worthy of the Master's observation in all the phases of his development, and nothing human was alien to him. In no way did he consciously hold aloof from the genre out of intellectual pride or prejudice in favour of 'beauty'. When Rembrandt, feeling his way, began, the ideals deriving from the schools, tradition and the spirit of the South as regards composition and invention were all against direct apprehension of the visible. Rembrandt's road runs from foreign style via nature to his own style.

If, for our instruction, we keep to the drawings, which say something personal like a diary, like a conversation with oneself, and to the etchings, which afford spiritual aspiration an easier outlet than does the toilsome labour of painting, then we shall find relatively little in the way of genre—in the stricter sense of the word. People low down in the social scale struck the Master as paintable, in coarse, worn-out clothing: individual figures, oddities, characters stamped by misery and suffering. Unsociable, too, those morose heads framed by a shock of hair. Seldom occurrences rich in association, seldom genre-like narrative unless biblical illustration. The Scriptures as read by Rembrandt teemed with traces of sheer humanity. The psychological relations between man and woman, mother and child, father and son, master and servant, teacher and pupil, engaged his imagination in the figures and events he had read of in the Bible. His genre is religious, inspired by compassion, just as his religious pictures are genre-like, because unhistorical and unecclesiastical. Beggars seen in the streets of Amsterdam are admitted by him into the holy precincts. Rembrandt is a pessimistic Christian as Rubens with his almighty altar-pieces is an optimistic pagan. The Roman Church was heathenish compared with the puritanical Reformed one. Rembrandt lifts dailiness up to the religious sphere without idealizing it in form.

He shared the 'melancholia ingenii' which, although coming to the full only in the work of his late period, sharpened his eye for suffering and long-suffering creatures at all times. More and more he veers away from mummery towards tragedy. If the *Ganymede* in Dresden can still, at a pinch, be called genre, done about 1635, nobody would be rash enough to apply the word to the *Jewish Bride* or the *Blessing of Jacob*. Rembrandt was most successful in uniting the biblical and the genre in his middle years, especially in his Holy Families, those in Cassel and Leningrad.

We have occasion to wonder at the overwhelmingly large number of biblical themes in Rembrandt's work, in the drawings, etchings and paintings. But opportunity, commissions, requirements of patrons hardly ever, in themselves, drew the Master to the field of the biblical. A review of the whole of Dutch production in the seventeenth century tells us that, where it was animated by any receptive interest in the religious picture, this was Rembrandt's *personal* achievement or was at least set in motion by him. It was Rembrandt who, from spiritual predilection, bequeathed the non-ecclesiastical religious picture to the reformed North, which was ready to only a very limited extent to accept this present with gratitude. Rembrandt's loneliness in old age can indubitably be explained by the change of taste and ascribed to the incapacity of his contemporaries to understand the last and highest utterances of genius. It is certain that the content, the austerity and sublimity of the themes was disagreeable to the comfortable optimism of the satiated bourgeoisie, while Rembrandt's religious performances may well have struck the orthodox as disquietingly real and offensive. Apart from Rembrandt's own work almost all the religious pictures in Holland were done by his pupils and successors who, the further they get from their Master, turn more to the portrait, to landscape and genre, like Livens, Bol, G. Flink and others.

The altar-piece was expelled, the iconographic tradition cut. The Church that held the field in Holland was nonsensuous and neither willing nor able to symbolize its doctrines. Cranach's frigid allegories lay bare this incapacity on the part of the Lutheran Reformation as well. Rembrandt, without the help of tradition and without being moved by puritan orthodoxy, found the way to an unconfessional Christianity of love, of compassion and was first understood at his deepest by Tolstoi's contemporaries.

If Rembrandt went beyond the genre or exalted its status, Rubens did not stoop to the genre because, in the spirit of the Baroque, he raised given reality to heroic proportions. In him, Flemish sensuality was kept within bounds by the civilized cult of form, draped itself mythologically, bacchantically. Rubens overcame banality in the body, Rembrandt in the spirit.

Of the painters who derive from Rembrandt, Gerard Dou, born 1613 in Leyden, is a genre-painter in the strictest sense. He was a tractable and conscientious pupil, although he felt no whisper of his Master's spirit. With him there begins that virtuosity of specifically Dutch colouring, an innocuous virtuosity, a painstaking finesse cultivated by him and many imitators all the more assiduously since it met with rich success and suited the taste of the times, particularly during the second half of the seventeenth century. Treatment, format and the scale of the figures harmonize with the subject chosen. A narrow intellectual horizon, a decorous world, modest pretty maids, well-behaved children, kindly school-masters and hermits who are more worthy than holy. Dou's faultless and never-failing precision, rightness and subtlety of execution, draughtsmanship, lighting were highly admired, and this peaceful, unworried, spick and span sort of existence ingratiated itself. As a painter Dou is an honest pedant; as a narrator an amiable philistine.

Round about 1630 the man, the male, doughty of deed,

the good fellow, comes loudly to life in the genre-picture; about 1650 it is the woman, quiet and unassuming, the diligent maid, the careful house-wife, the pious old granny. From the encampment, the guard-room, the tavern and the fête, painters turned to the sheltered coign and the domestic scene. The Treaty of Münster—1648—brought Germany peace, the peace of the graveyard 'tis true, and for Holland the security of all that she had fought and won.

The change can be seen in Haarlem, in the work of Adriaen van Ostade who was born in this town about 1610 and continued to work there until 1685—the town where the virile Frans Hals was permanently, and the domesticity-hating Adriaen Brouwer temporarily, active. There is little trace of Frans Hals having been Ostade's teacher. Brouwer was in Haarlem when Ostade was taking in, intelligently, his first impressions. Ostade's early pictures have some share in the rowdyism which Brouwer depicts in figures more sharply individualized, in events and situations that go deeper, than his, but more and more in the course of his long career he turns peaceable and seeks 'kindness in a corner'. He is listed as a peasant-painter. One asks oneself whether these thick-set, unwieldy men, good-natured, dullards and sharpers at once, can possibly be peasants. At any rate one never catches them doing any land-work. So far as they have a recognizable profession they are village musicians, beggars, cobblers, tinkers. Generally they are hunched up in the pub smoking, drinking, gaming, and sitting peaceably with wife and child in the house or in front of the house.

Busying himself as an etcher, like no other genre-painter of the seventeenth century, Ostadc was naturally referred to the outstanding model he had in Rembrandt. Etchings of Rembrandt's may have stimulated him to make use of this medium. Both as an etcher and in some ways as a painter he was dependent on Rembrandt in the period after 1640. His middle-period paintings please by their warm colour-harmonies and pellucid chiaroscuro. The field of his vision, as regards themes and motifs, had fast and narrow bounds to it, save that his village community with its small joys and pleasures grows cosier, cleaner and tamer as time goes on. The memory of Brouwer's spurting vitality pales with the years, just as the ageing Master's sense for pictorial and coloristic values becomes progressively feebler. He moves away from Rembrandt and Brouwer alike. His late pictures and aquarelles take on a gay colourfulness. He remains true to the phlegmatic optimism with which he never tires of describing a petty-bourgeois world well satisfied with its lot.

The genre-painter's penchant for the typical led Ostade to extremes. The sedentary men with prematurely aged and furrowed brows, the rotund women, the globular children, all look alike as though from village in-breeding.

From Rembrandt various currents go out, in 1630 to Dou, 1640 to Ostade, 1650 to N. Maes, 1660 to Aart de Gelder. The source which Maes tapped when he attached himself to Rembrandt was no longer the source Dou had drawn on, since the lofty prototype was changing all the time. Especially the drawings indicate that Maes was a skilful imitator who, like a forger, has been able to fox knowledgeable connoisseurs. A thoroughly studious pupil at first, then a truant, this Master, who was born in 1632, lived until 1693 as a successful portraitist in Amsterdam. He has kept his prestige in our eyes thanks to a number of genre-paintings which he did in his youth, between 1650 and 1660. He was not, however, a born genre-painter, as is evident from the fact that in later years he confined himself to portraiture. The quietistic soft-heartedness which he instils into his girls, mothers and pious-minded old women is derived—in watered-down form—from Rembrandt's humanity. The world of the nursery and Homes for the Aged is insulated against all virility and active life. The piety of the poor in spirit, women's patience in housework and handiwork—to all such, especially on a small scale, he gives convincing expression in individual figures, using his Master's pictorial and coloristic technique, showing himself a successful follower of Rembrandt more or less independent in his own narrow field. But since he lacked inventive imagination he fails the moment he tries his hand at narrative. An old woman praying at table, while a cat is about to pull off the table-cloth and food. A footling conceit, maddening in its tastelessness. And life-size at that! No less offensive the oft-repeated scene with the inquisitively listening maid, her forefinger raised to her lips. Maes is a highly gifted painter of limited mentality, sedulously courting applause.

Carel Fabritius distinguishes himself from among the Rembrandt pupils as a painter of rich gifts and very fair promise. His art did not get a chance to degenerate with the times, since, born about 1620, he died in 1654, hence in the period of general excellence. It is difficult to assess his significance in the historical context, because little of his work has been preserved and what we do know of him is, thematically, unequal and fragmentary, affording no all-round view although great things might be expected. Since he moved from Amsterdam to Delft about 1645, the town where Pieter de Hoogh and Vermeer were to begin their work soon afterwards, he seems, as a lively-minded Master given to experiment with the problems of perspective and lighting, to have stimulated not only the go-ahead Vermeer but the sluggish Pieter de Hoogh as well. Whereas in Amsterdam Rembrandt's chiaroscuro congealed, in the work of imitators, into convention and manner and was opposed to the development of space, in Delft there grew up a sense for light, air and open local colour in happy accord with that specifically Dutch quality: contemplativeness inclining to still-life.

Pieter de Hoogh, born 1629 in Rotterdam, came to Delft about 1653 and went later to Amsterdam. The years he spent in Delft were crucial for the growth of his work. He began with unremarkable, impersonal genre-pictures, not much above the level of average Haarlem production. Berchem is reputed to have been his teacher. There is little trace of this. All the same, this tradition may find confirmation in the fact that Berchem was active in Haarlem about 1645, where at about this time de Hoogh received his first training. De Hoogh's fame rests on not more than 40 pictures, while at least 170 from his hand have been preserved, and the master-works, which form a compact group, were all done in Delft between 1655 and 1662. After that comes at first a slow but soon increasingly rapid decline until the Master's death in Amsterdam in 1683.

Pieter de Hoogh is one of the great Masters despite the narrowness of his intellectual field of vision, because his eye discovered a new sort of beauty. For him the object is not the mother or the maid in the home, but the inhabited room, parlour, courtyard or garden. The emotional note which his work conveys to us echoes out of the room. You can blot out the figures—it still echoes, not only because the architecture is based on a clear ground-plan, convincing in perspective and vivid in its materiality, but also and even more because the room, cutting it off or letting it in through door and window, regulates the play

27. PIETER DE HOOGH, THE BEDROOM
Washington, National Gallery of Art (Widener Collection)
(*p. 187*)

of light and with it the tone and colour-values and finally the psychological atmosphere as well. His observation is concerned with sunlight and the wealth of colour it magically conjures up, no matter whether it falls on roofs, walls, brickwork or a human face. His human beings are dependent on the locality which, however, is far from being a stage or set-piece waiting for something to happen.

Just as the Dutch, from 1630 on, regarded the countryside with pleasure as the home they had fought for, so, about 1650, they looked with satisfaction at the protecting city-walls, the clean houses, the well-tended gardens, the thrusting churches, the comfortable residences. The Dutch art of living developed in this happy time, delighting in assured possessions; and Pieter de Hoogh is the first to speak of it in pictures. A warm, mild light floods into the clean rooms, heightening the sense of well-being. An open door gives us a glimpse of a sunny room at the back of one all twilit. Gentle gradations of light and dark make the atmosphere alive, while the mistress of the house, busy but unhurried, the well-behaved child, the capable maid come and go without fuss, in polite silence. The men are outside, they appear only occasionally as courteous guests and are regaled with friendly attention. The master of the house does not permit himself to be seen; the woman, the mother rules the house, unless it be that the house rules her. An art-lover who is fond of putting keen judgments wittily, albeit a little tastelessly at times, once remarked that de Hoogh partakes of the nature of cats, which display more loyal affection for the house than for its inhabitants (Pl. 27).

De Hoogh is never sentimental or garrulous or anecdotal in his paintings of the Delft period. He is not an inventive narrator nor, in his youth, does he try to become so.

Defects can be spotted in the drawing of the figures even in his masterpieces, but nobody thinks of that, spellbound by the harmony of colour which symbolizes a happy accord between the inhabitants and the room. This accord is a Northern ideal, prematurely realized in Jan van Eyck's Arnolfini portrait, then in Dürer's *St. Jerome in his Study*.

Had Pieter de Hoogh, in that fateful Amsterdam period when he sank below the level of his imitators such as Pieter Janssens, Esaias Boursse, Jacobus Vrel, had he then followed an inner voice he might yet have produced something of significance as a painter of church interiors and town views. The highest, the incomparable achievement of Delft art is—and this is no accident—the town view. The decline of public taste must bear the blame for de Hoogh's fate, but a personal lack of stamina, character, self-criticism is nevertheless obvious. In his late genre-pictures we find numerous figures in sumptuous dress, in pretentious palatial rooms. The colouring has become flat and drab. The weakness of the drawing comes to light as, with distressingly spiritless, facetious ideas and amorous motifs he tries to keep abreast of the modish genre-painters. De Hoogh is not a thinking artist, not a psychologist. So long as his creative fancy was youthful and fresh he created works that look grown rather than made; but he had no knowledge to fall back on, no hard-won ability, no resources which, once the warmth of his feelings had abated, might still have given the late works a bearing and a dignity. The loss of naïveté and originality was not offset, as he grew older, by experience and wisdom.

It would be hard to find a painter who, by character and disposition, is so exactly predestined to be a genre-painter as Jan Steen. A sanguine optimist, he had no misgivings about the way of the world, at least no moral ones. Life for him was an amusing spectacle. His love of story-telling pours out in such an extravagant spate that it often hampers the patient execution of the individual picture. Steen worked unequally. Active for a time in Leyden, The Hague, Haarlem and Delft, he had at his finger-tips all the attainments which Holland had to offer in the way of high pictorial culture about 1650, but nowhere did he strike root, nor did he go at all deeply into any foreign art. His style shows no definite development, so that the experts have not had much success in arranging his undated pictures chronologically. A connection with Knupfer, with Isack van Ostade, with Frans Hals can sometimes be detected. For Steen painting is a means and it always adapts itself to the idea.

A single work of Vermeer's is enough to convince us of the greatness of this Master and to justify his fame, but to appreciate Jan Steen one has to get a bird's-eye view of his extensive work. A publication containing all his pictures would increase his prestige and astonish us with the multiplicity of themes and, even more, the ingenious modulation of one and the same theme.

Jan Steen never fought shy of any task, painted biblical and mythological stuff without compunction, not with intent to travesty but always in such a way as to make even the most serious theme the occasion for some entertaining spectacle. Samson, unmanned and deprived of his adornment of hair, has to look on while a cavalier is sporting with his spouse, and a small child is able to tie him up with a chain. In the rare cases where the project does not admit of humour and wit, the Master falls into conventionality. His brawls are never so bad or dangerous, sickness is never so grave but somebody present manages to extract amusement from it. And this jollity is infectious.

Jan Steen is unsurpassable when the theme is in complete harmony with his view of the world—in revelries when high good cheer holds sway at a banquet with music, when the actors can let their humour rip, temperamental, daring, full of the joy of living. He is at home with the naïve instinctiveness of the child, and grown-ups with their delight in fun and games and innocent mischief have kept something of the child about them.

Jan Steen is a Shakespeare *manqué*, an inhibited Shakespeare—*manqué* because he does not know the seamy side of life, inhibited because he cannot extend the limits of pictorial art. Comedy and fun insist on verbal report. At his best the painter brings off his point in the single incident, the anecdote. 'The Lovesick Girl', a favourite theme of Steen's, is a short story. The daughter of the house, in love, appears agitated. The symptoms of her behaviour, the change that has come over her, are interpreted as sickness by her parents. She is put to bed. The doctor is called. He examines the girl with mock gravity, knows well enough what the matter is, but writes out a prescription with the solemn charlatanry of a professional while the look and manner of the grinning members of the household betray partly sorrowful sympathy, partly insight into the real cause of her condition. Inasmuch as the painter supplements the report of the picture with the inscription: 'Daer baet geen medisijn, want het is minnepign[1],' he veers towards the literary. Another time a festive board is explained with the saying: 'Op de gesonheyt van het nassauss basie in de eene hant het rapier in de andre hant het glaesie[2].'

Steen's knowledge of men does not go deep, but it runs wide. It embraces expressions of mood ranging from gaiety to wantonness. With all their weaknesses his men

1 'No medicine helps where there is love-sickness.'

2 'To mine host's health: in one hand the sword, in the other the glass.'

remain sympathetic in their frank and healthy activity. We would not mind associating with them—a wish which is definitely not evoked by Brouwer's murderous toughs or Ostade's witless peasants.

The pictorial idea, as an end, leads the genre-painter to the type, while observation, as the means, leads him to the individual. Born genre-painters like Brouwer or Jan Steen, who are acute observers at the same time, have to set about reconciling two divergent ways. For example: in the Steen picture entitled 'Soon won, soon gone', the happy winner is being mulcted of his winnings by the rapacious inn-keeper and complaisant femininity. The cavalier has an individual stamp to him, but what dominates the impression is the human type, the good-humoured, scatter-brained man of the world as seen in a mood conditioned by the situation. At any rate the portrait element subserves the narrative, the entertaining lesson. If we collected together all the portraitesque genre-figures which Frans Hals did and related them to one another, we would get close to Jan Steen's ideal.

Prodigal of his powers, Steen undertook all kinds of things—biblical, landscape, mythological. He is most himself with the average sensual man among his fellows. The individual figure—but only seldom does Steen content himself with that—betrays his sociability by turning towards the spectator and thus establishing the contact.

Steen's fancy does not throw up ideas which he then illustrates—it throws up pictorial ideas straight away.

The effect his paintings have on us may stimulate us to meditate on the mystery of the comic. Anybody who, like Schopenhauer, holds that boredom is the root evil which increases in strength to the degree that physical need and the struggle for existence grow less pressing, can well understand the joy we feel in the sudden emergence of the unexpected, the interruption of normal, rational, regular occurrences. We see a man walking, but our attention is not fixed; he stumbles and falls, and the spectacle of this arouses that innocent *Schadenfreude* which is peculiar to the comic. The moment the certainty dawns: We are above such silliness, such weakness—amusement and the desire to laugh set in automatically.

Where humour is concerned, it is a sign of superficiality to laugh at everything always, but of spiritual freedom to be able to discern what is funny, to laugh at human failings like Shakespeare, who most certainly was not always laughing. Whether and how far this spiritual superiority, creative in poetry, retains the same potency in the visual arts is another question.

We can only judge from our own contemporary standpoint, caught in a theory according to which humour, the comic and the witty prevent a pleasurable assimilation of the artistic phenomenon and thus are 'unaesthetic'. So that we may put the opinion that prevails today in the following hard sentence: Jan Steen was a great painter as far as a comic poet can be a great painter. Art, however, has not climbed the heights by adhering to dogmas that grew riper and riper as time went on—on the contrary, every valid aesthetic derives from the art that happens to be effective at the moment, and it changes with our mode of vision, not with our knowledge. Bearing this in mind, we are afraid that we are somehow not being just to the Master when, gazing down from the supposed eminence of our artistic understanding, we hesitate to admit a certain pleasure in this clever and amusing art. Goethe, finding pleasure in Feti's genre-paintings in the Dresden Gallery, felt impelled to excuse himself. Feti, he said, was 'an excellent artist, although a humorist, therefore not in the first class'. The enlightened art-lover of today judges rather like Goethe, albeit his aesthetic prejudices are completely different from Goethe's. Taking the historian's standpoint we incline to the belief that Jan Steen's fruity, warm-hearted humour, his explosive wit must have loaded his contemporaries with acceptable gifts, and we are amazed to find out that pecuniary success was not his portion. The peaceable cast of mind of the well-fed Dutch bourgeoisie may have been better content with G. Dou, Terborch and Frans Mieris.

For very different reasons Vermeer of Delft scores over Jan Steen today. Figures, the prices paid, do not lie. In the judgment of the art-market Vermeer is rated far higher than Steen, and not only because his works come up less often. Fame was late in coming to this Master—only when genre-painting had grown suspect. He is now accounted a great painter, not in spite but because of his not being a genre-painter. His connection with human beings is neither one of sympathy nor interest in the joys of life nor sense for humorous situations nor concern with psychological relationships. He observes the living as a still-life painter. A copy after Steen is at least an amusing illustration of some sort, a copy after Vermeer—characteristically enough, there are hardly any, only forgeries—is nothing at all (Pl. 28).

For him the human being is a model that keeps still in order to be painted. Individual women or heads of individual women, sometimes two figures, mistress and maid in impassive relationship. Seldom any move in the direction of genre-like narrative. The figures silent and unemotional. Vermeer did not paint children, although he had eleven in the house. Probably they did not keep still enough. One of his master-works: the painter and his model. He turns his back on us, so that we do not get to know him, only his professional activity. He must have worked as slowly as Jan Steen worked quickly, self-critical and with conscious aspiration, whereas Steen let himself go. He chose simple motifs so as to concentrate all his powers on the execution. Movement disturbed him, while it was precisely in action that Jan Steen saw the force of life and hence reality at its most characteristic, and was able to evoke the illusion of movement as hardly any other painter could. Vermeer is conspicuous among his countrymen because of his method of work and fastidious, delicate sense of beauty. His open local colour seems un-Dutch, reminds one of the South, almost of something exotic. In his youth he may have been inspired by Utrecht, the Dutch Rome. Terbrugghen, a native of Utrecht, would appear in his best efforts to have been a forerunner of his. But the essential in Vermeer he owes to himself.

Rembrandt—an artist. It sounds inappropriate, almost like blasphemy. For Jan Steen, too, we look round for another title. But Vermeer, with his conscious, thoughtful, supercharged mastery, his artful subtlety, we call an artist without misgiving. In his early paintings, depthless and gobelinesque in effect, the pigments occasionally remind one of the run glaze of Asiatic ceramics. Looking at the *Head of a Woman* in the Mauritshuis Jan Veth remarked that it was as though painted with crushed pearls.

Out of tune with his age, emphatically turning away from the warm chiaroscuro of the Dutch, he strikes us as if his ears had already caught the battle-cry 'l'art pour l'art!' as decidedly modern. And his modernity is confirmed by the fact that it was only a contemporary of Manet's, namely the Frenchman Burger-Thoré, who discovered him. He is not romantic, not pathetic, not mysterious, or rather he is 'mysterious in broad daylight'. His art is objective and betrays little of his personality.

28. VERMEER, MASTER AND MODEL. DETAIL
Vienna
(*p. 193*)

A picture by Vermeer is like a 'living picture' or tableau, yet without the disturbing or disquieting effect of rigidity. The painted figures do not, like the real ones in a tableau, evoke the painful question of why they don't move.

The only dated picture, the *Procuress* in the Dresden Gallery, which Vermeer did in 1656 when he was 24, is fairly large, warm-toned and chiaroscuro-like, depthless, containing four figures and a comparatively lively narrative. Soon afterwards, probably stimulated by the example of the Delft Master Carel Fabritius, Vermeer took pains with spatial depth, light and air. His colouring becomes cool, with yellow and bluc. Thc pigments shine rather than glow. The Master acquires a colour treatment all of his own by analysing the surface and breaking it up into splashes and points, following the play of sunlight on matter. The later pictures please with their silvery, nacreous shimmer. Everything that came from his hand beguiles the senses like jewellery.

Every Master is threatened by the reverse side of his virtues. In Vermeer's case degeneration is at most hinted at, not actually perceived. Perhaps his early death—he died when he was 43—forestalled cold-hearted artistry.

Like Pieter de Hoogh, Vermeer belongs to the great Masters because he discovered a new beauty, with the difference that he systematically worked for what fell into the other Master's lap. Vermeer, exciting preciosity; Pieter de Hoogh, delicious, suavely enfolding intimacy.

The more painters like de Hoogh and Vermeer succeeded in feeling the beauty of appearances and conveying this feeling to us, the weaker grew the need for the proceedings and the situations to be interesting as such. The dish no longer required spicing with dubious condiments or with various alluring, infamous, waggish and sentimental touches. The significance of the subject was in inverse ratio to artistic value. The What of a picture is to the How as the text of a song is to the melody; and the more potently the music works on the feelings the feebler the effect of the text on our understanding.

Gerard Terborch, born in Zwolle in 1617, came to Haarlem in his early years and attached himself to the painters of guard-rooms and saucy soldiery—the sort of genre that was being cultivated with success about 1635. From the very beginning he distinguishes himself by his select colouring, his harmony and his comparatively quiet interpretation of the events and situations. Gentility is the negative virtue that maintains itself throughout the whole of his work, in the form of controlled effect, discretion and allusive language. He would rather be indistinct than loud. In later years the leading light among the 'elegancies', he eschews the vulgar luxury of the *nouveau riche* and never departs from the dignity he was born with. On his trips to London, Rome and Madrid he consolidated his man-of-the-world attitude and found, in Münster, the welcome task of painting the portraits of diplomats of many lands. He gives Dutch phlegm the reflected glory of Spanish *grandezza*. His version of a tinker looks like an aristocrat who has sunk to coarse manual work or is playing the workman.

Terborch has prudence, worldly experience, taste and tact. Taste is nothing but tact in the realm of aesthetics. Format and scale of figures are, in this Master, consistently kept within modest bounds. He observes individual traits delicately and surely, but never pointing, never accentuating. His mastery never degenerates into virtuosity. His much admired interpretation of silk has not the effect of a technical trick, is rather the outward and visible sign of a refined style of living. These ladies, who may not always have been ladies, cannot be dressed otherwise; they move in these costly stuffs in the most natural way.

Now and then, even in his mature period, Terborch condescended to paint a boy de-fleaing a dog, or a mother combing a little girl's hair; but in such pictures treatment seems to conflict with content. He is wholly and inimitably himself as chronicler of 'good' society, or the society that behaves as though it were 'good'. Seldom more than three figures, lazy women of a somewhat lethargic charm who know no other occupation save that of music-making, letter-writing and receiving; youthful cavaliers of a mannerly demeanour who betray no amorous inclinations. The composition balanced to a degree, mild light, a grey all-over tone with local colour sparingly introduced, little development of space, tender but not exactly smooth colour-work, the atmosphere crepuscular, lit up with reflections, shimmering stuffs, no obtrusive plasticity of body: everything completely adapted to the psychological climate.

Terborch only died in 1681 but kept on top of his form more surely than Pieter de Hoogh, who lived two years longer. His resistance to the general decay of taste he owes to his staunch, conscious expertise, perhaps, too, the circumstance that he grew old in Deventer and not in Amsterdam. For him it was a good thing that, in contrast to de Hoogh, he was a zealous portraitist, compelled to observe the facts of individual form. This continuous exercise guarded his genre-painting against carelessness even though he probably took great care not to overstep the limits of the typical in his genre.

A trace of weariness and apathy lies on Terborch's creatures. Gentility is hard put to escape boredom. Just as in the life of the individual, struggle, victory and enjoyment of the spoils leads in the end to blaséness, so and no different is the fate of a nation. And Terborch represents the autumn, the valedictory phase of the golden century.

Beside the finished personality of Terborch that of his rival Metsu appears protean, chameleon-like. This Master, born in Leyden in 1630, seems to have appropriated to himself all the values which G. Dou, Terborch and Vermeer bequeathed to the Dutch genre. He is a master draughtsman, tells, like Terborch, of music-making or letter-writing women, also of other non-committal undertakings, and sometimes lights up a room like a Vermeer. The sensational prices paid for his *Sick Child* at the Steengracht auction, as also the companion-pieces —letter-writing cavalier and letter-receiving lady—at the dispersal of the Clinton-Hope Collection, would seem to prove Metsu's high rank. Nevertheless, examining his masterpieces with a critical eye and surveying his work as a whole, we feel the weaknesses of eclecticism despite the fact that biographical data do not show him an imitator. He was born a little earlier than Vermeer and died in 1667, hence some time before Terborch. His work lacks the unity that is rooted in personality. He was studious and receptive to a high degree, and that explains his affinity with Vermeer. He brings nothing new, nothing peculiar to himself, apart from the sentimental note he strikes on occasion, in which respect he is in advance of his time, since this note had many reverberations, more particularly in the nineteenth century. A maid drying her tears at the sight of her sick mistress. The worried mother with a sick child on her lap. Vermeer has no time for children, Steen's are all fit as a fiddle, and Steen would not let the woman be really ill and would have put in somebody to make fun of the howling maid.

Metsu lacks the unfailing tact with which Terborch brings the What into line with the How and keeps within

29. METSU, THE MUSIC LESSON
London, National Gallery

(*p. 199*)

the bounds of his talent. A coquettish animation of form fights against psychologically vapid ideas. Metsu is no story-teller. Not because he is close, like Terborch, but because he hasn't much to say. This would not in itself be a reproach. Vermeer, too, is no story-teller, but unlike Vermeer, Metsu tries to indicate psychological relationships or to become arch like Jan Steen. Take the *Music Lesson* in the London National Gallery, faultless in drawing and colour. The woman sits at the piano, shows the gentleman, who sits facing her with a glass of wine in his hand, a sheet of music. The dialogue fails to become audible in gesture and look. How differently Jan Steen got the amorous element peeping through the paedogogic attitude and, with his psychological acumen, brought out the *double entendre* of the situation! (Pl. 29.)

The interest of the Dutch went out to the busy, active doings of human beings; particularly in the second half of the seventeenth century they liked to regard their country as densely populated. The painters of church interiors, streets, squares peopled these spaces with a profusion of genre-like figures. What a perfect accord, what a happy balance between countryside and humanity reigns in the pictures of Avercamp, A. Cuyp, Adriaen van de Velde or Ph. Wouwerman! Outdoor creatures, horses and grazing cattle, mediate between landscape and man. Of course, the Masters of the nation's landscape, Jacob Ruisdael and Hobbema, are, in contrast to their Italianizing contemporaries, fond of solitude, unwilling to let the human voice interrupt the still solemnity of nature.

A survey of the whole rich harvest of Dutch art begets the idea that in the field of genre, as far as interpretation and technique are concerned, all healthy possibilities had been exhausted in the work of Ostade, Dou, Pieter de Hoogh, Steen and Terborch, and that afterwards there was no room for anything but imitation, variation and eclecticism. By and large three stages can be distinguished: about 1603 the man of action, about 1650 the woman, caring and careful, and about 1670 the lady and gentleman in some sort of erotic relationship. The more the century tends to its end, the more pomp and luxury come to the fore. Many painters moved to Amsterdam, the seat of fashion; but the fountain-heads continued to be Haarlem, Delft and, above all, Leyden. From Ostade we get Bega and Dusart; from Jan Steen: Brakenburgh; from Pieter de Hoogh: Pieter Janssens, van der Burgh, Vrel, Bourse, Lud. de Jonghe, Ochterveld; from Terborch: Caspar Netscher; from G. Dou: P. v. Bosch, van Tol, Abr. Pape, Toorenvliet, Frans Mieris, Slingeland. The sort of fine painting indigenous to Leyden was cultivated right into the eighteenth century by Egl. v.d. Neer, Verkolje, Schalken, A. v. Boonen, Ph. van Dyck and Adr. v. d. Werff. Q. Brekelenkam, a native of Leyden, keeps a modest corner all to himself. Often he visits artisans at their work and favours a comparatively crude and open technique.

About 1670 the successful and representative painters are Frans Mieris and Caspar Netscher, both about the same age; and Adriaen v. d. Werff in 1690. Mieris is only a sumptuous and elegant edition of Dou. Like other painters he is fond of taking over the interior framing of the picture introduced by Dou, the window-composition, which gives rise to strongly modelled figures picked out in great detail by the light and dark backgrounds. The fact, of course, that cool, diffuse light would have to fall from in front is passed over unnoticed. They stick to warm interior lighting. The opportunity to fill out the intellectual paucity of their ideas with hangings, still-life-like extras, marginal vegetation, carved stonework underneath the window and so forth is eagerly seized, and a lot of technical tricks strenuously put on view in order to create the illusion of material textures—silk, fur, metal, stone.

Dexterity was gazed at open-mouthed, like magic; verisimilitude—of the sort that still 'worked' under the magnifying-glass—admired; the smooth, polished surface relished not only by the wealthy Dutch burghers but even more by foreigners, German princes in particular, who acquired 'cabinet-pieces' and sometimes attracted painters to their courts. The fame of these Masters who served up banalities like something precious and significant, even sacred subjects like gew-gaws, was soon contested, although every now and then it was promulgated afresh, somewhat shamefacedly, in modern times. One shakes one's head as one reads that the serious-minded and strictly educated Grillparzer, visiting the Gallery in Dresden, found eloquent words of admiration to jot down in his diary for but one picture: Adr. v. d. Werff's *Expulsion of Hagar*. It is true that he corrected himself afterwards, tipped by art-lovers who must have raised an eyebrow at his admiration.

Caspar Netscher, somewhat behind Frans Mieris and Adr. v. d. Werff as a virtuoso of the subtle technique, became the fashionable portraitist in The Hague contemporaneously with N. Maes in Amsterdam. His genre approximates to the portrait. Rounded, richly dressed children, the pampered darlings of their parents, rather too conscious of their childishness. The gentlemen, luxuriously apparelled, living images of self-satisfied prosperity. The merchant prince with one eye on the French Court.

The South of the Netherlands with Antwerp, the capital, proved to be unfruitful soil for the genre in the seventeenth century for more than one reason. The Church of the day had a lien on all resources for altar-pictures. Southern form-ideals were within easy reach and made native reality look petty and vulgar. Rubens, because of the superiority, the incomparable success of his work, inspired all the painters who came under his spell—even those with clipped wings—to soaring flight. His big format and big scale were enough to go against the spirit of the genre. Theodor Rombout's groups of life-size half-figures done in the Italianate manner strike us as empty and pretentious. Jordaens, earthy, with a streak of humour in him, was drawn by the time and place—but against his better nature—to the ecclesiastical, the mythological, the decoratively monumental. His spirit does not fill out those mighty bodies. He seems to creak in his efforts to hold his own beside Rubens. Of the esteemed and influential painters of the Flemish School only David Teniers was sober and common-sensed enough to keep his feet on the ground, cultivating the genre in small-figure compositions. In his long career of mechanical production he satisfied the needs of the private house and of the export-market with sprightly pictorial wares, and acquired a prestige that is out of all proportion to his talent. Festivities, outdoor games, dancing country-folk, guard-rooms, taverns, often the identical themes that Ostade, Brouwer and other Dutch painters had favoured, but done without psychological interest, without humour, with affability at most. Constant types, which nevertheless give no clear expression to the popular Flemish spirit. Hardly ever a situation grounded in character and circumstance or an event that actively convinces. The figures as though thrown together haphazard, and rarely any common action or psychological relationship that would guarantee the connection. The success of this sort of manufacture may be explained, perhaps, by the unobjectionable niceness of the 'small' folk, who presented a comfortingly friendly picture to the higher classes, like a dutiful staff, like contented domestics. But Teniers' international effect rests on the fact that the Netherlands world of pictures, eagerly sought after in the South and even in France, was more acceptable in the mild form of the Flemish School than in that of the Dutch; moreover exports to the Latin countries were easiest from Antwerp. In his early period Teniers (who was born in 1610) copied Brouwer's warm colouring and chiaroscuro; then he slips more and more into a light, cool, over-all tone suited to the open air and develops a routine of smooth-running hatching, so much so that in the end you get the feeling that he could have painted, as one can write, with his eyes shut.

France was chary of the genre. Here lively invention, fluent composition, heightening of effects were demanded as appropriate to and conformable with the dignity of art. Prepossessions in the matter of 'beauty', ecclesiastical, academic and courtly convention put limits to straight observation, so that pictures reveal little of the conditions and manner of life of the French people. Aesthetic doctrines imported from Italy were rationalized in France and became law. The attention that has only very recently been devoted to the extensive work of the brothers Le Nain has brought to light a large number of genre-pieces of French extraction from about 1640. In the work of these painters Flemish and Italianate elements appear to have mixed. First impression: these pictures do not look French. Now, our somewhat questionable idea of what is 'French' derives from the art of the eighteenth century. The brothers Le Nain are distinguished neither by Gallic sparkle, nor by wit, nor by temperament; they are anything but eloquent or erotic. Since French landscape-painting bloomed on Italian soil, it is expected that French genre should have arisen if not exactly on Netherlandish soil then at least as the result of stimulations coming from over there. This is not quite true. All the same, the brothers Le Nain do get close to their contemporaries in Antwerp, painters like G. van Herp or the third Rijkaert. An honest serious-mindedness can be felt. While Brouwer's beings are intensely wrapped up in what they are doing, and Teniers at least gives his the appearance of doing something, those of the French, men, women and children, stand or sit about in groups, or indeed, in rows, like pipes of an organ, so as to keep still for the painter, not coquettish, if anything rather shy and embarrassed. No use is made of spatial depth for figure-composition, a relief-like order is preferred. The Latins are hardly interested at all in the rooms people live in. Lower in the social scale or in the stuffiness of the bourgeoisie there is an oppressive, sullen atmosphere which emanates from the drab or sombre colouring. So far as the brothers Le Nain go in for pathos or 'beauty' of form we can feel indirect contact with Italy, more particularly with Caravaggio. One fancies that one can detect the pressure put on the people by their autocratic rulers.

More or less contemporaneously with the resuscitation of the brothers Le Nain, Georges de la Tour was discovered. A gratifying achievement on the part of stylistic criticism. This Lorrainese distinguishes himself from all followers of Caravaggio active this side of the Alps by the determination and earnestness with which he realizes his personal vision. Crass reality is observed with a keen, incisive eye and, through uncanny effects of lighting, sublimated into something mystical, pathetic and monumental. Several of his pictures were catalogued as Spanish before his personality became known.

It may be that somebody will feel that the type of person depicted by de la Tour and the brothers Le Nain is more Spanish than French and will think he has spotted the emotional approach with which, on a higher level, he is familiar in the popular types created by Velasquez. In them the sinister side of the French is deepened into Spanish dryness and gravity. I am far from wishing to add to the number of attempts at solving the already overloaded Le Nain problem by putting forward a new hypothesis—if new it be—and saying that I regard a connection with Spain as probable. The most we can surmise is similarity of mind, similarity of vision coming from racial affinity. A widespread prejudice always expects gaiety and a readier endurance of hard living conditions in the 'sunny South', and melancholy in the chill and misty North. The world of pictures shows, at least in the seventeenth century, the exact opposite, since it is precisely among the Latins that open-heartedness, gay abandon, bourgeois comfort, rustic joviality, uninhibited expression of feeling seem to be lacking. The bridges which the Netherlanders, and particularly the Dutch, used to make contact with common everyday things, i.e. sympathy, good intentions and humour, on these bridges the Southerners set foot with the greatest reluctance. Even Dutchmen like Pieter de Laar seem to lose their good humour in Italy. As to Spain, a ceremonial ranging from the court down, pervades all social strata. The very beggars are not wanting in reserve and dignity. The cavalier, eyeing the lower orders without pity and without contempt, encounters no humility and no complaint, and certainly not modest contentment; what he does encounter is proud resignation and sombre melancholy.

Of all the genre-pieces coming from the South, Murillo's street-urchins enjoy the greatest renown and win the favour of sensitive spirits despite the rudeness of the theme. The treatment, the colouring, the scale, not essentially different from those the Master employed in his altar-pieces, may be felt as out of key with the subject. Genuine Andalusian folk-life—even though, to the Northener, these beggar-boys look like the offspring of an impoverished nobility that has come down in the world. Murillo's fame as the painter of the resurgent Church has paled somewhat, but now and then over-zealous attempts have been made to bolster up his prestige by pointing to the 'naturalness' of his genre.

As regards Italy, the classical art tradition weighed too heavily on the seventeenth century for the small human joys and sorrows to be worth painting. Pathos, bigness and invention were deemed indispensable ingredients of all artistic endeavour. Naturally the 'Realists' revolted against the academy, but their ruthless observation concerned itself with clothing, flesh, lighting, texture, still-life and did not inform the interpretation, the idea, the motifs of movement; they were not in the least inclined to give up pathos, the heightening of visual data. Their inclination aimed far more at adding a further touch of illusion to what they saw and conceived in the grand manner, at marrying tragedy and reality. On us this *mélange* of large scale, mighty gesture and flimsy motive has a distasteful effect. The 'small' Masters who devoted some care, particularly in North Italy, to still-life, landscape and genre, generally keep close to Netherlands models. The fusty melancholy and astringency with which the French and the Spaniards observe the life of the people, the Italian changes into something spookish. It is with such dodges as unnatural proportion, fitful lighting and hysterical animation that Magnasco contrives to make daily life interesting.

IX

GENRE IN THE EIGHTEENTH CENTURY

From the standpoint we have taken up, interested in the fate of genre-picture, we have been looking all the time at the Netherlands; and, where the sixteenth and seventeenth centuries are concerned, few of the salient features can have escaped us. In the eighteenth century, France holds the field and in France the Court. To begin with, painting portrayed concentrated monarchical power, then followed a sumptuous and *galant* period inclining to erotic frivolity. More and more the lady, whether mistress or queen, sets the taste. The Court and the classes which copy Court style move ceremonially. Convention, social discipline stiffens the deportment, makes the gestures stilted. Along with the Court the Academy ruled art, like as not guiding it away from the Court on occasion. But both ruling powers were unanimous in their rejection of everything natural as unseemly. The villainous and famished mob at the lower end of the social scale was not permitted to dim the glitter of the pictorial stage. The further the century advanced, the more an intimation of danger looming ahead may have induced the idle rich and the privileged consciously to shut their eyes to misery and indigence.

In the Netherlands, so far as the genre-picture informs us, people ate, drank, smoked, danced, made music, brawled, sometimes even worked, with a spot of hearty love-making thrown in. But in the French epoch the only one of the mainsprings of human action that appears to have functioned is love. Dancing, playing and music were all subservient to *l'amour*. This indicates certain limits. Within these limits and in the territory permitted, at least three Masters were able to develop personally and in freedom: Watteau (b. 1684), Fragonard (1732), Boucher (1703). The instrument that set the tone was fashioned by the social culture of the day and place, but the music played on this instrument was wrought by the Masters on their own resources.

Watteau, born in Valenciennes, headed for Paris where, with his *Pilgrimage to Cythère* done in 1717, he struck a note that had not been sounded either in France or anywhere else. He was taken up indulgently by the Academy and had the good fortune to find understanding patrons. There is a widespread idea that the spirit of the French people is manifest in his work. We draw conclusions from him, whose lustre eclipses all else in our eyes, about the spirit of his nation and his time. National vanity is always inclined to ascribe the merits of individuals to the 'genius' of the nation. It is always a dubious thing to regard great Masters as representatives. The overwhelming majority of his contemporaries were far from finding, in Watteau, the illustrator of their worries, sorrows and joys. And, had the overriding taste of the Court appreciated him, he would be represented more copiously in the Louvre than in Potsdam and Berlin. Since Watteau came to Paris from the borders of Flanders, since it can be demonstrated that he admired Rubens and copied the drawings of this Fleming, certain authors who can read and write but not see lay it down quite simply: French spirit in Flemish form—or, contradiction being *de rigeur*: Flemish spirit in French form. It is very likely that the sensitive Watteau gazed with alarm, perhaps with envy, at the robust Flemish vitality; but nobody who did not know the facts would think of Rubens in connection with any work of Watteau's.

Neither sociological interpretation nor art-classification contributes anything essential to our understanding in this case.

Artists make statements about the time, the place and the society for which they create—direct statements with the What of their work, indirect ones with the How of it. The What in Watteau's work is so little real that it betrays very little of time, place and environment, but all the more about the artist's personality. The concept of the genre does not really apply to his *fêtes galantes*. Naturally enough, he has nothing historical, nothing biblical, little mythological. Everything typical, characteristic of this human society and therefore genre-like, is imaginary and fictitious, and to that extent not genre-like. Watteau's society cannot be taken outright as *French* society.

His eroticism is spiritualized, clouded over with gentle melancholy; it expresses itself as an overture, a wishing, a desiring, a wooing, a longing. His creatures do not dally on the Isles of Love, they go there on pilgrimages. Liking, attraction animates their bodies and causes them to move gracefully. In the open, amid paradisal scenes, under the sky, not in secret closets, in another world in which there is no guilt—there the sexes seek and frisk with one another. By transporting these indolent, gallant couples out of the salon and into the wide, mysterious, awe-inspiring world, Watteau loosens the chains of convention and endues desire with something of the innocence of nature.

All through the centuries of poetry, from Virgil to Rousseau, we can trace how society, surfeited with culture, its natural instincts inhibited by binding norms, sought refuge in the bucolic idyll as though going on holiday in the country, feeling that humanity had kept its nature more unalloyed in the primitive life of rustic folk than in the civilized and intellectually more advanced strata. Disguised as a shepherdess the lady, enjoying the freedom of masquerade, thought she could 'dissipate'. Since people assiduously avoided and overlooked the poverty, wretchedness and neediness of shepherds and peasants, particularly in the France of the eighteenth century, a suspect idealization and affected simplicity made their appearance on the stage and in the picture.

Watteau's genius succeeded in giving plausible reality to a dream-world where human instinct accommodated itself to the demands of a refined and highly developed cult of form, without succumbing to the imminent danger of theatricality. However unreal and visionary, the world of these figures remains viable. Watteau's drawings, large numbers of which have been preserved, instantaneous impressions, transfix the multifarious movements of the feminine body with sure aim. But the study of the body's structure, the grain of the elastic flesh, subserves fantasy—to such an extent that everything individual, accidental is overlooked. The Master sees in his model—apparently it is always the same model—his ideal, a creature who, in virtue of her grace and charm, is worthy to belong to a society in which libertinage is ennobled, if not by morality, then by taste and a delicate sense of beauty.

In the eyes of the academicians Watteau appeared a realist. His drawings of the feminine body are truer to nature than those of any of his contemporaries, are not far behind those of Rubens or Degas. For us this 'realist' is a minnesinger whose sole task is to proclaim woman's sex-appeal. As against that it may be remarked—indeed it has sometimes been said—that he was a timid, peakishly continent and platonic adorer of womankind who held aloof from all frivolities (Pl. 30).

That judgments which contradict one another so sharply

30. WATTEAU, A LADY AT HER TOILET. DETAIL
London, British Museum
Drawing for the picture in the Wallace Collection

31. CHARDIN, THE WAY TO SCHOOL
Vienna, Liechtenstein Gallery

can be expressed with some show of justice may be explained by the fact that Watteau was able to fuse his heterogeneous inclinations, desires and requirements into the uniform whole of an inimitable and personal creation. Towards the end of his short career, waking as though from a dream, he produced one genre-picture—a special commission: the trade-shield for the firm of Gersaint. In accordance with the decorative nature of the task the treatment is lighter, more fluent, less draughtsmanlike in accent than usual. The colouring pleases with its silvery harmony. A real glimpse into a Parisian art-dealer's shop. The figures move with such confident nonchalance and unaffected grace that, compared with them, even Terborch's cavaliers and ladies seem stiff and phlegmatic. A vital breed, born of the longings of a man who was neither healthy, nor sociable, nor elegant.

Of the eighteenth century Frenchmen, Chardin emerges as a genre-painter with something of the contemplativeness of the Dutch about him. Nice, innocently occupied boys, good children, youthful mothers. An uneventful, well-mannered sort of existence, a tale told cautiously and amiably. Charm in its best behaviour, with no erotic excitements. Chardin is neither the courtier nor the libertine. He is a painter, not a draughtsman. Hardly any drawings of his have been found. If Watteau's eye penetrates to the structure, Chardin's contents itself with the texture. In Watteau's painting the drawing functions as the ground-plan, the scaffolding; Chardin's language avoids articulation and linear accentuation. The colour-surface, a tissue of select notes gently shading off into a mild harmony of pale blue, faint pinks, reddish brown—this is always the aim of his treatment (Pl. 31).

If I called Vermeer a still-life painter I can say the same thing of Chardin, and with less fear of being contradicted since he actually did paint still-life and achieved something perfect, unassailable in this category. That which endures, that which wears well is the object of his choice. He avoids the open, seems never to have gone out of doors. To reproduce fruit in its many tints and textures—that was his passion. And as a matter of fact the skin of children, of women, linen and woollen clothes all partake of the downy bloom of ripe fruit. His personal, unacademic technique, neither smooth nor rough, covering the canvas like a caress, seems to spring from the practice of the still-life painter.

Less personal than Watteau or Chardin, François Boucher also ministers to the spirit of the times. A past-master of his *métier*, he was able to solve his tasks—principally those of decoration—brilliantly. His eroticism, though not exactly bashful, is formal, unintimate and cold.

Always bent on avoiding triviality the Frenchman of the eighteenth century often glamourized familiar things only by sentimentalizing them. Chardin avoided this danger, but Greuze fairly wallows in pretty-prettiness, bogus innocence and lachrymose theatricality.

Pater and Lancret keep to Watteau. Lancret in particular translates Watteau's poetry into prose and for that reason gives a more factual account of the nature of French society. In Fragonard's case the dilemma of succumbing either to triviality or sentimentality does not apply, because his lively and inventive mind turned everything he took up—and what did he not take up—into a sort of playful turmoil, an erotic commotion. The motive source of his strength lay more in the nerves and senses than in passionate feeling, a little, too, in calculation and, finally, habit. Hailing from the south of France he had revelled in landscape scenes on Italian soil before ever he developed his astounding versatility in Paris—portraits, studies of heads, single genre-like figures, piquant anecdotes, scenes of bourgeois life and rustic idylls. Everything he set his light hand to dazzles and surprises at first glance. His eroticism is frank and saucy. For all that, his improvising technique veils the scandalousness of the situations and events, just as Watteau transfigures the erotic with his poetry and Boucher puts an academic chill on it.

If a loosening and attenuation of hard-and-fast form, and frivolity, are supposed to be characteristic of Rococo, they are so more particularly because they figure so impressively in Fragonard's work. As a painter Fragonard sipped everywhere, now with the Venetians, now with the Netherlanders, even with Rembrandt, taking over whatever he needed for his coquettish and fluent delivery. The Goncourts described Watteau and Fragonard as the only poets among the French painters of the seventeenth century. Compared with the lyric Watteau, Fragonard is at least a witty epigrammist.

The graphic arts of the French prove to be rewardingly instructive as regards the customs and way of life—in etchings, engravings and the colour-print, now developed to a masterly degree. Gabriel St. Aubin was a fanatical draughtsman, a reliable reporter and chronicler of daily happenings, who offers the historian more than the painters do. It is possible to trace, particularly in the engravings of Moreau le jeune, how towards the end of the century 'good' society grew more and more mindful of poise and dignified behaviour, and how finally, just before the social catastrophe, something like caustic criticism of luxury and idleness springs up in Dubucourt's colour-prints.

The Revolution, by putting an end to what was ethically objectionable, destroyed aesthetic values as well. The view from above of innocently contented country-folk, of a comely and sentimental populace, turned out to be a delusion, an hallucination now that a relentless foe was rising out of the depths. Nobody in France—although Goya did so in Spain—looked the hard and savage reality squarely in the eye, before which all amorous pleasantries, *fêtes galantes* and rustic idylls vanished at a breath.

In France the fury and terror of the upheaval and the political, economic and social rebirth made the genre, whether of the Court, the bourgeoisie or the country, whether sentimental or entertaining, seem otiose. The imagination pullulated with pathetic images, vast forms, heroic will. The Academy had kept up tradition enough to satisfy the requirements and demands of that stormy time. The frigid mastery, the spineless cleverness of a Louis David triumphed because he exemplified Roman virtue and did portraits of self-confident personalities athirst for power.

In England political and social conditions were different. Ideas which exploded with destructive violence in the French Revolution had been at work earlier in England, making for organic transformation. The slumber had not been so deep, and the awakening was less terrifying. England showed herself immune to violent hammerings at her political and social structure. Morality was perhaps no higher than on the Continent, but was esteemed. English art—in the main eclectic—kept more to the Netherlands than to France. Honesty and reasonableness as opposed to the ingenuities of the French with their cranky illusions. Hogarth strikes a new note about the middle of the century. An un-naïve painter who saw life like a schoolmaster, a satirist with outstretched forefinger. In order to put clear limits to the idea of 'satire' I lay it down that Jan Steen is, or would be, wrongly called a satirist. Jan Steen gives himself and us a good laugh, but he does not laugh at men and their doings, let alone moralize, instruct or accuse. Steen laughs and incites to laughter, Hogarth makes folly, vanity and vice laughable. Such a crass, tendentious and exaggerating vision, something of a novelty in the middle of the eighteenth century, had a powerful effect, particularly in the German Protestant countries. The pictures became widely known through copper-engravings, and a witty and intelligent German literary man, Lichtenberg, interpreted them.

Hogarth is a painter of high calibre so long as he is not preaching at men to improve themselves, and so long as he does not recall his bizarre aesthetic theories.

The average run of English genre-painting during the second half of the eighteenth century sticks close to portraiture, then at its peak. Aristocratic gentlemen had themselves painted as happy fathers of families, landed proprietors, preferably in the open and with their dogs and horses. Eroticism was hushed up, sport and healthy energy put on view, with marked success in the case of George Stubbs (1724-1806), Ben Marshal and Wheatley.

Holland produced one more painter of significance in the eighteenth century, not a late birth but a Master whose freshness and gaiety freed him from tradition, now grown very weary and dreary. Cornelis Troost is often regarded as spiritually akin to Hogarth, who was born in the same year as he—1697—and was likewise at home in the Protestant North. Common to both the Dutchman and the Englishman is the need to communicate, a predilection for picture-sequences and a dangerous leaning towards the literary. Troost keeps up the advantages won by his nation's pictorial culture. He is no tendentious satirist like Hogarth, and no comic poet like Steen, rather an illustrator of plays written by others. However eloquently he tries to express himself, the meaning of his vivacious scenes often remains hidden for those who do not know certain Dutch comedies which have since disappeared. As a painter he is at his best when he is not illustrating, not telling a story. The What of the thoughtful painter begins to impair the How.

Italy's relations with the genre in the eighteenth century were not so very different from what they were in the seventeenth. The renown of classical art was still operative, with the result that ardour, grace, shapeliness and ingenious invention continued to be demanded as essential and indeed indispensable. On top of this there was none of that middle-class cult of the living-room which fathered the genre-picture in the North, since this did not fit in with the capacious palazzos of the South. Decoration of extensive areas of wall was demanded and fulfilled by Tiepolo in an inexhaustible spate of production. Venice, city of painters, of oriental brilliancy of colour, felt herself comparatively free from the pressure of monumental classical art, sculpture and antiquity generally, and enjoyed a late blossoming in the work of Tiepolo and Francesco Guardi. Here, too, the production of modest genre-pieces could go forward, with scenes from the salon, the boudoir. Venice was a city of festivities, operas, comedies, masquerades. Here it was that Dürer had attempted to learn how to dance. In Pietro Longhi's description Venetian society appears in a Sunday mood of contentment and its inevitable gallantry harmless and polite, if we think of France.

No doubt the eyes of eighteenth century Italians, even outside Venice, occasionally rested on the common people, but, though they may not always have transmogrified reality into witches' kitchens and madhouses, in the manner of Magnasco, they still see in it mainly wretchedness and oppression. What is unearthly is now winged and astir, while the earthly plods on in dull quiescence. Once upon a time it was quite the contrary: in Heaven everlasting stillness reigned, while on earth men—and the devil—raged. Life now seemed a serious thing, and art lost its serenity to the extent that it participated in life. Sporadically, even in the eighteenth century, social criticism looms.

X

THE GENRE: PRESENT AND FUTURE

In the world of politics, philosophy and pictorial art the nineteenth century presents a confused spectacle, shot with harsh contrasts—at least, that is how it appears to us. It may be that earlier periods, seen in closer perspective, had just as much the devastated appearance of a battlefield. Let us try to pick out the spiritual forces struggling for mastery, and exercising it, with a view to explaining and arranging the manifestations of art in those terms. A virile and serious century, then, a century of democracy, of the middle-class now feeling the threat of the worker. Technological advance, science, historical-mindedness, materialism, and by way of reaction to all this, an excessively idealistic dogmatism. The power of the churches on the wane. Man's longing for the unearthly, no longer canalized by orthodox belief, pours into poetry, philosophy, pictures, music. Schopenhauer's theory of pity was Christian, was interpreted by the philosopher himself as Christian, but was turned down flat by every sect, even by theism. His pessimism is far more hopeless than the pessimism of Christianity ever was. For the orthodox there was not only the Fall, original sin and this earthly vale of sorrow, there was also confession, absolution, redemption, a just Judge and bliss everlasting. The pious, the saints and the martyrs may have suffered, but were rewarded for it and triumphed over pain and death. The religious art of the Church is not monotonously melancholic like that of Millet, where religious feelings are mixed up with social sympathy.

Schopenhauer's doctrine of immortality and the conquest of evil remains, to say the least of it, obscure, and is a poor counterbalance to the meaninglessness, pointlessness and questionableness of earthly existence so indefatigably described by him. Tolstoi, another formidable and influential representative of the spiritual movement of the times, took possession of the intellectual edifice Schopenhauer had erected but not occupied, and ended tragically. Feeling a profound need of faith the wealthy aristocrat, the renowned author deviated more and more from the orthodox Church and fetched up against a comfortless blank.

Nietzsche superseded Schopenhauer as the fashionable philosopher. In a continual whirl of utterance, now rationalistic, now ecstatic, he endeavoured to fight free of Christian pessimism and pity, alternately pointing to Voltaire, to Goethe, to the Greeks, to the 'South'. Finally, a way out of the labyrinth of philosophical systems was found in resolute sensualism, in resting under the shade of sensible appearances.

The idealistic view of things which Kant worked up into a doctrinal system denies the reality of the sensible world in so far as it assumes no object to subsist, or even to be perceptible, without a subject. But for that very reason it proves that a supposititious 'thing-in-itself' is not only invisible but also unseeable; that for the 'subject', that is to say the creative artist, nothing exists but the 'representation' or 'idea': that which appears to him. Thus it comes about that idealistic theory leads to realist practice. If it had once been an altogether feasible task to represent the invisible with the help of the visible, now all attempts to represent the unseeable had to be abandoned. Even Courbet with his trite demand: 'How can anybody paint an angel when he hasn't seen one?' could have appealed to Kant, just as he could have appealed to Darwin. Darwin would have corroborated that fauna possessed of human corporeality have no wings and cannot fly, and that a hybrid of man and bird would be an unnatural monster.[1]

Cézanne certainly uttered Kant's name on one occasion, as reported by Joachim Gasquet, though he expresses himself as unintelligibly as any Hegelian. He himself, he says, appears to himself 'like the subjective consciousness of the landscape, while the picture is its objective consciousness'.

As far as concerns artistic creation, easier travel, the spread of reproductions, the literature of aesthetics and the history of art, museums, exhibitions on a scale unknown before, all threatened to produce eclecticism. And this danger threw up a craving for originality. Characteristic marks of art particularly in the first half of the century: lack of naïveté, high-flying aspiration coupled with little craftsman-like tradition. The clean break with the 'frivolous' eighteenth century is taking its revenge.

In former times the artist stood face to face with certain exacting but stimulating forces: the Church, princes, rich amateurs, then a solid bourgeoisie in Holland, society in England, the Court in France. The fact that these authorities invariably determined the form and content of art-production with their requirements and wishes is one that hardly ever receives sufficient attention, since people think too exclusively of the will and desires of the producers. In the nineteenth century the artist saw himself faced with 'the public'—both a patron and an enemy. The public is a hydra-headed monster, better furnished with ears than with eyes. Once upon a time the valuable

1 He also calculated that an angel would have to have a sternum projecting to the length of some six feet. Trans.

was what people liked; in the nineteenth century, after the public had repeatedly shown itself up, the valuable—at least in the eyes of those who set the tone—became what the public did not like. This criterion, however, proved to be untrustworthy. Not even the tastelessness of the public could be relied on. The man of ambition turned away with defiant contempt from the likings of the crowd who had the purchasing-power, often after he had wooed their favour in vain. Right judgment and good taste are not creative. In Germany in particular the type of the cultivated, enlightened, cerebral painter emerged, fruitlessly tormenting himself in his efforts to realize his ideal. The letters of the German painters are conspicuously good in comparison with their pictures. The press, praising and condemning, increased the confusion with its multiplicity of voices and its hectic tempo.

In the course of the nineteenth century genre-painting fell into a disrepute from which it finally perished. But for some time the requirements of the untutored public kept it alive.

Reality, looked squarely in the eye, no longer seemed harmless or diverting. For the nature-worshipper every phenomenon, even the most ordinary, was rich in mystery and, in the pantheistic sense, divine, with nothing amusing about it; but for the materialist nothing was profane because nothing was holy, nothing earthly in the sense of being base because nothing was higher; there was no Here because there was no Hereafter. The world of the senses, which once seemed familiar, innocuous or comic by contrast with the unearthly, was now taken seriously, regarded pessimistically, critically, or with injudicious neutrality. The intellectual pride that came to the top in Germany in the first decades of the nineteenth century, despised the genre. Cornelius, who was the German

Master for a spell, said that genre was no business of his. Three phases of change may be distinguished, not exactly periods, because late-born painters could still remain at the level of those born earlier.

First: genre in the proper sense, indulging itself to the full (Waldmüller, b. 1793; Knaus, b. 1829; their forerunner the Englishman Wilkie, b. 1785). Optimistic view of things, sentimental or entertaining in effect. The painter begins with an idea, e.g. family happiness, childish innocence, rustic jollification, human goodness, or he thinks up some curious or piquant situation. He then looks round in his visual memory and in his folios of 'studies' for suitable motifs, selects the model that befits the theme, finds the various props and prospects. He succeeds in bringing off a piecemeal trueness to nature. But where this manipulative procedure fails is in the convincing trueness to nature of the thing as a whole. The painter sets to work like somebody organizing a 'tableau'. We are reminded of the theatre. The actors on the stage speak louder and articulate more clearly than people do in life; they say what the author has told them to say, move as the producer arranges. And what is so 'produced' expresses the painter's thoughts and feelings with forced distinctness. The use of professional models alone entails a certain amount of theatricality. Menzel is certainly an honest, impartial and keen observer. And yet— let us examine a justly admired masterpiece of his, the *Procession in Gastein.* The procession of pious local inhabitants is seen without bias. But Menzel was a visitor from the rationalist North, depicting the contrast between the religious peasants and the enlightened, free-thinking, elegant strangers as the point of his genre-picture. And the spectators chattering unconcerned in the foreground and turning away from the strange local custom strike us as more thought up and invented than actually seen. The painter is interested not only in the proceedings but also in the impression the proceedings make—that is, he is passing judgment.

Genre-painting in the nineteenth century fits on to the peak-period of this category, the seventeenth century, save that enlightenment, sentimentality and education throw anecdotal, emotional or tendentious elements into sharper relief. Nobody longs so avidly for the naïve as the sentimentalist.

The child catches our notice with its innocence and drollery. Genre-painters begin to fight shy of life's seriousness, of which children alone know nothing, and seek refuge in the world of children as a supposed paradise.

Second: the genre-concept becomes problematical (Millet, b. 1814; van Gogh, b. 1853; Israels, b. 1824; Daumier, b. 1808). Tragic, satiric view of things. The worker who, in the seventeenth century, had mostly smoked, drunk or played cards, is made a hero, pitied and honoured at once for his heavy physical labour. The worker as hero: an idea that came up in the second half of the nineteenth century. The ordinary is larded with pathos, touched up with religion, everything agreeable cut out so as to express suffering and patience. The pessimistic view turns into satire, scorn of human frailty, stupidity and bourgeois philistinism. Man is an object of pity or mockery, a cause of complaint or accusation. Daumier, who towers above the satirists of all ages in the extent and depth of his knowledge of human nature, pilloried and exposed to ridicule the folly of the rulers, the pettiness of the ruled in 4000 lithographs, and with stinging wit laid bare the miseries of his time and of life in general. With satire there goes a large measure of political freedom, which England reached in the eighteenth century, France in the nineteenth and Germany still later. Hogarth, Rowlandson, Gillray are sober caricaturists compared with Daumier, who gives his work weight and verve as a child of French Romanticism, and a grim bitterness all his own.

Third: the movement that set in about 1860 in France and was to gain widespread currency round about 1880, listed under the somewhat empty term 'Impressionism'. In the programme, theory and technique of Manet and Renoir there is no place for the genre. The motifs can still be called genre-like but not the interpretation and way of looking. The war-cry 'l'art pour l'art' with which these painters burst upon the scene is, strictly speaking, not altogether apt. After all, any painter, even a Piloty or a Makart, could say: I work for art's sake; invention, composition and staging minister to what I understand by 'art'. An apter slogan might be: appearance for appearance's sake. In the negative sense this means suppression of all intellectual interpretation, verbal interpolation, arrangement. The reality is not sought, the object not selected from intellectual inclination, it is rather taken in from a reverent distance. The man who knows most sees most; he sees more than is actually visible to him in a given instant and from a given standpoint. The Impressionists, however, were at pains to forget what they knew so as to notice only what fell within their field of vision. Though this principle could not be carried through consistently since nobody can see anything completely unbiassed, nevertheless the intention, so directed, became the distinguishing mark of Impressionist art. In effect, the personality of the creator with his likings, his temperament would appear not to be excluded in the least. A happily affirmative, lover-like attitude to life determines the choice of standpoint and theme. Yet at first sight it is as though a slice of reality were addressing us; the painter seems to keep silent. Something is there without appearing to be put there or put on view.

The procedure of work in keeping with the programme is different from that described in the first 'phase'. The painter now sticks to the point of view from which he can see the whole; he does not work by thinking and piecing together, he sets about it spontaneously. Everything phenomenal is of equal value for him, working long-sightedly, to a big scale. He does not stress, does not accentuate. Here we see people, not play-actors; processes, not scenes. What was once a sketch, design, first impression is now the picture. Despite the distance, indistinctness, paucity of detail the artist manages to convey to us—so far as he is successful in realizing his vision—the feeling that animated him when looking. He obtains wholesale trueness to nature, whereas formerly only piecemeal trueness to nature resulted. That no historical pictures could be born of this kind of vision is a foregone conclusion, as is proved by Manet's attempt to depict the execution of the Emperor of Mexico. A group of soldiers firing. The meaning and purport of the event, place and time, consequently *everything* essential to the incident, remains in the dark. The Master was bound to fail in the attempt to illustrate something that he had not seen as a whole with his physical eye.

Indictment, mockery and scorn as applied to conditions and events are by no means silent, but are directed to the drawing, the poster, the periodical, the funny paper. Painting holds aristocratically aloof from the battles, questions, problems and worries of the day, intellectually neutral, cultivating its palate, delighting in the senses. The Impressionists, deliberately forgoing all criticism and judgment in respect of the phenomenal world, appealing neither to sentiment nor to sense of humour, absorbing the prismatic glitter of things with a sort of positive neutrality, mark the visual art off from the art of poetry, from history, from satire, as also from the affecting, entertaining, instructive or informative type of narrative. The picture is no longer the exemplar of an idea, does not point beyond the visible, strikes us as something unique, individual, like a portrait. A dancing couple, a picture of Renoir's does not tell us: This is how people danced in Paris; rather evokes the question: Who was this gentleman and this lady?

I began by defining the term 'genre' negatively as the sphere of the not-important, what is not historically memorable. In the same way as superior things ceased to rule the imagination, so everyday things lost their inferior character. The contemplation of the earthly as specific of the genre stipulated a belief in the unearthly, man viewed in contrast to the divine. When the pantheistic outlook lodged everything inexplicable and every mystery firmly in the world of the Here and Now, the pleasure of viewing the bustle of life as a familiar comedy abated.

The painter who starts out unintellectually with a visual experience does not regard himself as bound to the limitations deriving from a time when painters started out with an idea. Objects of this kind or that, fruit, landscape, an individual personality, all these still exist of course; but they no longer govern, as each in its kind once did, the spiritual approach, the technique, the format. Hence the categories of painting have ceased to have firm limits.

If a division can be made—it can never be quite complete—between style as determined by the individuality of the artist, by his technique and material, by place and time, and lastly by the object, then the fourth determinant lost more and more in strength in the course of the nineteenth century. In terms of his way of observing and way of looking Manet is a portraitist, no matter whether he has his eye on a bundle of asparagus, a personality or any other object. The direct apprehension of nature leads to the individual, hence to the portrait, and away from the typical, hence from the genre.

Historians, among them one as high-ranking and far-seeing as Carl Justi, condemned Impressionism. Many of them, however, became converts and, true to their profession, hailed even this change as a development, even this development as an advance—rightly, in so far as 'painting from nature' produced an additional touch of illusion and unlocked a new beauty. But: every organ that is not engaged constantly and forcefully, degenerates and atrophies. Surrender to the particular phenomenon stunts the visual memory, weakens the activity of creative imagination. Were an honest painter of our day to plunge into the Old Masters he might find little indeed that he would have wished to create, but much that he would feel incapable of creating. The performance, even of the averagely gifted Old Masters, is bound to strike him as incomprehensible. Faculties which were once general have now got lost. The artist who carried what he had seen in the store-house of memory was probably a keener observer than the one who realizes the phenomenal direct, in much the same way as people used to read better before the invention of printing than afterwards.

About 1860 Impressionism was received as something alien and prejudicial to current taste; about 1880 it was recognized by the spokesmen and it was not long before dealers, collectors and finally the public—and the market—saw in Manet's art and that of his companions the legitimate painting, the painting that was both appropriate to the age and true to nature, and valued it as such.

It was only to be expected that ambitious, originality-seeking painters of the 1910 generation should find that what everybody saw and everybody had learnt to see from Manet, was banal. One of them once said: We cannot reproduce nature better than Manet, therefore we must try to reproduce something other than nature—thus revealing that, lacking originality himself, he saw as Manet did but merely wanted to see something different differently. Every artist gifted with original vision thinks that his predecessors reproduced nature inefficiently and incorrectly. The tortuous movement that rose in revolt against the past, changing with fashion and actuated by snobbery, expressed itself in various mutually contradictory styles and forms, the only thing they had in common being the excruciating attempt to bring forth something peculiar, novel, *épatant*. They may be distinguished more or less as follows:

Ecstasy, real or pretended. Life is observed in a state of frenzy ('Expressionism').

Freakishly anti-natural form and colour. The cheapest brand of originality.

Conscious stylization, geometrical consolidation, abbreviation, optic music. Manet went looking for nature and found his style, but the style-seeker finds only manner.

Real or simulated primitivity (the Douanier Rousseau).

Pedantically punctilious, still-lifeish groping after reality, the 'New Objectivity', panopticon plus symbolism.

Not infrequently the attempts to get round appearances remind one of those passages where Lichtenberg castigates certain writers of his time: 'Stupidly affected eccentricity . . . becomes the criterion for originality, and the surest sign that a man has a head is for him to stand on it a couple of times a day . . .' He goes on: 'Indeed I will not deny that a clever head can even contrive a certain brand of art which may delight another head of similar cleverness, and may thus be capable of a certain degree of perfection.'

In all these unwearying and solemn efforts, in spite of arid calculation and the mania for bamboozlement, we must rate as something positive the urge for spiritual, masculine, constructive activity as opposed to the sensuous, spiritually inert, feminine receptivity of the Impressionists. What will the future bring? Perhaps a new sort of monumentality, hardly a new art of the genre.

Familiarity and sympathy as between the seer and the seen was the well-spring of the genre, an attitude to life which was productive above all in the sixteenth century, say in the woodcuts of Hans Weiditz or in Brueghel's work. Today we feel existence too much as a dangerous liability, hence we cannot lightly give ourselves up to any understanding with the visible world as it is. In the nineteenth century the factors working against the genre were intellectual ambition and the shift of interest from the picture's content to its form. In the twentieth century visual art would like not only to show something but to say something. It struggles with forms and symbols for the sake of the unsayable; it treads many paths, none of which leads to the genre.

XI

SOMETHING OF THE PRINCIPLES AND HISTORY OF PORTRAITURE

Lessing, a teacher of the Germans, banished the portrait from the domain of art. He found portraiture incompatible with his aesthetic principles. Winckelmann, another teacher of the Germans, started like Lessing with the idea of 'Beauty' and he, too, was unable to fit the multiplicity of individual appearances into his system. He was less logical and acute than Lessing, but his artistic experience was greater and he was at pains to bring 'Nature' and 'Art'—or what he understood by art—into harmony, whereas Lessing, who was totally lacking in visual experience (he had not even seen a cast of his *Laocoon*), had no artistic recollections of any kind to disturb him in his uncompromising deductions. The dialectician and the enthusiast drew their judgments from a fragmentary—in Lessing's case literary—knowledge of classical art, which, compared with the art of their own day, seemed superior and exemplary. They were anything but historians. You may say: What have the prejudiced aesthetics of a rationalistic, classicistic age to do with us? But—ever since the fifteenth century the idea of that sempiternally valid and exemplary art of our forefathers has guided aesthetic theory and, indirectly, aesthetic practice not only in Italy but later in the whole civilized world. The rule of theory always rises in proportion as creative power falls. It rose to the utmost limit in the work of the Saxon, Raphael Mengs. We have to wonder why a non-Italian living on Italian soil should have gone to the last extreme in the worship of antiquity, just as in the seventeenth century the Frenchman Poussin was far more of a classicist than any Italian of his time. The Renaissance was rich in self-confident creative talent. The art of the Greeks, not so much a visible prototype as an ideal, produced no eclecticism to begin with. The eighteenth century doctrine of 'Beauty' as the goal of all desire, proclaimed as law, especially by the Germans, hampered the observation of the individual and hence the growth of the portrait. There is only one Beauty, and no two individuals are alike. Winckelmann toyed with the presumptuous idea that the task of the artist was to create 'Man the beautiful' by observing the unfortunate efforts of nature. The Greeks were supposed to have done this. It was a doctrine that taught a most prejudiced observation.

From the fifteenth century the awakening of personality tended, in Italy, in the direction of the portrait, whilst the rigid ideas as to the nature of art led, under the influence of those venerable forefathers, to the type. 'No man was afraid to be striking, to be and seem different from the others,' says Burckhardt even of the Italians of the fifteenth century. And to the 'discoveries' of the Renaissance the same author adds the 'discovery of man'. The craving for fame was frank and articulate in those days, and became one of the motive forces of portraiture.

The history of portrait-art as running parallel with the history of biography, and that of the self-portrait parallel with the history of autobiography: this is what we would expect. I do not know if a history of biographical literature exists.[1] A sketch of it can be found in Burckhardt's *Civilization of the Renaissance in Italy*. If, as this shows, the

[1] A *History of Autobiography* by Georg Misch is announced by Messrs. George Routledge. Trans.

literary description of individual personalities was undertaken earlier in Italy than elsewhere and more brazenly, more elaborately, more thoroughly than in the sculpture and painting of the day—and often undertaken successfully—then the reason why the visual arts of Italy lagged behind language, prose and poetry, other reasons apart, may be sought in the widely prevalent idea of the function of visual art, which was obliged to hold aloof from fallible, imperfect nature.

The heightening of self-consciousness, so favourable to the development of the portrait when found in the object, became a stumbling-block to it in the subject, i.e. the creative artist. Cornelis van Haarlem, the Dutch academician, is supposed, according to van Mander, to have painted magnificent portraits, but with reluctance, because he could not unfold his spirit in this kind of work. Falling from such lips the dictum sounds showy and arrogant. Nowadays people would probably be of the opinion that a portrait from the hand of the Haarlem Master pleases precisely because he did not give free run to his spirit. But if Pieter Brueghel, Bosch or Michelangelo had based their objection to the portrait on the reasons given by Cornelis van Haarlem, we would certainly find it intelligible, just and self-evident. The job of painting a portrait entails something akin to obsequiousness, against which creative power puts up a fight.

Apart from the fact that the object, the appearance as given, demands to be observed accurately and objectively, thus limiting the artist's freedom, his imagination, his spirit, the portraitist is quite specifically in a subservient position to the patron—who, even if he does not consider himself knowledgeable in matters of art, still thinks he knows himself better than the artist and therefore feels entitled to pronounce judgment on the portraitist's performance. From the degrading pressure exerted by the pretensions, wishes, vanity of the patron no successful portraitist—apart from the greatest, like Holbein, Velasquez or Frans Hals—could escape.

More or less fruitfully we may distinguish as follows: portraitists who make use of the medium of painting, and painters who make portraits. Frans Hals belongs to the first group, Titian to the second. In Italy there is scarce a Master to be found who put forth his strength exclusively in portraiture, save perhaps Moroni. Everywhere and at all times the portrait was a school of objectivity. The portraitists are 'Naturalists', so far as this term may still be used. Even so one is often tempted to contradict this thesis, not only in the South where ideals of form limited the assimilation of individual traits, but also in the North where the subjectivity of strong personalities intruded or social convention hindered observation, as in the work of such successful portraitists as van Dyck and Gainsborough.

In the North things were different from what they were in the South. At the beginning of the fifteenth century painting broke away from tradition in the Netherlands, alienated itself from its parents without—as in Italy—clinging to the invigorating if sometimes hampering example of its grandparents. Whether Jan van Eyck was greater than Masaccio is a question about which one may wrangle, pointlessly enough; but it is certain that Jan van Eyck drew far more impartially on what he could see with his own eyes than did the Florentine. When Canova, a classicist of the first water, made, in a moment of lucidity, that astonishing remark as reported by Schinkel: 'Every step forward on Raphael's art demolishes it, but on van Eyck you can go on building indefinitely,' the historian will find his dictum corroborated, particularly where the portrait is concerned. Art is something other than imitation of nature. But to know of this difference and to think of it when working, proves to be dangerous.

The Middle Ages were not so mediaeval as we read in books. It was an unavoidable error that the new age formed its ideas about the mentality of the Middle Ages from the monuments that had been preserved. In them, the artist seems as impersonal as his subject. He was in the grip of the iconographic tradition of the Church. The sublunary mortal he was depicting appeared in the shape of a supplicant, a contingent creature, a member of the community, as a rule dimensionally small in proportion to the celestial figures. The individual physiognomy of the donor, with eyes devoutly upturned, received little attention, particularly as the obligatory task of portraying divine and unearthly things led the Masters to a type-style, holiness and venerableness being presentable only through comeliness.

On coins, as sometimes in book-miniatures, the object was to portray a ruler or emperor. But in all essentials artists were content to render majesty and sovereignty visible by the man's poise, or perhaps through certain attributes, rather than make this or that emperor recognizable.

The question of capacity or incapacity may be disregarded. The crucial thing is that in the range of commissions set to mediaeval art no need, no requirement of any kind, aroused or stimulated the capacity to interpret individual characteristics.

There is a romantic, sentimental and ingenious legend about the 'invention' of portraiture. The young man in love fixes the silhouette of his girl. Love the incentive, drawing the instrument, profile the result. After the fifteenth century artists in Italy called the ancient world to mind when engaged on a portrait. Little was known of ancient portrait-painting. Not much is known even today. Apart from busts and statues, all that could be seen was the coins of the Greeks and Romans. They were collected quite early on and admired, so that here were indications which induced artists to copy on a small scale, in low-relief and in profile. The portrait-medallion developed apace as an achievement of the Early Renaissance, spurred on by the cult of personality and thirst for fame. Durable, handy, the medallion could be cast by the thousand and gave the head in question something like immortality. Antonio Pisano, a contemporary of Jan van Eyck's, a pioneer as a draughtsman and Master of the portrait-medallion, imposed low-relief on painting. Even in the second half of the fifteen century the pure side-view was preferred for women's portraits, above all in Florence, e.g. Botticelli and Ghirlandaio. Portrait-medallions only came into existence in the North in the sixteenth century, with the impact of the Renaissance movement. Jan van Eyck, like all the Netherlands portraitists of the fifteenth century, avoided the profile.

Wherever man, the contingent creature, appears portrait-wise in the mediaeval church-painting, he shows himself for the most part in profile, to one side, at the edge, a humble adjunct to the holy, praeternatural figures presented full-face in the centre of the picture. The profile as opposed to the front-view is, as a form of portraiture, appropriate to the vision of the draughtsman as the front-view is appropriate to the vision of the painter. In the profile we have the 'thing-in-itself', in the front-view the 'phenomenon', contingent on conditions of visibility. I must apologise for the frivolous abuse of philosophical terms. In the front-view the sitter is turned towards us, addresses us; in the profile he inhabits another sphere than we. Here aloófness, aloneness; there intimacy; here something permanent in his idiosyncrasy is caught with pencil and line; there, where the margins are less distinct in their utterance, the psycho-physical being manifests itself more openly, more in the instantaneity of mood. The profile is as it were the ground-plan of the physiognomical building and is to the front-view as map is to landscape.

The profile makes a fragmentary statement. The child drawing a face will not omit to give, as best it can, the marginal line of nose, forehead and chin, but would feel there was something missing if only one eye and half a mouth were visible. It will make awkward attempts to combine profile and full-face. The solution of this difficulty —in the three-quarter-profile—was successfully achieved when artists learnt to master the perspective foreshortening that went with it. In the front-view the face *is turned* towards us; in the three-quarter-profile it *turns* towards us and the illusion of movement, of action, of life is evoked, particularly when a look at variance with the position of the head meets our eye.

The historian can see that, on the whole, the individual entity was absorbed more and more in the totality of the figure. We can follow the process step by step, aside from occasional jumps: first the face, the uncurtained portion of the body, a sort of shop-window, against a neutral background; then the bust together with the hands, sticking up over the edge of the frame; then the half-figure, with talking hands; then the three-quarter length, finally the whole figure. First the personality dissolved out of its locality and surroundings; later as something indigenous to this spot, since landscape-background or domicile or interior is developed along with it. The more the figure becomes visible as a whole, the more solidly entrenched the sitter seems in his station, his profession, his social class, and the more his local and temporal ties will govern the impression. Especially the costume betrays something of the Where and the When.

To begin with, it was the sharply defined physiognomy of the man that was seized, later the less sharp one of the woman. Moreover, the painter was a man and, faced with a woman, preferred to see shapeliness and symmetry rather than individual departures from the ideal of beauty. The child received attention last of all and then mostly in connection with the family-portrait. Initially the task of portraiture was bound up with the bias in favour of honour and excellence and confined to princes and other outstanding personalities—a bias that determined vision and style; until finally every human countenance without respect to position and intellectual significance seemed, as a unique phenomenon, worthy to be held fast in a picture.

Pisanello was roughly contemporary with Jan van Eyck, the Italian working in direct contrast to the Netherlander. Pisanello did portrait-medallions in large numbers. The few portraits of his that have been preserved share the stylization of the medallion. Face and breast are embedded in the surface in strict profile and are so one with the surface that they create the illusion of monument-like permanence. The decided statement of the profile's lines is not vitiated or confused by any three-dimensional bodiliness lifting away from the picture. We feel less the presence of a living person than that the memory is conjured up of some immortalized personality—a memory that has preserved only the essential features, but these with concentrated sharpness.

In such portraits of Jan van Eyck's as we possess the sitter turns towards us in three-quarter-profile. The facial quarter averted from us is bathed in light, its outline detaching itself abruptly from the dark neutral ground. On the other, unforeshortened, portion of the face the light, falling from the side, throws the prominences of flesh into extremely clear relief. The head does not lie flattened and fixed in the plane of the picture as in the profile position—on the contrary it is animated by a three-dimensional bodiliness, so that an illusion of spatial depth is created despite the neutral ground-colour. Interest in the peculiarities of individuals makes for near-sighted, sharply-focussing observation. The hieroglyphs which life and fate have engraved on the face are read off. More than once the sitter's line of vision diverges from the position in which he holds his head, thus evoking the impression of fleeting movement, as in the portrait of the *Man with a Turban* in the London National Gallery.

The portraits of donors in the Ghent Altar as well as in Jan van Eyck's other religious pictures are, dimensionally speaking, equivalent to the holy figures and are not inferior to them in significance, taking the picture as a whole. Man confronts his God with a newly-awakened feeling of selfhood.

Once, in the portrait of Arnolfini and his wife, Jan van Eyck forges right ahead, developing the whole figures of man and wife in relation to each other, and the interior—in more than one respect a work of genius, far in advance of his time. No Master of the fifteenth century followed Jan van Eyck along this path (Pl. 32).

The fifteenth century Italians felt the superiority of the Northeners in their unswerving grasp of individual characteristics. Jan van Eyck's pictures were marvelled at in the South, Rogier v. d. Weyden did successful business in Ferrara, Justus van Gent was summoned to Urbino. The Sicilian Antonello adopted, together with the tech-

32. JAN VAN EYCK, ARNOLFINI AND HIS WIFE. DETAIL
London, National Gallery

nique, something of the portrait-interpretation of the North and passed on the Netherlands pattern to the Venetians. Neither Petrus Christus nor Rogier v. d. Weyden nor Memling, nor any Italian of the fifteenth century is so objective a portraitist as Jan van Eyck. The term 'objective' can easily be misunderstood. Here I take it as meaning: the apprehension of the individual phenomenon, and the ability to feel one's way into the spiritual being of the personality in question, are hardly hindered at all by stylistic habit, formal ideals, the taste of the times or subjective emotions. Van Eyck's portraits are less like one another than those of all other portraitists of the fifteenth century.

Rogier v. d. Weyden, the most powerful influence anywhere in the North about 1450, kept in portraiture to the bust, the three-quarter-profile and neutral ground. Petrus Christus sometimes made tentative attempts to depict the room or space in which the sitter happened to be. In the second half of the century the Netherlanders give a clear view of the landscape-background. Memling in particular, the most successful portraitist in Bruges towards the turn of the century, more or less regularly sets his busts against a clear sky and has a summery landscape showing in the distance. Laterally he likes a frame of columns, indicating the room. He was led to this form of picture not so much by thirst for space nor by the desire to heighten the illusion of reality in this way, as by his own weakness for a mild over-all harmony. In a benevolent, optimistic frame of mind his eye rested on the sons of men, the weather good, the sky clear, the countryside friendly. Since Memling did portraits of a number of Italian merchants staying in Bruges, his style may have been somewhat coloured by the cultivated taste of his patrons. Portraits from his hand went to Florence quite early, and here and there in Italian portraiture we see traces of his influence (Pl. 7).

Botticelli painted but few portraits, relatively few, that is to say, in proportion to his prolific work as an inventive Master. His aesthetic sense puts its mark on his portraits. The draughtsman's vision favours the profile. Even in his front-views and three-quarter-profiles the operative factor is a linear boundary. Space is rather hinted at than developed. A system of architectonically straight lines running upwards or downwards parallel to the frame sometimes gives his pictures a sort of skeletal stability and enhances, by contrast, the effect of the undulating, curvy lines of head, hair or draperies. Details of individual physiognomy are sacrificed to his overriding desire to express chasteness, sublimity, spiritual grace. Botticelli would rather create a human being in the likeness of his ideal than reflect the human being standing before him, purely, like a mirror. What is true of Botticelli is also true of his Florentine contemporaries—Uccello, Domenico Veneziano, Pollaiulo. Everywhere you can feel, more or less distinctly, the influence of the medallion and *relievo*.

Domenico Ghirlandaio was nothing of a pioneer. For all that, he strikes into the future on one occasion: in the portrait of the old man with the abnormally out-of-joint nose and a boy looking up at him tenderly—the picture now in the Louvre. A double portrait, the relation between old man and child conceived in a warm-hearted, almost genre-like way, the landscape-background in the frame of a window, perhaps after the Flemish model. A notable exception to the Florentine quattrocento in more than one respect (Pl. 33, 34).

Leonardo da Vinci was born only a few years after Botticelli, and his development falls within the Florentine

33. GHIRLANDAIO, OLD MAN AND BOY
Paris, Louvre

34. GHIRLANDAIO, OLD MAN AND BOY. DETAIL
Paris, Louvre

quattrocento, though his genius bears him into another world. He was to pave the way for the High Renaissance, cut loose from his native soil and, as a creator and teacher, find opportunity in Upper Italy and in France to spread his influence far and wide. Whilst his scientific observation of nature paralysed the somewhat doubtful consequences of his pre-conceived theories, the thinker in his rich make-up was nevertheless at odds with the artist, and the very diversity of his aspirations prevented individual works from maturing. Leonardo was an empiricist, and each of his creations has the appearance of a bold venture. He never rested with what he had done, never repeated his successes. Always he strove to produce something that nobody had done before him, that not even he himself had done so far.

Three portraits of women from his hand are known to us: the Ginevra de' Benci in the Liechtenstein Collection (1474); the Cecilia Gallerani in Cracow, in the Czartoryski Collection (1483?); and the Mona Lisa (1503). Outwardly, in technique, these paintings differ from those of his Florentine predecessors. The outward difference is closely allied to an inner one. A prismatic layer of air envelops the object, vibrating light plays over it, so that the statement about the sitter does not sound naked, bald, definite—it thrums like a lyre.

Mona Lisa's notoriety, still further increased by the sensation of the theft, has become tedious. The art-lover wants to discover merits, he would like to show his superiority by being the first to see something nobody has ever seen before. But he cannot succeed in this in front of the Mona Lisa, at least not with positive appreciation. Only in the negative is there any hope of an independent, original opinion. Thus people speak of 'rigidity', of a 'mask' or, driven to despair, the connoisseur explains the 'bad state' of the picture as the reason why the first impression fails to come up to our tense expectations.

In connection with our observations the question arises as to whether we are really confronting a portrait, the likeness of a woman living in Florence round about 1500. For despite the pneumatic physical reality what seems to have been realized is a dream of mysterious, disconcertingly feminine allure. The veiled glance, the smile, invite sensational interpretation. The background with its fantastic turrets of bleak rock—a minatory world—stands in enigmatic relationship to the enigmatic woman. The visionary quality of the whole apparition is contradicted by the exceedingly precise execution, which gives the feeling of massiveness and weight. Leonardo, who left much incomplete, seems to have lost his sense for end, finish. On untrodden paths it was difficult to spot the goal. The Master may have worked too long on the Mona Lisa.

The two earlier portraits are more portrait-like. What makes the Cecilia Gallerani so peculiar and extraordinary is the movement. Leonardo expresses spiritual beauty in terms of bodily shapeliness and charm, that is to say grace of movement. The girlishly slender figure is turning three-quarters round with her body to one side, her head to the other—an elastic gesture. The motive for this action is supplied by the fact that in her hand, moulded most expressively, the woman is holding a singular domestic pet: a weasel.

In the Ginevra, whose hands are not visible, the bust detaches itself from a background which, flat and archaically decorative in part, opens out to one side into a distant landscape.

As with everything he undertook, so also in the portraits Leonardo is paving the way for the future.

35. RAPHAEL, PORTRAIT OF MADDALENA DONI. DRAWING
Paris, Louvre
(*p. 243*)

Raphael is not a pioneer like Leonardo, rather a fortunate legatee. He reaps what had been sown in Umbria and Florence. His development proceeds at an astounding pace, in one unbroken flow. With intellectual discretion and spiritual lucidity he brings all the aspirations of the Italian Renaissance harmoniously together. In one or two portraits he manages to marry the unique phenomenon as given to his ideals of form. The *Cardinal* in Madrid is at once the youthful, high-born, spiritualized Prince of the Church and yet an unmistakable personality. Although in his Madonnas Raphael sticks to an almost monotonous typicalness, as a portraitist, at least with men, he seems as objective as Holbein, even if the means he uses to reach the goal—to render an immortal account of the idiosyncratic—are different from those of the German. Just how receptively he was able to utilize the past and fuse it together may be seen from a drawing now in possession of the Louvre, done about 1505. Here, in poise and movement, the woman reminds one of Leonardo's model, whilst the landscape in the background and the lateral frame of the columns go back to the Memling pattern. As Raphael is continually acquiring without ever sacrificing he even adopts in the end something of the vision of the Venetian painters, without forfeiting in the least his Roman monumentality and clarity of form. (Pl. 35.)

In Holbein's nature everything was at the ready to produce the portraitist he became in England, whereas a good deal in Dürer's nature hindered the portraitist. The Master's change of abode from Augsburg via Basel to London, the travelling experiences all sharpened his eye. Holbein is objective in the sense that I called Jan van Eyck objective. If a single personality had been portrayed by him, Dürer, Massys, Raphael and Titian, and these portraits were now before us, Holbein's report would be chosen as the authentic, the reliable one. Holbein is neither passionate nor sentimental nor pathetic. Little that is autobiographical can be read from his work. Nevertheless the nobility, the decorum, the cool stateliness, the psychological poise, the spiritual elegance—qualities which his models all share, despite their individualization—come from his own nature, his temperament. Nothing is to be felt there of the conflicts, struggles, perils of time and place. Even his Henry VIII has hardly anything brutal about him. Holbein was faithful in his service, but not servile. By way of exception: when he did a portrait of his wife and children there is a slight feeling astir for the hard lot of humanity. This picture alone holds out material for the biographer.

In technique Holbein is not in the least progressive. He is a draughtsman rather than a painter. At least he catches the idiosyncrasy of his model direct, like a draughtsman. His painting, masterly as it is, is craftsman-like, done with local colour, near-sighted. The light does not dominate, it subserves the modelling.

With faultless tact Holbein always, in every case, hits on the pictorial form appropriate to the object: prince, lady, merchant, statesman. Now a bust, now the whole figure, profile or full-face or three-quarter-profile, neutral ground or richly finished interior. And always one believes that every other form would be unsuitable. Holbein never wanted anything he could not do. Other Masters may provide deeper effects, but hardly any of them produced a work that is as immaculate, as unassailable as his. Titian is *the* painter of the sixteenth century—painter in the stricter sense of the word. How does he acquit himself as a painter of portraits? Holbein's work shows how a Master with the vision of a draughtsman can solve this task. To Holbein in particular applies what Dostoievski demanded of the portraitist when he said: 'The painter seeks the moment when the model looks most like himself. The portraitist's gift lies in the ability to spot this moment and hang on to it.'[1]

Everybody thinks he knows what 'local colour'—or 'specific colour'—is, defining it perhaps as 'the colour of a thing independent of conditions of light'. Now there is, strictly speaking, no colour without light. The light does not produce the colour, but it awakens it, resurrects it. Moreover the light is not content with that, for it plays with the colour, transmutes it, indeed on occasion annihilates it. A green leaf hit by the light may appear white, colourless. 'Specific colour' is only known to us as the colour visible under normal, neutral, tolerant lighting as opposed to colour tyrannized by the lighting, as it were improper or 'non-specific' colour. It is not a matter of a hard-and-fast this or that, but of differences of degree. Light is to specific colour now more of a friend, now more of a foe.

These considerations apply not only to colour but to form as well. We can speak of 'local form' or 'specific form'. Form, likewise, is more or less assaulted by the invading light. The morphological fact which the sculptor refers to is only accessible to the painter as transmuted by the conditions of light and locality. The more unrestrainedly the painter surrenders to the phenomenon as given here and now, the less he will hit on specific colour and specific form, the catching of which may be—and by Holbein was—regarded as the duty of the portraitist. There are no drawings with portrait-sketches of Titian's. He caught form and colour at a single visual glance, whereas Holbein, working at the painting independently of unique visual experiences, crystallized specific form and

[1] *Diary*, 1873.

specific colour out of the chance context of place and light.

Contemporary vision is nearer to Titian's vision than to Holbein's. As a result the Italian's portraits strike us as being true to nature in a higher degree than those of the German. First impression of a portrait by Titian: a man living at such and such a time in such and such a place; of a portrait by Holbein: a personality caught in a lasting mood wholly characteristic of him. The opportunity to make portraits of members of the Imperial House lent fire to Titian's caesaristic spirit as, conversely, his gift for portraying princely grandeur recommended him to their Majesties. Undoubtedly, the painter saw the Emperor Charles face to face, but his vision was substantially coloured by his knowledge of the extent of the Imperial power as well as by his wish to honour His Majesty. Thus he was able to combine the momentary and the monumental to a peculiar degree and border on the historical picture in his portraits.

More than once the Dutchman A. Mor had occasion to set up in competition with Titian. Both Masters made portraits at about the same time—1550—of Chancellor Perrenot de Granvella. Mor's portrait is in Vienna, Titian's found its way into the museum in Kansas City—reproduced in a volume of 'Unknown Masterpieces' (1930, Plate 23). The comparison is instructive. Mor has obviously kept to the Venetian as a model and is not far behind him in expressing the dignity and spiritual significance of the statesman. He observes details of physiognomy more conscientiously, and his portrait seems to achieve a higher degree of individuality than Titian's, who has sacrificed detail in the interests of the whole, more particularly because, with the years, he grew both physically and psychologically long-sighted. (Pl. 36, 37.)

36. A. MOR, ANTOINE PERRENOT DE GRANVELLA
Vienna, State Gallery

37. TITIAN, ANTOINE PERRENOT DE GRANVELLA
Kansas City Museum
(*p. 246*)

An attempt—not a very successful one—can be made to distinguish two paths open to the portraitist, namely, on the one hand the unbiassed re-creation of the physical phenomenon and, on the other, feeling one's way into the psychology of the model, so that, in effect, the actual appearance is subordinated to an 'idea'. Particularly when it comes to doing portraits of friends the shaping of their exteriors is determined more or less strongly by knowledge of their inner being.

Schopenhauer says in his *Reflections on Physiognomy* that the portraitist can take in a personality that is strange to him, seen perhaps for the first time, more correctly because more objectively than that of a friend, an acquaintance or anybody with whom he has human relations. From this it might be inferred that the self-portrait provides the least reliable report—an interpretation which we must supplement and limit by pointing out that the road from within outwards can also lead to the goal.

To devote a whole chapter to the self-portrait is tempting to the psychologist. First of all the naïve expectation that the observer is here identical with the observed, that therefore the self-portrait is superior and has the advantage. The subject is the Master himself as a psychological entity, seen with his habitual vision; the object his physical appearance. The question as to how far a man can know himself I leave to one side. It is certain that the deeper his knowledge penetrates into his own interior self, the more prejudiced will be the gaze he turns upon his exterior, and, in the main, he will find what he expects to find. His eye is governed by ambition and vanity. Even an eminently objective mind has difficulty in remaining objective as regards itself. Moreover, the observer is not seeing a model that keeps still, inert, passive, somewhat bored; he has before him an intensely attentive, intellectually active face. Self-portraits strike us as pathetic, not to say theatrical; they are, as is to be inferred from these reflections and as experience itself shows, no whit more 'like' than any other portraits.

If we compare biographies with autobiographies we do not find that the autobiographies are in any way more truthful. In descriptions of our fellow-mortals a modicum of reliability can be attained which a man recording his own life cannot attain, since inclinations, volitions, tendencies colour his report, with the result that this finishes up as a *plaidoyer* rather than a judicial sentence. As with autobiography, so with the self-portrait.

Dürer does not, as draughtsman and portrait-painter, come up to Holbein's unswerving sureness and uniform mastery. He interprets appearances—the physical facts—from his knowledge of the psychological entity. Above all he expresses the temperament of his subject, intensifying, accentuating. The liveliness of his intellect, the diversity of his aims very often disturbed his equanimity and peace of soul when confronted by an individual strange to him. His portraits are unequal and unequally valuable. This is particularly true of the painted ones, thoughtfully executed; less so of those he drew, spontaneous impressions. Schopenhauer's idea applies here. Strangers are caught more objectively than the friends and acquaintances who were close to the Master.

Lorenzo Lotto, the leading North-Italian portraitist together with and next to Titian, borders on the genre as Titian on the historical picture. His creatures are all fairly bourgeois and a bit sentimental. Titian's men keep themselves to themselves, for all their vitality, while those of his rival address us jovially and convivially. As a portraitist Lotto is a narrator set on divulging something of his sitter's profession and way of life by means of attributes, symbolical bits and pieces. He is as fond as the Northeners of giving the eye clear access to a landscape in the background. His figures often incline to one side, bending their heads. He was inventive in devising solutions for the double portrait, the family picture, the affectionate group. With his sprightliness and confiding humanity, as with his light, decorative colouring he has a seductive effect on art-lovers in our day.

I have selected Mor, a native of Utrecht, from the array of Netherlands portraitists in order to compare him with Titian, and thus done him honour. After being touched by the Italian High Renaissance, Mor came to the top exclusively as a portraitist. The sound foundations of his rise lay in Holland. He was a pupil of Jan van Scorel's, whose friend Vermeijen was. Heemskerck, too, derived from van Scorel. Dirk Jacobsz, a son of Jacob of Amsterdam in whose studio van Scorel had worked for a while, was likewise influenced by the Utrecht Master. These Dutchmen were fond of travelling. Van Scorel visited Italy and the Orient, Vermeijen Spain and Africa, Heemskerck Rome. Only Dirk Jacobsz remained true to his homeland as the portraitist of the Amsterdam middle-class. All of them gain strength—like Antaeus as soon as he touches earth—when faced with a portrait.

In the south of the Netherlands as well, Romanists like Floris and Willem Key surprise with admirable performances in the field of portraiture. The Guild-piece, a peculiarly Dutch achievement, was founded by van Scorel and Dirk Jacobsz. The family portrait in Cassel is quite astonishing, claimed—probably rightly—for Heemskerck, with children that really do behave like children.

Desirous of making us familiar with the sitter as an active, living, communicative personality the Netherlanders, particularly in the period between 1520 and 1550, availed themselves of the gesticulating hand. Gossaert, van Scorel and Heemskerck make the hands talk, Vermeijen and Dirk Jacobsz even more so. Van Scorel's men move their hands with restraint, while Vermeijens' try to persuade the spectator of something, to talk him down, so that sometimes we have the uncomfortable feeling of being in a company of deaf-mutes. A. Mor, head and shoulders above his Dutch predecessors and contemporaries, avoids with the tact of a courtier all such aggressive frankness. His sitters are neither preachers, nor popular orators, nor convivial burghers; they persist in an elegant reserve and a diplomatic closeness. Their nature is seen from their physiognomy and comportment, without their making any visible effort to show it. Instead of sociability, intimacy, confidences we have the aloofness of the personality that distinguishes itself from the crowd.

Titian died in 1576 at a ripe age. Tintoretto became the portraitist of the Venetian patriciate even while Titian was alive, and after his death was without rivals. If all his many portraits were stood up in a row we should see not so much a series of sharply defined personalities as the picture of the society which, with dignified consciousness of itself, represented the Republic. Just as Tintoretto immortalized the Venetian character in his portraits, so el Greco immortalized the Spanish character. Whoever thinks of Spain thinks of Loyola, Don Quixote and el Greco. Precisely because el Greco came to Toledo as a foreigner, asceticism and ecstasy struck him more forcefully than they would a Spaniard. The gaunt, bloodless heads, all of one spirit, all alike as though from inbreeding, seem to border on the maniacal. The subjectivity of the painter has a large share in developing this kind of spirituality. Nonetheless the Toledans liked seeing themselves so reflected, they were agreeable to being seen as the Greek saw them. El Greco gave shape to a Spanish ideal if not to Spanish reality. His portraits are appreciated in our own day even by those art-lovers who eye his compositions with wonderment and mistrust. But to conclude from this that el Greco was a portraitist by nature would be beside the point. He lacked the objectivity of the born portraitist. His bold, unbiddable, creative energy appears more or less toned down in the portraits, therefore easier of access than in the compositions. This the reason why some art-lovers prefer the portraits and have found through them a way to his singular art.

Velasquez was the painter of the Spanish Court and dispatched all the tasks connected with his office to the complete satisfaction of his masters. One might expect to find his art at its best and most idiosyncratic in the portraits of the King and his ladies, the children of royal blood. For the art-lover, however, who recalls the Prado and the Velasquez Room, the protraits of dwarfs and Court jesters eclipse those of the princely personages, and that for more reasons than one. To begin with, the high-rankers were far from being patient models. Then the favourite, who was nevertheless a subject, was forbidden any penetrating observation, all impartial impressions when face to face with his King. And lastly Majesty, to portray which was his primary duty, could more easily be rendered visible by costume, insignia, princely occupations like hunting or the equestrian art, than in the face, especially as at the time of the painter the thin-blooded and worn-out Spanish Royal House lacked any forceful-looking ruler and individuality was strangulated by ceremonial. The Master's spiritual freedom excelled most of all when he was with men who were socially inferior to him, describing the comical existence of the Court jesters and dwarfs with telling sureness. (Frontispiece.)

The Doria Pope occupies first rank among the portraits, all the same. The extraordinariness of the occasion, the illustrious task of painting the portrait of the supreme head of the Church, the ambition to distinguish himself in Rome, commerce with foreign peoples—all these things sharpened Velasquez' eye with glorious results.

On the one hand Spanish autocracy and world-dominion, senescent, scenting decay but keeping up a stiff and shrouded presence, and on the other the Dutch middle-class, youthful, healthy, flushed with victory. Autumn and spring. One feels this contrast when one compares the works of the two greatest portraitists of the seventeenth century: Velasquez and Frans Hals. The object differs racially, socially and historically. If Frans Hals was able to depict the radiant vitality of the men and their community-feeling so happily in his first Guild-pieces, he must have sensed the heroic temper of the age very profoundly, himself in happy accord with the community. But in time he grew long-sighted, weary and, like all ageing optimists, disillusioned, while his fellow-citizens became bloated heirs and Philistines. His late, visionary, almost spectral group-portraits, rightly singled out for admiration today, met with little understanding from his contemporaries. Frans Hals experienced the tragic fate of the lonely genius just as Rembrandt did. And the enterprising van der Helst triumphed over Frans Hals and over Rembrandt.

Rembrandt, the obstinate cultureless genius: this idea, rooted in classicist art-theory, has given way to a deeper understanding and more spacious view of his work. He is now described as the representative of everything Dutch, a description which overlooks many elements in the broad and various thrust of his endeavour. He is not narrowly Dutch, was touched—though not tied—by the West and

South, by the international spirit of the time more powerfully than appears on a superficial showing. The richer a nature is, the more deeply hid what it assimilates. In his early years Rembrandt—quite un-Dutch in this—struggled for dramatic action; faced with a double portrait he depicted a process instead of a condition. The woman is subordinate to the man busy at his profession, as in the Ansloo portrait and in that of the shipwright. Later, having gained the first height, he shattered at one mighty blow the traditional form of the Guild-piece by substituting, in his *Night Watch*—much to the dissatisfaction of the patrons—flowing action for peaceful arrangement, military subordination for democratic equality. He builds, organizes and makes climaxes with light. Genius is by nature aristocratic, whatever its social position and political views.

Man as a human being engaged Rembrandt's imagination more powerfully than this or that man. If he created a long series of self-portraits in greater numbers than any other Master it was not vanity that impelled him, not the desire to immortalize the peculiar formation of his own head, rather the likeness in the mirror seemed to him a comfortably get-at-able model from which he read the symptoms of old age, expression and instantaneous mood far more than anything individually physiognomical. He saw in the mirror examples of human life guttering. He created the most complete autobiography in pictures, wherein we may read not merely the story of this painter but, over and above that, the common fate of the man of genius. The higher Rembrandt climbed the further he removed himself from his contemporaries in time and place, and the less he was considered their portraitist.

In contrast to Rembrandt, Rubens remained in successful accord with the world at large right to the end, not only because of his suavity of manner, his affable character but also because his art chimed in with the mood of the day, the internationalism of culture, as well in Antwerp as in Italy, France, England and Spain. He managed to bring tendencies, aspirations, loyalties which seem mutually contradictory, together: Flemish free-and-easiness, religious orthodoxy, Court service and a Dionysian, thoroughly pagan abandon. Naturally the harmony between him and his surroundings also rested on the fact that his contemporaries gladly followed the lead of the born ruler, whereas van Dyck's luck and success have a different explanation. Van Dyck's ambition, his pliable talent, met the wishes of society and readily fulfilled its ideals.

Van Dyck began as a collaborator in the Rubens workshop and fell under the sway of that organizing and editorial Master. In some cases connoisseurs are in two minds as to whether Rubens or van Dyck is the author of a portrait. Nevertheless the nervous, femininely receptive and slightly ingratiating nature of the younger man is noticeable in contrast to the powerful virility of the older. To feel his way into an individuality came much more easily to the younger man. Van Dyck visited Italy and chose Titian for his model, breaking away from Rubens by becoming enchanted with southern culture and the Venetian colouring. Following the law of his nature he took the road that was to get him to the top. Following the law of his nature he departed from his bourgeois homeland, headed for palazzos and later for the English court. In Genoa he conquered the local aristocracy. The type of the aristocratic portrait evolved, which remained valid and exemplary for a long time. The whole figure in broad perspective plane, taking in the spacious seignorial surroundings, the face relatively small, at a remove from the beholder. One feels oneself very much in the presence of a lady or a gentleman who stands on a social eminence and gazes down on the looker; the impression of class outweighs the impression of individuality. Cultivated poise regulated by convention limits personal utterance. Van Dyck struck the note of distinguished gentility and feminine grace with astounding sureness. Returned to Antwerp, he did portraits that seem a shade more middle-class in their cool colouring, finally on English soil, in the atmosphere of court and nobility, to develop aristocratic deportment more and more mechanically and schematically. The taker in Italy became the giver in England. It may be conjectured that, as master of ceremonies, the painter educated the somewhat rude and unruly British aristocracy into a semblance of dignified composure, that the model became a model indeed. However powerfully Rubens and Van Dyck were stimulated as painters in Italy, as portraitists they triumphed over their Italian contemporaries, just as the Frenchman Claude triumphed over the landscape-painters of the south.

Rubens died 1640, van Dyck 1641, Velasquez 1660, Rembrandt 1666, Frans Hals 1669. With them the age of the great was at an end, and a protracted, relatively empty period followed. Portraiture is to a peculiar degree and more than art-production at large dependent on political and economic conditions. Right into the eighteenth century there was impotence in Germany as a result of the 'great' war. In England, poor in native talent, nothing save the reflection of van Dyck's sun, now set. Italy still lived on the memory of her proud past. Even in Venice not much stirred between Tintoretto and Tiepolo, as in Spain not much between Velasquez and Goya. In Holland solid painting held its own under economically favourable conditions until the first decades of the eighteenth century, but the spirit grew more and more lethargic and lent a willing ear to the luxury requirements of the customers. Terborch kept up the honour of Dutch portrait-art the longest, giving the merchant a touch of diplomatic finesse and discreetly expressing personality in small format, small scale, with cool colour-harmonies. Only France seemed to be in the ascendant at a time when the autocratic power of the Throne was gathering strength. Largilière, Mignard, Rigaud and Charles le Brun provided models that had a wide influence, especially as their portraits were run off in large numbers by well-schooled engravers. Their academic mastery, more particularly in drawing, was a product of Italian teaching, even though the attempt to combine Flemish colouring and Italian form met with occasional success. Three of France's cultural phases bear the names of the reigning kings. First, at the time of aggrandisement, virile, self-confident, impressive dignity in representation. In the course of the eighteenth century the woman comes more and more to power, finally sentimentality, taking note even of the child. Everywhere the social ideal that happens to be in vogue triumphs, just as modish dress triumphs over personal foibles. The greatest French painters of the eighteenth century, Watteau, Fragonard and Chardin, only did occasional portraits. Court and nobility favoured the academicians.

The eighteenth century is the French century. Visual art paid homage to Eros, poetically and idealizingly at first, then more openly and brazenly. The optimism of the ruling class lives on in the portrait. All trace of worry, of intellectual work were overlooked. Gallantry and complaisance were *de rigueur*; ladies and gentlemen should not behave and comport themselves otherwise than in the salon. They confront the portraitist only on the plane of self-satisfaction.

England, strong economically, was late in coming to a native art of painting, only in the second half of the eighteenth century and then almost exclusively in the categories of portrait and landscape. Reynolds, Gainsborough, Romney, Hoppner, Raeburn, Sir Th. Lawrence appear as successful portraitists of the English aristocracy. Eros, under healthier political and social conditions than in France, behaves more politely. The English liked to keep more to the open air, to the garden and park than to the salon or boudoir. The whole figure was governed, in its bearing, by the dignity and elegance of a favoured society. Dress not so strictly *à la mode*, slightly idealistic, flowing round the female body. In France a binding tradition as regards drawing and painting, in England a fastidious eclecticism. The master-works of the older art which had reached the seats of the English nobility from the Netherlands and Italy—a foil for the paintings of the English portraitists—provided instruction and stimulus. Often indeed they had obligatory models before their eyes, particularly in the work of van Dyck, when they had to complete the series of ancestral portraits. Reynolds especially was an eclectic, but was protected from the worst consequences of such a procedure by intellectual superiority as well as by his self-confidence. His whim was that he could survey the whole evolution of painting—as a continuous ascent, feeling himself at the top of it since he believed that he stood at the end, the goal. Everything that his forefathers had won, he thought, was at his free disposal.

The English in the eighteenth century evince little talent for sculpture. London, like Venice, like Amsterdam, is a city of painters. The absence of scaffolding, of bone-structure, of solid build-up in their paintings is balanced by the colour-values of the surface, and in Reynolds' case by startling themes. And common to all as the demand of the age is a sense for shapeliness and grace. The individual is carefully merged in the type, in the ideal of a society living in an atmosphere of good breeding and under extremely favourable conditions.

Gainsborough's art has firmer and narrower bounds than that of the first president of the Academy, who garnished the portrait with genre-like and sentimental motifs, and is also more original. He developed his personal style with sensitive and undeviating taste, and stuck to it with quiet confidence. Feminine charm was spiritualized and refined; his caressing brushwork gave texture and skin a shimmering radiance, and to the picture as a whole an enchanting harmoniousness. Something autumnal, sublime, very choice, easy on the eye. That is how this Master's work lives on in the memory, and sometimes one thinks one can see in him a forerunner of Renoir. The Scotsman Raeburn solves the task of portraiture—the illustration of individual idiosyncrasy—with sure aim, a marksmanship reminiscent of Frans Hals; he is altogether more plebeian and virile than his rivals living in the aura of the English nobility. Hoppner and Lawrence keep to the model so successfully held out by Reynolds. Romney delineates what seems essential to his long-sighted eye, overlooking detail and arriving at a manner that is somewhat vapid.

In France artistic development broke off abruptly with the political and social upheaval, the great Revolution, while in England it ran on without sharp interruption.

With the nineteenth century a reaction set in against pretty-prettiness. The new age started off seriously and morally, more intellectual than sensual in tenor. As regards the portrait, pleasantness was offset by character, typical traits deriving from position and social class by individual traits. The new age, at a high level intellectually, was critical and pessimistic. Whether men were happier in the eighteenth century than in the nineteenth may be a moot point, but judging by the pictures they were happier. Careworn heads furrowed by intellectual labour or by hard fate were not to be seen before the first decades of the new century.

With the rising power of the middle-class, social conditions in France and Germany approached those which had developed in Holland as early as the seventeenth century. The artist was confronted by the 'public' as both patron and client—not, needless to say, a community with common aims as once in Holland. The many-headed public did not rightly know what it wanted, and put no such definite demands to art as the Church or the Court or the aristocracy had done. The stronger talents—or such as believed they were stronger—spurned the taste of traditionless monied power. Consequently the pressure of the time-style eased up on production, just as the increasing commerce between civilized countries loosened the artists' ties with their homeland. Germans above all had a second Fatherland outside the land of their birth, be it Rome or Paris.

The nineteenth century was an age of growing scientific knowledge, historical as well as empirical and philosophical. Science and art can never be kept apart wholly successfully. The artists may never have read either Kant or Schopenhauer, may barely have taken note of the results of scientific research, nevertheless they breathed the same air as the leading thinkers and scholars. Love of truth, the mainspring of scientific endeavour, was felt equally by artists in the nineteenth century as a duty, a virtue. In poetry, particularly in the novel, the inroads of the scientific spirit were most clearly apparent. The term 'belles lettres' sounds inappropriate for the psychological literature of Flaubert, Tolstoi, Dostoievski, hence for the writers representative of their times and most esteemed today. An eighteenth century reader would acknowledge that kind of writing more as science than as literature. Painters in the nineteenth century, who otherwise had nothing in common, met in their struggle for truth. The result is that ethical values encroach on aesthetics. By the devious route of pity for the hard lot of the wronged, art turns back to religion, coming close in this to the greatest Dutchman of the seventeenth century. Understanding for Rembrandt is one of the spiritual achievements of the nineteenth century.

The craftsman's link with the immediate past was broken, but knowledge of the whole older practice of art was deepened. In master-works of the fifteenth, sixteenth and above all the seventeenth century painters who visited museums saw their ideals realized. It was elective affinity and not force of tradition that led Manet to Velasquez, Max Liebermann to Frans Hals, and some English painters to Botticelli.

Seeking truth, the portraitists of the nineteenth century stumbled on the Spaniard Velasquez and the Dutchman Frans Hals. In their efforts to reproduce the peculiarities of physiognomy as given, without prejudice, they expressed their own subjectivity. Conscious striving for originality paralyses the danger impending from knowledge of other artists' work.

What was new, peculiar to the nineteenth century, began most clearly in drawing, and especially in Germany, who, after a long silence, at last made her voice heard again in art. In France drawing dominated fitfully, in the work of Ingres. Averting his eyes from colour the portraitist caught the permanent sub-structure underneath the spiritual or psychological idiosyncrasy. I am thinking not so much of the sketches or designs as of the meticulously drawn portraits, completely valid as such, which Ingres did.

The sort of painting that blossomed in the course of the nineteenth century, most of all in France, shows very clearly the change that came over portraiture, away from the abstract and intellectual to the sensuous, to the coloristic illusion of matter.

During the final decades the so-called Impressionists were in the lead and, after overcoming heavy resistance, exerted an influence as models far beyond the borders of France. Their programme, announced as universal law, seemed favourable to the portrait in so far as the Impressionists really did nothing but paint portraits. Even their landscapes are, so to speak, portrait snapshots. They do not invent, do not tell a story, at least not intentionally, not by programme; their vision begins with the particular instance as given, resolves itself into the unique phenomenon. But—they are long-sighted. Their eye, more synthetic than analytic, is completely claimed by light and colour. As regards anything human they are pretty well indifferent. A bundle of asparagus is just as interesting to Manet as a human face. This puts a limit to their portrait art. Only Degas, who kept somewhat apart from his comrades, was, particularly in his youth, a first-class portraitist, perhaps the greatest of his time. And he revered Ingres and was a passionate draughtsman. Cézanne, the very antithesis of Degas, a painter in the strictest sense and consistent impressionist, is anything but a good judge of men and not really a portraitist at all.

About the middle of the century, photography made its

appearance, became the rival of portrait-painting and, economically speaking, a dangerous rival. Artists looked with contempt at the mechanical and subordinate labours of the photographer and thought that there was no relation, no contact, between art and photography. The relation was a complex one nonetheless and worked out in various ways. Just as in the fifteenth century the thirst for book-knowledge caused the invention of moveable type, so in the nineteenth century science and love of truth called for the reliable pictorial report of the photographic camera. It offered painters a yardstick, an aid, a control of which many availed themselves, generally without wanting to admit it. Inevitably, of course, 'correctness' became suspect to artists—they wearied of 'correctness'. As a result they shifted the focus of their effort to a region where the camera could not compete with them. This is the region of colour and consciously subjective interpretation. The rage for colour can, other causes apart, be explained by the painters' repugnance to being mistaken for photographers. And the revolt of stubborn subjectivity has a similar interpretation. Photography, steadily increasing in proficiency, disgusts painters with imitation of nature and invites stylization. If they surrender to what they actually see they are naturally afraid of succumbing to the pedestrian prose of the photographic statement. In the twentieth century subjectivity broke away from all obligation and servitude, to autonomous creativity, wilful deviation from the object as given. This threatens another servitude, of course: attachment to art-fashion. Powerful artists have at all times wrestled with nature and acquired a style, each man his own; in the twentieth century they fight for style, with manner as the result. In portraiture they struggle to avoid reportage by means of periphrasis or aphoristic exaggeration of characteristic features.

XII

RELIGIOUS ART AND THE HISTORICAL PICTURE

Artistic judgment and artistic creation have always affected one another reciprocally, and this cannot be otherwise. In our day art is proud of its freedom to go where it lists, its sovereignty and isolation. We try in our judgments to make a clean division between the artistic experience and all other emotional experiences, thus getting ourselves into a false relationship to the art of the past. The further back we look, the further we trace the process to its roots, the less possible it is to crystallize out the pure artistic element, or what we count as the artistic element. For long stretches of time there was only religious art; here ethical and intellectual values deriving from the subject or project ally themselves with the artistic impression. Art began by making images. The barbarian confused the image of the demon with the demon himself and turned with fear and desire to the idol, which afforded him no trace of that pleasure the philosophers define as aesthetic or 'disinterested' pleasure. For centuries art was in the service of the Church. The faithful in the Middle Ages looked up at their altars with other feelings than did the savages at their idols; they could, more or less definitely, distinguish between the image and the divine or sacred being so imaged. Nevertheless, in the contemplation of images they felt themselves in the presence of supra-terrestrial powers. Visual art offered a way, a ladder to Heaven. Gratitude, remorse, hope, happiness and anguish of faith all mingled with the artistic sensation.

Treading the precincts of the Church, the believer left the noise, the unrest, the battlefield of workaday existence behind him; a pause, a spell of meditation presented itself. His mind could concentrate in holiday exaltation.
So ministering, art spread over the walls and windows of the churches. The magnificence, the glow of colour, the wealth of form, raised the churchly interior above earthly want. Mindful of how cramped and wretched accommodation was in the mediaeval cities, we can measure the impression which the house of God made on the community.
Whether decoration, symbolism or instruction predominated in the artist's task, trueness to nature was in all circumstances out of place and objectionable, because appertaining to everyday worldly existence. The Christian, his spiritual eye on immortality and eternal bliss, had little regard for ephemeral reality. However, it would not do to disregard verisimilitude altogether, since the spiritual could only be rendered visible in the bodily, the divine in the human, the unearthly in the earthly. Nature had to be observed, but it was more a case of taking something from her than of accepting her, of surrendering to her. Illusion of reality was not an end—it was rather a means. Time and place, the historical and the spatial did not fall within the working field of the mediaeval artist, since Godhead dwelt in the imagination as a deathless and ubiquitous presence. Christ had not taught and suffered there and then; rather he taught and suffered continually and everywhere. Men experienced the fate of the martyrs with their eyes, without asking the When and the Where. Holiness was outside all temporality and locality. The gold background, a negation of spatial depth, was not mere surface ornamentation—it also symbolized the absence of the locative.

As to the 'incapacity' of the artists, we should not speak of it without being clear in our own minds how far the task in hand demanded capacity and what sort of capacity. There was no other way of embodying something holy or divine, or spiritual purity, virtue and innocence, save by making them shapely. The deeper the faith and the stronger its devotional effect, the more typical and hence uniform the realization. The Masters were faced with the necessity of sifting out everything individual as being all too painfully human. There is only one perfection, as opposed to an infinity of deviations from it. Again, the lack of perspective cannot be interpreted as incapacity. The sacred proceedings were not played out in actual space. The altar panels, pews, Church-equipment had to be decorated, and while engaged on this task the artist no more thought of depth than did the Greek vase-painter.

Further, the force of iconographic tradition hampered the observation of nature and the personal approach. Neither the artist nor the community had ever seen John the Baptist. But it was necessary to know and recognize him, hence the necessary delusion that somebody had actually seen him and left a true likeness behind. The authentic image, or the one held to be authentic, was copied and adhered to so as to make recognition possible. The most ancient pictures of Madonnas were in high regard because people believed that St. Luke had done them from the life.

As handmaiden of the Church art was not free, but despite this limitation she was busied in the happiest possible way—an hallowed, exalted handicraft.

The orthodox sensed that art threatened two dangers. The command: 'Thou shalt not make to thyself an image' was aimed at the danger of worship degenerating into idolatry. This commandment was followed to its logical conclusion in the sixteenth century, in the North, by the iconoclasts. The other danger consisted in profaning the religious picture by shapes drawn without compunction from visible reality.

In the course of time art freed herself from menial service. Not that some genius or other caused the break on his own, say Giotto or Jan van Eyck. Neither can we see any continuous movement; it is more an incoming tide, when the first wave advances and retreats, likewise the second and third, with the result that in the end the whole beach is flooded under.

A glance at art-production in the sixteenth and seventeenth centuries makes us wonder at the tolerant attitude of the Church to the profanation of the altar-picture. Of course the Roman Church was a worldly power. A person like Calvin may well have felt the orgy of carnality in Michelangelo's *Last Judgment*, which did not disturb the Pope in the least, as repulsive, in the same way that the Dutch Reformed Churches later on found it hard to stomach the splendour Rubens displayed in his altarpieces.

In Jan van Eyck the historian sees a pioneer, and rightly in so far as this Master took a great step forward in recording reality. The individual, the richness and diversity of which attracted him, is mortal, ephemeral, subject to change, whereas the typical symbolizes the immortal and the unchanging. To reconcile the religious commission with the heightening of illusion, with the observation of space, air, light, matter, terrain, vegetation, was not at all easy. We can feel the crisis in van Eyck's work, most of all in the multipartite Ghent Altar. The lack of unity is not really explained by the famous inscription which speaks of two authors, i.e. the brothers. It has even been conjectured that this singular whole is compounded of two altar-pieces. With the joy of adventure Jan van Eyck forged ahead on untrodden paths, occasionally overstepping the limits of the iconographic programme, a triumphant discoverer and conqueror. It is chiefly the naked figures of the first human pair that do not quite fit the work as a whole. In his conception of the Fall Jan van Eyck hazarded a most disconcerting display of carnal reality. Not puritanical prudery alone but well-reasoned reflection was later to remove these panels from the altar and out of the Church.

Illusion breeds the need for illusion. A commemorative portrait, executed by Jan van Eyck, required a Madonna who looked every bit as viable as the donor. The Mother of God had come down to earth and visited the patron in his house. The ecclesiastical gentleman in his costume, reproduced accurately and in detail, binds the imagination to a definite period, the landscape in the background to a definite place.

All religious sensibility flows from the sense of dependence, the awe of some supernatural power which worship and ritual bid fair to propitiate. The weaker and more miserable man felt himself to be, the more fervent the tone of his supplications, and the smaller and sorrier he seemed—in his own eyes—in proportion to God. Jan van Eyck, who was employed by princes avid for power, had to juxtapose his benefactor to the Madonna as a figure that was formally her equivalent. Proud and ambitious were the laymen and ecclesiastical gentlemen who bequeathed devotional pictures—not for devotion's sake merely, as well for their own commemoration. The realist illusions which satisfied Jan van Eyck's exalted patrons probably shocked the more humble believer. The 'realist' was more of a Court painter than a servant of the Church.

Reaction was not lacking. About the middle of the fifteenth century Rogier v. d. Weyden came to the top and enjoyed more of a following than Jan van Eyck, typifying instead of individualizing, austerely spiritual instead of sensuous.

Speaking broadly, the evolution of art may be conceived as the road from the icon to the portrait. And Rogier's art is a retrograde step on this road.

The zealous preacher was succeeded by a kindly pastor of souls. Rogier gave way to Dirk Bouts, who harmonized love of nature and religious faith more easily than did the genius of Jan van Eyck. The uplifting stillness of his pictures is broken by no worldly echoes. His saints suffer in dogged immobility, submitting to the will of God. Whatever his lively sense for natural life accepted in the way of landscape and vegetation becomes an integral and subordinate part of the biblical or legendary events he is relating.

Hieronymus Bosch stands by himself. In his case the What produces the How, his imagination creates form and language. He does not observe with the tenacious patience of his Netherlands contemporaries. Neither does he feel any conflict between spiritual vision and sensuous visual experience. He creates boldly from visual memory. His Paradise has nothing in common with any earthly garden. Neither his flora nor his edifices are of this world. His space is in the likeness of a dreamy Beyond. He harps with maniacal glee on the seamy side of Christian doctrine. In spiky, weightless atomies, quick of movement, he brings out the verminousness of the Devil and his works—maliciously tormenting the damned and cunningly tempting the saints—so convincingly that succeeding generations were unable to visualize hell in any other form. Whoever thought of hell and the Devil remembered

Bosch. The terrors of the Middle Ages, exposed so freely to the light of day, raise doubts as to the stability of their faith. The cruelty and savagery of the Passion is depicted in one of his pictures in terms of grotesque physiognomical caricature.

So far as pictures bear witness to the state of religious feeling in any age—inasmuch as the painter's success confirms that his message was intelligible to his contemporaries and received an attentive hearing—Memling's work would indicate a friendly and comparatively lax relationship to the Powers that be: a confiding address after the comminations of Rogier. The abatement of religious zeal and above all of fear of God on the one hand, and a more relaxed view of nature on the other, these were the factors that produced Memling's mild, amiable and temperate art.

In the South things were different. Historians of Christianity busy themselves more with theological points of dispute than with the question of the spirit in which such and such a people, in accordance with its race and fate, received the holy teachings and lived up to them. Here as there we find festive solemnity, but in the North more solemnity, in the South more festivity. Symbolic of the saint in Italy: gravity, stateliness, sublimity. The heritage of classical sculpture which the Renaissance came into, contained form-ideals regarding the human body little suited to a pessimistic and ascetic view of the world. The Southerners felt the deeper piety of the religious pictures done in the Netherlands. Communities living in the vicinity of the Papal Court, which had been growing more worldly ever since the fifteenth century, were more attracted by the glittering garment of Church ritual than by the substance of its religious doctrine. Looking at the altar-pictures they gazed on a more patrician world.

After 1500 the Latin cult of form pushed northwards as a model and a criterion—to the detriment of originality. Compared with their fathers and grandfathers, successful and influential artists like Quentin Massys and Jan Gossaert are virtuosi. They exhibit their mastery as a personal performance. We hear how they speak before we perceive what they say. Quentin's emotional debauches are no less artificial than Gossaert's acrobatics.

In the sixteenth century the Bible, now printed and accessible in translation, was read. Illustrators worked more freely and independently. Saints were humanized. The Madonna was regarded less as the Queen of Heaven or chaste virgin than as a happy and solicitous mother, caressing or feeding her child. Landscape, genre, even still-life invaded the religious picture, loosened and weakened its content. In its struggle for sovereignty art compromised with the Church.

The sixteenth century is the age of the Reformation. The far-reaching change, the schism of the Church is described as the action of one or two personalities, so prone are we to regard events as acts. The success and victory of Luther and Calvin cannot be explained save on the assumption that here and there communities were ready prepared to understand the teachings of the Reformers and follow their commands. Certainly it was a considerable time before dissatisfaction and disunity in matters of faith, piling up underground, grew powerful enough to erupt and men dared to launch an open attack on the centuries – old Roman Church. Had Geneva or the majority not been Calvinistically-minded the fanatic would have been hard put to it to escape the fate of Savonarola. Luther's militant passion, the seriousness of his faith is apparent in pictures, but in pictures done before the reformer's outburst: in Dürer's *Apocalypse*.

Rome set out to impose her forms on the civilized world, just at a time when the universal rule of the Roman Church was collapsing. The nations went different ways philosophically. The Germanic peoples in particular adopted the new teaching.

To purge the 'universal' Church of abuses was the first goal of the Reformers, since their attack was directed against the combination of pretensions to wordly power and the rule of souls. Faith alone, not good works, gifts, endowments, confessions, indulgences, helped the Christian on the way to bliss. Calvin, more consistent than Luther, banned the picture from his Church as an integral part of sensual pomp, and based worship exclusively on the word. Personally, Luther was tolerant of visual art, but his doctrine as elaborated could infuse no life into the picture. The more spiritualized faith became the more it fled from imagery to music. German Protestant art produced Bach, not Cranach. So far as there was any specific Protestant imagery it was more allegorical than symbolic.

In the seventeenth century visual art received a great many commissions from the Roman Church, whose religious zeal had been intensified in the Counter-reformation. Murillo's painting expresses tender devotion, glorification of the Madonna with the means appropriate to the age. Outside Spain, in Italy and the South Netherlands, the Church Militant announced its victory in huge, tumultuous altar-pieces. Rubens conceives the martyrdom of a saint almost in the spirit of a lion-hunt. (Pl. 38). He passed for a true son of the Church, actually believed he was and acted so; but in his sculptural imagination, his delight in healthy carnality and heroic action, he was more of an optimistic pagan than a pessimistic Christian. Dutch orthodoxy was hostile to imagery and had no need of visual art. Without receiving any impulse from the Church Rembrandt penetrated to the heart of Christian teaching, in so far as compassion and loving-kindness are its heart. The Reformation had replaced the image by the word; Rembrandt once more drew on the word to create the image. He made man holy, while the Netherlanders in the sixteenth century had made the holy human. Whatever his conscious position was to the questions of theology and whatever the creed he professed, his imagination was filled with the figures and happenings of the Old and New Testaments. To begin with it was the exotic, legendary, adventurous quality of the Bible story that fascinated him, later the human element. In his own fate he experienced the Passion. The barriers between Reformation and Catholic doctrine break down for him, who reverted to primitive Christianity. He fashioned the Saviour in such a way that his image would have inspired devoutness in any place of worship, though he himself was seldom called upon to paint a Church-picture. Creating spirituality in images that grew ever purer and more limpid, he stood at the end on a solitary height, and everything in the way of religious art that came to birth in Holland is in essence nothing but imitation, derives from him. In the whole field of art we can find no work that limns the spirit and sense of the gospel as purely and perfectly as Rembrandt's *Hundert Guldenblatt*.

The philosopher can always satisfy his metaphysical needs in the abstract; not so the painter, who requires symbolic form for his deepest experiences. The intellectual pantheism of Spinoza satisfied the seventeenth century artist as little as the non-sensuous theism of the Reformed Church. Art, having become emancipated, turned from an inner necessity back to religion. Banned from the house of God it became religious in Rembrandt.

Museum Boymans/van Beuningen

38. RUBENS, MARTYRDOM OF ST. LIEVIN

Rotterdam

Sketch for the painting in Brussels

(*p. 271*)

The eighteenth century was worldly, proudly conscious of being 'enlightened'. At least this is the verdict of the pictorial monuments—witnesses which, of course, point exclusively to the spirit of the upper classes. The Catholic Church did not abate her need of ornamentation. But if we recall the outstanding painters of the age—Watteau, Fragonard, Chardin, Gainsborough, Goya—we find none, with the possible exception of Tiepolo, who did religious work. And how little religious Tiepolo's altars pieces are! The best work was private in character, was destined for the salon and boudoir, gratifying the taste of fastidious amateurs and no longer the community—not, as yet, a middle-class society. After the other-worldly vision dried up as a source of strength, creativity lost in grandeur, seriousness and pathos.

The nineteenth century turned away from the immediate past which now seemed flimsy and frivolous. The Revolution overthrew the rule of French courtly culture. Broader and deeper-lying strata became vocal in the democratic age. The Germanic countries gained in importance, England not only by reason of worldly expansion, Germany by intellectual deeds. The heroic pathos of the Napoleonic era passed quickly. The rise of the masses on the one hand, the increasing wealth of the middle-class on the other, caused the threat of the 'social question' to loom. The poor, the needy, the wronged were observed with a mixture of fear and pity. Pessimistic metaphysics, though far from theistic, consorted with primitive Christianity. The German efforts to resuscitate the Church-picture did not get beyond drab and pedantic imitations, since education and historical sense produce sterile eclecticism. Pantheistic belief, however, deepened the feeling for landscape nature, and dailiness was lifted to a higher plane by a sense of earnest obligation, most conspicuously in

Millet's work. In the older art there was heroism and there was genre-like ordinariness. The combination of heroism and plain workaday activity is an achievement of the nineteenth century. The German Romantics came, via poetry, to a somewhat problematical piety, whereas formerly faith had produced poetry. Painters in the nineteenth century, feeling in their own hearts the hard human lot, inglorious heroism, passion without resurrection, arrived at an emotional experience of religion, whereas formerly faith had produced art.

Religion and art have this in common: that understanding and reason fail in the one as in the other, that in the one as in the other feeling is prompted to plunge into the inscrutable. This affinity explains why religion and art got on so well together for so long. Only in the sixteenth century was the marriage between spiritualized dogma and sensuous creativity dissolved. The affinity was ultimately re-established by art taking the place of religion in a faithless age. The wonder that was sought in another world pushed its way into this, since to deepened scientific insight the near and the seen became mysterious and incomprehensible. If created nature had once led men to infer a divine Creator, now creative nature aroused religious intimations.

The historical picture in the stricter sense of the term—the portrayal of significant incidents—came to luxuriant and unwholesome flower in the nineteenth century. The art-lover thinks with distaste of Piloty, of whom it has scathingly been said that he painted 'famous accidents'. Wallenstein's death is, like Christ carrying the Cross, an historic incident. It is not the theme itself that decides—the decisive thing is the artist's relation to the theme. The believer's emotionality prevents him from viewing the carrying of the Cross like a knowledgeable eye-witness.

Biblical events could become true historical pictures only in ages weak in faith. A painter in the nineteenth century, shall we say, visits the Holy Land, assimilates the landscape, studies the costume from the time of the Saviour, determines to break away from the iconographic tradition and portray the carrying of the Cross 'correctly'. In such an undertaking he can satisfy neither the believers nor the art-lovers nor even the scholars.

The profane historical picture which put in a pretentious and theatrical appearance, above all in Germany, had a past. The beginnings, the germs of it, can be discovered, as for instance in illumination, the woodcuts and tapestries of the fifteenth and sixteenth centuries. In the written and printed book the text guarantees intelligibility to the picture. The modest format and in the woodcut the nonsensuousness of black and white prove more appropriate to the 'once upon a time' feeling than the bodily actuality of large-scale painting. In tapestry-pictures the technique itself spread a gracious, veil-like indistinctness over the factual report.

During the fifteenth, sixteenth and seventeenth centuries there were opportunities for the monumental and decorative profane historical picture in townhalls and on triumphal archways at the state visits of princely personages. In the townhall in Brussels people could see Rogier v. d. Weyden's, in Löwen Dirk Bouts', drastic examples of strict justice, worldly counterparts to the Last Judgment. Festal decorations depicting historical events were done as early as 1468 in Bruges. In the seventeenth century Rubens staged brilliant displays to the glorification of a ruler or a dynasty, whether permanent decorations in palaces or on gateways erected *ad hoc* for the festivities connected with some reception. If paedagogic or monitory tendencies predominated in the townhalls, in the castles renown had to be proclaimed in fanfare tones. Rubens mostly covered up the naked facts with sumptuous mythology and allegory, more court-poet than historian. Of the 'Old' Masters it was Velasquez with his *Siege of Breda* who best created an historical picture in our sense. In contrast to Rubens he had the chronicler's love of truth. But even his picture was, in content and to a certain extent also in form, determined by the ambitious desires of his royal patron and destined for a definite spot. Meanwhile, in those Homes for Homeless Art—the exhibitions and museums—the historical pictures of the nineteenth century await the interest of the 'cultured,' and comply with book-knowledge. (Pl. 39).

In the last phase of art-development—or is it already the one before the last?—the melody outweighs the text. Interest in the object and in anything intellectually remarkable diminishes; with it the historical picture departs. The marked tendency to take the object as a whole direct from nature comports ill with that stage-managing arrangement without which the historical picture cannot come into being. The higher knowledge and education climbed, the less satisfying the historical picture became. Manet's *Shooting of the Emperor of Mexico* proves that this category is dead rather than that it could ever be revived.

Sure enough there is already a reaction against the de-intellectualizing of representational art. As William M. Ivins has tellingly remarked: 'If, as we are sometimes assured, story-telling lies outside the province of art, then so much the worse for art.'

39. VELASQUEZ, THE SURRENDER OF BREDA
Madrid, Prado

XIII

CONCERNING THE STILL-LIFE

The thoughtful art-lover, particularly if he is more given to thought than to art, may find it astonishing that a lemon, a herring, a wine-glass can be regarded as objects worth painting in themselves. When and how did it happen? What change of artistic sense, of outlook, indeed of social conditions must have come about that production and demand turned to such simple, insignificant objects?

Still-life blossomed late, most richly in the Protestant and Germanic part of Holland, whereas the Latins, especially the Italians, hung back in regard to this young category. But wherever the Church became hostile to imagery man's eidetic hunger took possession of the whole range of the visible world. To the painters who were now free of the obligation to edify and to inspire devoutness, everything phenomenal seemed worthy of being preserved in an image. The scale of value according to the spiritual significance of the object went out of force.

For more than one reason man as a living organism continued to be the favoured, indeed the indispensable vehicle of art in Italy. Interest in heroic or idyllic, religious or mythological events still governed artistic production there, even after the bonds of service to the Church had been loosened. Tradition, resting on the oppressive grandeur of the ancient world and, in connection and also in conflict with this, Christian teaching, together gave rise to certain requirements as regards the intellectual and spiritual content of the picture and its formal size. The dimensionally small panel-picture was unable to thrive in the South as it did in the North for the additional reason that in the South comfortable living conditions, so far as cultivated at all, demanded palatial spaces.

I cannot gloss over the paradoxical fact, however, that the oldest pure still-life known to us—in Munich, dated 1504—comes from a Venetian, Jacopo de' Barbari—a degenerate and deracinated Venetian, it is true, who executed his picture on this side of the Alps.

The broad stratum of the middle-class in Holland provided a market for an astonishingly wide range of profane pictures—genre-paintings, landscapes and also still-life. If in the other Germanic Protestant countries the still-life found a less ready market, economic and social conditions must be taken into account as the principal causes. In Germany, the impoverishment following the 'great' war; in England, the exclusiveness of the society whose taste determined the subject-matter of art. Still-life met with an even less friendly reception among the English than in the French Court and the German *Residenzen*, with their eyes fixed on Versailles.

That the English painters who did such great things in the eighteenth and nineteenth centuries in portraiture and landscape showed no interest in still-life despite a decided gift for pictorial vision, constitutes a problem calling for some reflection. This lack of interest is observable in England's extraordinary wealth of art treasures, even in the universal National Gallery where, though Dutch painting is brilliantly represented, Beyeren and Kalf are absent. Apart from the causes noted it is possible that the vigorous character of the people and their outdoor life turned away from any attentive concern with 'dead' things.

If still-life was cultivated with passion in France rather late, chiefly by Chardin, then in the nineteenth century by the so-called Impressionists, this only goes to show that it was to the advantage of this category to have developed in its own right just when and where art was practised 'for its own sake'. And again, in France, now that capitalist society had superseded the courtly, the heroically-minded monarchical society, the bourgeoisie had a liking for still-life. Peace and democracy and satiety promoted its cultivation. Peace is all the more peace when it follows on grave conflicts, on the Dutch struggles for freedom, on the Napoleonic War, on revolutions and *coups d'état*.

The change in art-sense and art-theory which made the emergence of still-life possible, in conjunction with the social re-alignment, may perhaps be clarified by the following antitheses:

Autocracy: Democracy,
Art subordinate: Art autonomous,
Intellectual form: Sensuous rcceptivity,
Energy: Need of rest,
Sculptor's vision: Painter's vision.

The historian can trace the germination of still-life through the Netherlands painting of the fifteenth and sixteenth centuries. First of all the introduction of dead things in the religious picture as attributes—say St. Catherine's wheel or St. Dorothea's basket. Then the welcome chance to rouse a slumbering delight in still-life within the Church-picture. Jan van Eyck, portraying St. Jerome, illustrates the erudition of this Father of the Church by detailed description of his study, his library. Later, about the middle of the sixteenth century, for instance in the case of Pieter Aertsen, the biblical design is used as a pretext for displaying kitchens and market-places

with vegetables and hunks of meat unashamedly occupying the foreground. Finally, in the seventeenth century, still-life emerged without apology and without disguise.
How strong the urge for still-life was in Holland after this category had emancipated itself can be judged not only from the exceedingly rich production of specialists in this field but also from the occasional incursions of Masters like Albert Cuyp, Salomon Ruysdael and Jan v. d. Heyden. Conscientious patience welcomed the object that cannot move. The live model, even if it keeps still, distresses the observer precisely because it might move. Vermeer, one of the greatest, is by vision a still-life painter even though no proper still-life from his hand is known.
On a superficial view the still-life attempts nothing save the true-to-nature portrayal of familiar things. But deeper insight does not miss the symbolic and the decorative function. All art symbolizes or decorates in one way or another. Blossoming flowers, ripe fruit remind one of the gifts of creative nature, of increase, growth and genesis; the death's head warns of transience, the vanity of earthly things. Still-life functions decoratively in so far as the picture's surface is artfully filled and the objects appear grouped, organized, built up to please the eye.
The graphic arts—drawing, black-and-white—can enter into serious competition with painting in portraiture, landscape and the genre, but not at all in the category of still-life. A flower, a fruit means little without colour, without its material idiosyncrasy. Still-life is the painter's affair in the strictest sense. The sculptor can, as it were, translate the human body, also, perhaps, the animal's, into matter alien to it—bronze, marble—but hardly any other object created by nature, least of all a man-made one. The human body can be strongly reduced or praeternaturally enlarged; but in inanimate things something

essential goes with their natural proportions, as also with their colour and substantiality. Michelangelo the sculptor, and Cornelius the draughtsman, certainly despised still-life.

If all still-life with its play of form and colour can, more or less aptly, be called decorative, in the South of the Netherlands as opposed to Holland it was decorative in the narrower sense, namely decorating. This difference becomes obvious when we compare above all the flower-pieces. The Fleming makes borders or garlands of flowers and fruits, he adorns something; while for the Dutchman the flora as such are completely valid as pictorial content and are in no way mere trimmings and ancillary ornamentation. The Dutch decorative sense is architectonic, the fanatical love of flowers a Dutch passion. The leading Master in Antwerp, Daniel Seghers, b. 1590, felt himself a servant of the Church, adorning altar-pieces and devotional pictures with garlands of flowers. And many Flemish painters followed his example. Frans Snyders, b. 1579, and his successors Jan Fyt, Paul de Vos, Pieter Boel differ from their Dutch contemporaries in their bigger format and spaciousness; they excel in the portrayal of living animals. So far as they paint dead matter at all it proves to be hunting booty and makes one think of animal vitality, human strength triumphant. Their still-life does not symbolize stillness and duration like that of the Dutch. The Dutch citizen closes his house against the tumult, the noise, the restlessness of human action; he recuperates by contemplating the things that belong to him, are there for his use and enjoyment, that, mute and will-less, do not set any volitions going in him.

The contrast between the South of the Netherlands and the North, a contrast based on differences of race, religion and political conditions, works out very clearly in the course of the seventeenth century. Round about 1600 the frontiers were still open. Impulses from the South governed Dutch creativity at that time. We can follow in the history of still-life how almost all the Masters born in the sixteenth century came from Antwerp, how in content and form still-life, so keenly cultivated after 1630 in Haarlem, Leyden, Utrecht and Amsterdam, goes back to the Flemish pattern. Jan Brueghel, born in 1568, starts off as the founder of the flower-piece. After him comes Roelant Savery of Courtrai, born 1576. Many Flemings left their home-country about 1600, some moved to Holland. In Utrecht Ambrosius Boschaert, born 1570, devoted himself to flower-pieces. But he, too, is a Fleming by descent. The Dutchmen Hans Bollongier and B. van der Ast follow him.

As regards the 'luncheon-piece', the table covered with food and eating gear—a type of picture elaborated quite in the Dutch spirit in Haarlem after 1620 by Heda, Pieter Claesz and others, and brought to a high pitch of perfection: for this, too, there are Flemish precedents. The Antwerp artist Hieronymus Franken, born 1540 (or, in the case of the younger of this name, 1578), painted a crude picture dated 1604 with bread, a herring and table utensils, now in the museum at Antwerp. And there is a similar-looking picture which appears in a number of replicas and is ascribed—probably wrongly—to Pieter Brueghel the Elder. The seed comes from the South but finds most fruitful soil in the North.

Keeping our eye on the leading Dutch Masters and disregarding the numerous hangers-on and followers-on, we can distinguish three periods. In the choice of objects, in composition and colouring three generations distinguish themselves in the course of the seventeenth century, and the economic trends are clearly reflected in them.

40. W. KALF, STILL-LIFE
Amsterdam, Rijksmuseum
(*p. 283*)

After modest contentment there comes, with increasing prosperity, fastidious taste, then epicurean luxury. First bread, cheese, a herring, earthenware, then lush fruits, glass, pewter, finally choice silver. To begin with, a pedantic arrangement of objects, later a slanting build-up, along the picture's diagonal, the whole ingeniously woven together. Weak local colour with rich gradations of tone gives way to chiaroscuro, an open palette, lambent shimmer (van Beyeren) or glow and sparkle (Kalf). The Masters of the best period—about 1650—are I. D. de Heem (b. 1606), van Beyeren (b. 1620), Kalf (b. 1622) and Willem van Aelst (b. 1626). (Pl. 40).

The flower-piece, which cannot do without strong local colour, was cultivated in the botanist's manner by Ambrose Boschaert about 1610, the vertical medial axis being stressed; about the middle of the century it takes a back place only to reappear towards its end and in the following period in the work of Mignon (b. 1640), Rachel Ruysch (b. 1664) and Jan van Huysum (b. 1682), when it satisfied the Dutch mania for flowers. Heda, active about 1630, was a contemporary of Frans Hals; Kalf, about 1650, of Rembrandt; Ruysch, about 1680, of van der Werff.

In Italy, imported from the North or at least inspired by the Northern example, still-life continued to be a subordinate category. Hardly any of the respectable Italians stooped to this. It was tolerated for the sake of its decorating function. The single object, rose, tulip, apple, failed to command close and devoted attention as regards its coloristic and textural idiosyncrasy—it only counted as a formal colour-value in the picture as a whole. Objective interest, possessive joy and scientific scrupulosity did not, as in the Netherlands, give the still-life an equal place in the community of the categories of painting.

The seventeenth century Spanish shared the Netherlands sense of reality more than did the Italians, and thus a certain leaning towards still-life even though the range of commission afforded them little opportunity for its pure cultivation. The greatest, Velasquez and Zurbaran, painted dead things within the framework of figure-composition—culinary ware, books and suchlike—with grave objectivity. What was symbolized from the ascetic point of view was the astringency and hardness of earthly life. The Spaniards lacked the heritage of antiquity that bound and inspired the Italians, hence they lacked a gift for sculpture. This lack benefited their painting, just as it did, in another way, that of the Venetians. The autocratic, ceremonious nature of the State banished harmless, homely pleasures and gave the still-life a sombre look. Everything ornamental, friendly, blossomy was absent. The term *nature morte* is Latin. (Pl. 41).

Though German education in the nineteenth century freed itself but slowly and toilsomely from the aesthetic dogmas which Winckelmann and Lessing had derived from antique sculpture—an art theory that did bare justice to painting and to still-life none at all—it was nevertheless a German thinker who finally understood the meaning of this latter category and put it in a way that cannot be surpassed. Schopenhauer praises 'those excellent Netherlanders who turned such a purely objective eye on the most trivial matters and raised up a lasting monument to their objectivity and tranquillity of soul in the still-life, which no aesthetic observer can view unaffected, since it brings home to him the quiet, still, undesiring frame of mind of the artist necessary to so objective a contemplation of such insignificant things'.

Cook Gallery, Richmond

41. VELASQUEZ, KITCHEN SCENE. DETAIL

London

INDEX

Achenbach, Brothers, 146
Aelst, W. van, 283
Aertsen, P., 159 f., 163, 279
Alsloot, D. van, 84
Altdorfer, A., 66 f., 83
Amstel, J. van, 59
Antonello da Messina, 238
Ast, B. van der, 282
Aubin, G. de St., 213
Avercamp, H., 89, 199

Barbari, J. de, 278
Barbizon-School, 119, 132
Bega, C. P., 200
Berchem, N., 96, 100, 186
Beyeren, A. van, 278, 283
Blake, W., 169
Blechen, C., 148
Bles, Herri met de, 56, 57, 59, 62 f., 70, 80
Bloemaert, A., 86, 87, 88, 171
Böcklin, A., 142, 145, 149
Boel, P., 281
Bol, F., 181
Bol, H., 80 f.
Bollongier, H., 282
Boonen, A., 200
Bosch, H., 42 ff., 53, 54, 58, 64, 71, 232, 268 f.
Bosch, P. van den, 200
Bosschaert, A., 282 f.
Both, J., 100, 107
Botticelli, 115, 235, 240, 260
Boucher, F., 126, 208, 212
Boursse, E., 188, 200
Bouts, D., 31 ff., 39, 46, 268, 275
Brakenburgh, R., 200
Brekelenkam, Q., 200
Bril, M., 85
Bril, P., 85
Brouwer, A., 103 f., 166, 174 ff., 179, 183, 203, 204
Brueghel, J., 79, 84, 89
Brueghel, P., 44, 70 ff., 79, 88, 102, 138, 159 ff., 163, 166, 169 f., 174, 176, 229, 232, 282
Brueghel, d. J. P., 74, 282
Brunswick Monogrammist, 59, 62, 160
Burgh, A. v. d., 200
Buytewech, W., 87, 88, 93, 171, 173

Canale, A., 123
Canova, 233
Caravaggio, 102, 204
Carpaccio, 115
Carracci, A., 85, 103
Carstens, A., 139
Cézanne, P., 17, 129 ff., 136, 138, 144, 220, 261
Chardin, J. B. S., 211, 256, 273, 279
Christus, P., 34, 239
Claesz, P., 282
Claude, 74, 85, 100 f., 107, 109, 111, 116, 124 f., 255
Cleve, J. van, 47, 56 f.
Cleve, M. van, 163
Cock, H., 71, 74, 76
Cock, J. Wellensz de, 75f., 67
Cock, M., 67, 70, 73, 75
Codde, P., 177
Coeck, P., 46, 62, 71, 73 f., 163, 174
Coninxloo, G. van, 81 f., 86, 89
Constable, 115 ff., 118 f., 132
Cornelissen, C., 86, 171
Cornelisz, J., 65
Cornelius, P., 19, 139, 222, 281
Corot, C., 104, 117 f., 144, 148
Courbet, G., 117, 119 f., 124, 131, 140, 142, 219
Craesbeek, J. van, 176
Cranach, L., 66, 80, 182
Crome, J., 116
Cuyp, A., 65, 94, 96, 106 f., 111, 125, 199, 279

Dalem, C. van, 80
Daubigny, Ch., 117, 144
Daumier, H., 134, 169, 223
David, G., 38 ff., 48, 54
David, L., 214
Degas, E., 15, 122, 124, 126 f., 131, 133, 153, 210, 261
Delacroix, E., 119, 133
Diaz, N., 117

Dou, G., 64, 182, 184, 200
Dubucourt, 213
Duck, J. A., 177
Dupré, J., 117
Dürer, A., 21, 46, 48, 49, 66, 75, 80, 169, 188, 216, 243 ff., 248, 270
Dusart, K., 200
Duyster, W., 177
Dyck, A. van, 111, 233, 254 f., 257
Dyck, Ph. van, 200

Elsheimer, A., 82, 85, 93
Engelbrechtsen, C., 65
Everdingen, A. van, 99
Eyck, H. van, 23, 25, 27, 28
Eyck, J. van, 17, 19, 23 ff., 53, 70, 158, 162, 188, 233, 235, 237 f., 243, 266 f. 279

Fabritius, C., 185, 195
Faistenberger, A., 115
Feti, 192
Feuerbach, A., 140, 149
Fiammingo, P., 85
Flémalle, Master of, 30
Flinck, G., 181
Floris, F., 74, 164, 174, 249
Fohr, 117
Fragonard, H., 109, 208, 212, 256, 273
Franken, H., 282
Friedrich, C. D., 114 ff., 144, 148, 150
Frühauf, R., 66 f.
Fyt, J., 281

Gainsborough, Th., 111 f., 233, 257 f., 273
Gassel, L., 57, 59 f., 66
Geertgen tot St. Jans, 40
Gelder, A. de, 173, 184
Gent, J. van, 238
Ghirlandaio, 235
Gillray, 224
Giorgione, 69, 70
Giotto, 120, 266
Goes, H. van der, 35 ff.
Gogh, V. van, 119, 134 ff., 140, 146, 150, 223
Goltzius, H., 86
Gossaert, J., 46, 68, 69, 250, 270
Goudt, H., 93
Goya, F. de, 169, 214, 255, 273
Goyen, J. van, 89 ff., 98

Greco, El, 133, 250 f.
Greuze, J. B., 212
Grimer, J., 80 f.
Grünewald, M., 66
Guardi, F., 216

Haarlem, C. van, 232
Hals, D., 173, 177
Hals, F., 124, 134, 170 ff., 176, 183, 189, 233, 252, 258, 260
'Hausbuch' Master, 162
Heda, W. C., 282
Heem, J. Dz. de, 283
Heemskerck, M. van, 46, 80, 164, 174, 249 f.
Helst, B. van der, 252
Hemessen, J. van, 56, 160 f., 163
Herkomer, H., 134
Herp, G. van, 204
Heyden, J. van der, 108, 280
Hobbema, M., 107, 199
Hogarth, W., 214 f., 224
Holbein, H., 140, 172, 233, 243 ff., 248
Hoogh, P. de, 96, 186 f., 195, 197, 200
Hoppner, J., 257 f.
Huber, W., 66 f., 75
Huysmans, 103
Huysum, J. van, 283

Ingres, J. A. D., 19, 261
Israels, J., 119, 137, 223

Jacobsz, D., 249 f.
Janssens, P., 188, 200
Jonghe, L. de, 200
Jordaens, J., 160, 202

Kalf, W., 106, 278, 283
Kaulbach, W. v., 140
Keuninck, K. de, 85
Key, W., 249
Kick, S., 177
Klinger, M., 145
Knaus, L., 222
Knibbergen, F., 94
Knupfer, N., 189
Knyff, W., 94
Koch, A. J., 115
Koninck, Ph., 105, 173

Laar, P. van, 205
Lancret, N., 212

Largillière, N. de, 256
Lawrence, Th., 257 f.
Le Brun, Ch., 256
Leibl, W., 140 f.
Lenbach, F. von, 121
Leyden, L. van, 65, 69, 162
Leyster, J., 172
Liebermann, M., 119, 137, 144, 260
Lievens, J., 105, 173, 181
Lombard, L., 63, 164
Longhi, P., 216
Lorrain, le, s. Claude,
Lotto, L., 248
Luini, B., 115

Maes, N., 173, 184 f., 201
Magnasco, 206, 217
Makart, H., 139 f., 148
Mander, C. van, 39, 40, 47, 56, 62 ff., 68, 70, 73, 81, 86, 171, 232
Manet, E., 114, 121 ff., 127, 129, 132, 134, 140, 144, 224 f., 260 f., 276
Mannerists, the, 57, 58
Marcanton, 69
Marees, H. von, 140, 149
Marshal, B., 215
Masaccio, 233
Massys, C., 47, 60, 70
Massys, J., 56
Massys, Q., 46 f., 54, 56 f., 162, 243, 270
Master of Female Half-figures, 161
Master of Flémalle, 30
Master of the Virgo inter Virgines, 45
Mauve, A., 134
Max, G., 148
Memling, H., 35 ff., 239, 243, 269
Mengs, R., 230
Menzel, A., 136, 142, 145, 169, 222
Metsu, G., 198 f.
Meunier, C., 137
Michelangelo, 19, 69, 164, 232, 266, 281
Mieris, F. van, 64, 200
Mignard, 256
Mignon, 283
Millet, J. F., 113, 117, 119, 134 f., 137, 218, 223
Mirou, A., 84
Molanus, 34
Molenaer, C., 84
Molenaer, J. M., 172
Molijn, P., 89, 92
Momper, J. de, 80
Monet, Cl., 17, 122 f., 124, 127 f., 144
Monogrammist, *see* Brunswick
Mor, A., 246, 249 f.
Moreau le jeune, 213
Moroni, 233
Mosscher, van, 94
Mostaert, F., 56, 63
Mostaert, G., 80, 82
Mostaert, J., 65
Munkaczy, M. von, 113
Murillo, 205, 271

Nain, Brothers Le, 203
Neer, A. van der, 106
Neer, E. van der, 200
Netscher, C., 200 f.

Ochtervelt, J., 200
Olivier, 117
Orley, B. van, 46, 75
Ostade, A. van, 103, 166, 171 f., 183 f., 200
Ostade, I. van, 189
Ouwater, A. van, 40

Palamedesz, A., 177
Panini, 109
Pape, A., 200
Patinir, H., 56, 62, 63
Patinir, J., 47 f., 50 ff., 74, 83
Pater, 212
Picasso, P., 121
Piloty, K. von, 140, 148, 274
Pisanello, 237
Pisano, A., 235
Pissarro, C., 125
Pollaiuolo, 240
Post, F., 100
Pot, H., 172, 178
Potter, P., 105
Poussin, N., 85, 103, 109, 115, 231

Raeburn, H., 257 f.
Raphael, 119, 164, 243
Rembrandt, 70, 87, 96, 101 f., 104 f., 119, 172, 179 ff., 213, 252 f., 260, 272
Renoir, A., 122, 127, 224, 226, 258
Reynolds, J., 111, 257 f.
Ribera, G., 102
Rigaud, H., 256
Robert, H., 109
Rohden, 117

Rombouts, Th., 202
Romney, G., 257 f.
Rosa, S., 103
Rousseau, H., 228
Rowlandson, Th., 224
Roymerswaele, M. van, 56, 161
Rubens, P. P., 70, 74, 101 f., 172, 180, 182, 202, 208, 210, 253 f., 266, 271, 275
Runge, Ph. O., 117
Ruskin, 115
Ruysch, R., 283
Ruysdael, J. van, 95, 97 ff., 107, 113, 124, 199
Ruysdael, S. van, 92, 94 ff., 280
Ryckaert, 204

Saenredam, F., 105
Saftleven, C., 179
Savery, R., 84, 282
Schalcken, G., 200
Schaubroeck, P., 84
Schinkel, F., 233
Schongauer, M., 162
Scorel, J. van, 65, 66, 69, 249 f.
Seghers, D., 281
Seghers, H., 87, 89, 104
Seurat, 138
Siberechts, J., 103, 111
Sisley, 125
Slingeland, P. C. van, 200
Snyders, F., 160, 281
Sorgh, H. M., 176, 179
Steen, J., 96, 188 f., 200, 215
Stubbs, G., 215
Swart van Groningen, J., 66

Teniers, D., 103, 176, 200 ff.
Terborch, G., 172, 196 f., 199 f., 211, 256
Terbrugghen, H., 194
Thoma, H., 145
Tiepolo, G. B., 216, 254, 273
Tintoretto, 70, 115, 250, 254
Titian, 69, 70, 77, 233, 243 f., 248 f., 254
Toeput, L., 85
Tol, van, 200
Tons, Willem (?), 75
Toorenvliet, J., 200
Toulouse-Lautrec, H. de, 169
Tour, G. de la, 204
Troost, C., 215
Turner, W., 115 f., 119

Uccello, 240
Uden, L. van, 103

Vadder, L. de, 103
Valkenburg, F. van, 85
Valkenburg, L. van, 74, 81
Veen, O. van, 74
Velasquez, 103, 124, 134, 165, 172, 205, 233, 251 f., 260, 275, 284
Velde, A. van de, 108, 199
Velde, E. van de, 87, 88, 92, 93, 171, 173
Velde, J. van de, 93, 170
Velde, W. van de, 105
Veneziano, D., 240
Verkolje, 200
Vermeer, J., 106, 186, 193 ff., 211, 280
Vermeyen, J., 249 f.
Vinci, Leonardo da, 240 f.
Vinckboons, D., 84, 170
Vos, M. de, 74, 164
Vos, P. de, 281
Vrel, J., 188, 200
Vroom, C., 98

Waldmüller, F., 117, 222
Wassmann, 117
Watteau, J. A., 208 f., 256, 273
Weiditz, H., 72, 229
Werff, A. van der, 200, 201, 283
Weyden, R. van der, 20, 24, 29 ff., 162, 238 f., 268, 275
Wheatley, 215
Wildens, J., 103
Wilkie, 222
Wilson, R., 107, 111
Witz., K., 67, 75
Wouwerman, Ph., 199

Zurbaran, 284